For Andy Paulson —
After all that Chaucer,
Shakespeare and Blake. With
here is my poem.
Love —

Michel Oesterreicher

December 17, 1998

PIONEER FAMILY

Life on Florida's
20th-Century Frontier

Michel Oesterreicher

With a Foreword by
Daniel L. Schafer

Cypress cabin built by the author's grandfather in 1876. Photograph by the author's son, Anthony Nettuno, reproduced courtesy of the J. T. McCormick family.

The University of Alabama Press

Tuscaloosa and London

Copyright © 1996
The University of Alabama Press
Tuscaloosa, Alabama 35487-0380

Manufactured in the United States of America

∞

The paper on which this book is printed meets the minimum
requirements of American National Standard for Information
Science—Permanence of Paper for Printed
Library Materials, ANSI Z39.48-1984.

Library of Congress Cataloging-in-Publication Data

Oesterreicher, Michel, 1939–
Pioneer family : life on Florida's 20th-Century frontier / Michel
Oesterreicher ; with a foreword by Daniel L. Schafer.
        p.   cm.
        ISBN 0-8173-0783-4
    1. Frontier and pioneer life—Florida.   2. Florida—Social life
and customs.   3. Oesterreicher, Michel, 1939–   —Family.
        4. Oesterreicher family.   I. Title.
                F316.O36   1996
    975.9' 1061—dc20   95-15202

British Library Cataloguing-in-Publication Data available

People living today don't know.
They have no idea what a hard time is.
We have lived through it, I mean.

—Hugie Oesterreicher, 1984

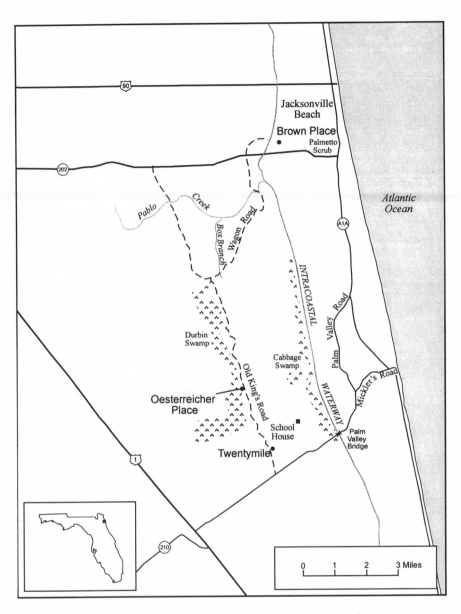

Northeast Florida, near the old Oesterreicher and Brown places

Contents

Contents

Foreword

MICHEL OESTERREICHER'S *Pioneer Family* has a valuable lesson for those who would know our nation's history. It is that we cannot fully comprehend our past by focusing exclusively on the experiences of our most influential citizens; we must consider ordinary Americans as well, even if the evidence of their lives is often difficult to find. *Pioneer Family*, an oral history of Michel's parents, Huger and Oleta Oesterreicher, is also a compelling portrait of twentieth-century frontier life in Florida and a guide for the study of America's ordinary people.

Readers will meet Hugie as he rides on horseback through the Diego Plains of northeast Florida, driving cattle through the pine woods and wetlands that are now the setting for golf courses and resort housing. They will share his life as a trapper and hunter in the snake-infested wilds of the Durbin Swamp and will learn how he survived the depression by chopping trees and squaring timbers and by setting up an illegal still and selling moonshine. In the decades before World War II, Hugie risked his life daily in confrontations with snakes, bears, wild hogs, alligators, floods, drought, and disease.

Oleta also learned to tend cattle, to garden, grind sugarcane, and make syrup, and to butcher hogs and preserve the meat in smokehouses. Like her husband, Oleta would find little time for school. After finishing the eighth grade, she joined her siblings and widowed mother as the workforce at the Brown family dairy. She too would face death in the woods and swamps and in childbirth. Always, it was family that could be counted on and sacrificed for. And in family, Oleta and Hugie found joy and abiding values.

The Oesterreichers, like countless other settlers before them who had struggled to establish homesteads and families in such distant places as Shenandoah and the Dakota Territory, were pioneers who continued the American frontier tradition in twentieth-century Florida. Readers of Marjorie Kinnan Rawlings's fiction will associate Hugie and Oleta with the vanishing "cracker" culture of the region;* like the author of *The Yearling*, Michel Oesterreicher has captured the authentic flavor of life among northeast Florida's rural people, a generation removed.

---

*The short stories by Rawlings mentioned here were collected in *When the Whipporwhill—* (New York: Ballatine Books, 1975, c 1940).

Pioneer Family has a special meaning for me. During a journey through a dense marsh to the site of a 1780s rice plantation, I met Huger Oesterreicher, long after he had traded woods and swamps for a snug suburban cottage. I realized that day, and was reminded by this book, that although my own parents had been born far from northeast Florida (in rural southern Minnesota and two decades after Hugie and Oleta), their family and educational experiences were not greatly different. My great regret is that I have not recorded their histories and charged their lives with meaning, as Michel has done for her parents in these pages.

Daniel L. Schafer
Professor of History
University of North Florida

Preface

HUGIE OESTERREICHER (1898–1987) and Oleta Brown (1908–1986) were born in northeast Florida when there were no paved roads between St. Augustine and Jacksonville and no automobile bridges over the St. Johns River. They lived in houses without electricity or indoor plumbing and drew water from wells curbed with hollowed-out cypress trunks. Hugie's home was a cypress log cabin built by his father in 1876 at the edge of Durbin Swamp. He made his living hunting hogs and deer, trapping fur-bearing animals, and raising range cattle. Oleta's home was a dairy farm near the little settlement of Pablo Beach.

Hugie and Oleta Brown Oesterreicher were my parents. Some of my first memories are of sitting on the front porch of our home listening to them share stories of that rural area in the early 1900s. Northeast Florida was pioneer country then, and they were twentieth-century pioneers.

In the spring of 1984, I taped interviews with my parents for an independent study with Professor Daniel Schafer of the University of North Florida History Department. All of the incidents in this book are based on actual events discussed in those interviews. At no time did I introduce emotions or responses to those events other than the ones Hugie and Oleta said they had. At all times, I strove for an honest, clear narrative, true to my parents and free from my own sentiments.

I believe the value of their story is, first, in its universal theme of the unending human struggle to be more than circumstances would seem to allow. Second, these stories are valuable because they are a firsthand account of a way of life that has almost disappeared in America. Hugie and Oleta and most of the others like them are gone, as are the answers to all the questions we always meant to ask them. I hope you enjoy their stories.

Michel Oesterreicher

Acknowledgments

I WOULD LIKE to acknowledge Dan Schafer of the University of North Florida History Department for recognizing the value of these stories. From the beginning, he prodded me to see this project to its culmination. Dan gave hours to reading various drafts and making important recommendations.

The writing of this book has been a work of faith, my faith and the faith of friends and relatives. My special thanks to Dan Schafer for believing in Hugie and Oleta's story; to Allen Tilley of the University of North Florida Literature Department for believing I could write their story; to my brother, sisters, nieces, nephews, and friends for catching hold to my own personal vision for this book, for not letting go, and for believing it with me. And finally, to my children, Tony, Anna Lee, Vicky, and Greg—my darlings—I thank you for always, always believing in me.

Pioneer Family

The Doll

When I was between three and four years old, Papa went off and bought a bunch
of cattle. I remember I seen them coming, driving them cattle down the road,
bringing them home. . . . Up until that time, we had no cattle. Had a horse. Two
horses. . . . From then on, we had cattle, and we had cowpens, and we would pen
our cattle every spring. Gather and bring them all home. . . . From that time on,
I was a cowboy.

—Hugie, 4 February 1984

IN THE EARLY fall of 1901, a little boy holding a rag doll and wearing a white
cotton dress sat on the cypress planks forming the steps of the Oesterreicher
cabin. Hugie was three years old, and his head was filled with dreams of being
a cowboy. Through the black fringe of his thick lashes, his clear blue eyes stared
deliberately across the clearing down the white sand road in front of him. He
listened intently, only moving occasionally to wipe the blond curls away from
his damp forehead.

His father, Tom Oesterreicher, and his older brothers had left early that
morning on horseback to travel some twenty miles on the old highway past
St. Augustine to buy cattle, a big investment for a man who made a scant living
out of the northeast Florida woods. The cattle would be turned loose to range
the swamps, forests, and marshes of Duval and St. Johns counties. After they
had fattened on the grass and Spanish moss, Tom would sell some of them at
a profit. The rest he would keep to build a herd.

The boy waited, holding the doll, while vague ideas of cowboys, patched
from the conversations of his older brothers, flitted in and out of his mind.
"We're going to be cowboys," he said to the rag doll with the black button eyes.

Behind him, beyond the sloping field separating his home from the dark
Durbin Swamp, the sun was setting on the northeast Florida woods. The shadows of the tall Durbin cypress reached across the furrows of the field toward
the cabin. When the sun had disappeared behind the cypress swamp, his mother
stepped quietly out onto the porch behind him. With one small hand, she pushed
the wet ringlets from her face and listened for some sound that might indicate
the approach of her husband and the cattle. At first, there were only evening
sounds of frogs and crickets and birds settling in for the night. Then she
straightened her back and said, "Shh, listen. Hugie, come here, son! Your
daddy's coming with the cattle."

Clutching the doll, he stood up and saw nothing but the sand road extending in a curve from under the shadow of the oak trees. Then he heard them in the distance, men whooping and whistling and cracking whips, as the lowing cattle complained mournfully of their long hot journey. Hugie stood breathlessly listening while the sounds of men and cattle grew louder and louder out beyond the gathering shadows of dusk. Then with a splash of movement they broke into the clearing in front of the cabin.

Ella, with her daughters and two young sons, stood on the safety of the porch as Tom and the older boys drove the cattle past—a flurry of animals and men, sweat and dust, hot breath and thunder—moving toward the new split-pine pens a quarter of a mile beyond the house. When the herd neared the pens, the children jumped from the porch and ran toward them. Ella followed. Reaching the wooden fence, the little boys and girls climbed to the top and let their arms and heads hang over as they gazed in wonder at the cattle. Tom walked to Ella grinning, beads of sweat streaming from his felt hat down his dusty face and into his red mustache and black beard.

Later that evening, beneath the light of a kerosene lamp, Tom Oesterreicher and his family gathered around the table for supper, eating greens, grits, and fresh biscuits. Tom talked about his plans for the cattle. He would keep them penned for about three months in the spring and early summer. During that time, he and the boys would move the pens every three weeks. That way, the entire ten-acre field to the north of the cabin would be fertilized by July, when it was time to let the cattle loose to range Durbin Swamp and its surrounding forests. Each of Tom and Ella's nine children listened intently, hopeful of more prosperous days ahead.

Little Hugie was the Oesterreichers' youngest son. The boy rested his head on his mother's arm as he strained to stay awake and be a part of the "man talk" in which his father and older brothers were engaged. He gazed with admiration at the menfolk around the table. The golden lamplight flickered on their suntanned faces, and when they talked of deer or cattle, their blue-green eyes sparkled, and Hugie thought the men in his family were very wonderful.

Minutes later, Hugie had fallen asleep, and Dora, his nineteen-year-old sister, gathered him in her arms and carried him to a cot in his parents' room. The handmade mattress stuffed with cornhusks engulfed his little body, and he dreamed of cattle and horses and deer and buckshot and bows and arrows. Outside the open window, the moon was rising, and faintly, from across the field somewhere in the swamp, a whippoorwill was calling.

The next morning, it was still dark when the aroma of coffee boiling on the wood stove in the kitchen drifted through the open bedroom window. Hugie rolled out of bed, still clothed in yesterday's white cotton dress. The little boy wore dresses because Ella had discovered that keeping a young child in dresses was less bother for her and cooler for the child, male or female. And although she had thought several times recently that it was time to make trousers for her young son, she had not yet done so. The child wandered sleepily out the back door, across the raised walkway, and past the cypress curbing of the well to the kitchen, which was built a safe distance from the main house because, in those days, sparks flying from the wood burning in stoves and open hearths often set kitchens on fire.

Tom sat drinking coffee and eating last night's biscuits, which had been fried with bacon grease. He was joined by his oldest sons, eighteen-year-old Jake, sixteen-year-old Clarence, and thirteen-year-old Thomas. Hugie padded in, picked up the rag doll he'd dropped the night before, and climbed to the bench. The dark night had done little to relieve the heat, and the blazing fire in the wood stove made the little kitchen seem like an oven. Tom already had sweat glistening on his brow. Although he said nothing, he noticed his youngest son, who sat clutching that rag doll with the black button eyes, and he thought about it as he rose and left the kitchen. The older boys followed him. There were cattle to tend and fields to plow and plant.

The fire in the wood stove dwindled, and Hugie walked to the front porch and sat quietly on the cypress steps as the morning sun rose above the live oaks and cabbage palms lining the eastern horizon. Sometime later, though, George, Hugie's eleven-year-old brother, came out, and the two boys began their day. They ran to the cow pens and climbed on the new split-pine fence. They chased birds and squirrels through surrounding groves of trees. They pulled thick clusters of dark grapes from vines behind the cabin and ate them. And every place Hugie went, he carried the doll.

The two boys ran to a stretch of palmettos, fell to their knees, and entered paths made through the foliage by the wild hogs that ranged the woods eating the plant's juicy berries. Hugie and George cautiously followed the tunnels through the sharp sawlike stalks that held the thickly matted silver-green fronds over their heads. They crawled around the winding curves and over the knotty roots bulging from the ground. Minutes later, when they heard their sister's voice calling for them across the wide expanse of green fans, they quickly scooted down the winding path beneath the palmettos to the outer world.

Little Ella stood there with her hands on her hips as the boys scrambled from beneath the prickly fronds. She was eight years old and looked like her mother—small with dark curly hair and dancing black eyes. "George, you know better than to go into those palmettos. I ought to tell Papa on you. A rattlesnake will get you." And then to her youngest brother she said, "Hugie, snakes as big as you live in those palmettos." The statement impressed the younger boy. He had seen one of their dogs die from a rattlesnake bite. The dog's death had been quick and horrible. "Come on, you two!" the little girl said, "Let's walk to the north field and see Papa before he comes home for dinner." The girl smiled with secret pleasure when she noticed the rag doll dangling from Hugie's hand. She had made that doll, stitched together those bits of rags and straw for her little brother.

Inside the cabin, Ella made ready to fry squirrel for the noon meal. She reached through the narrow door of the wood stove with an iron poker and stirred the smoldering embers. Then lowering her face to the opening, she took a deep breath and blew gently at the flame. The fire blazed.

Meanwhile, the three children and the rag doll made their way to the north field. Leaving the main road through the Oesterreicher land, they headed across a high scrub of scattered palmettos, low-lying blackberry bushes, and small blackjack oak trees. Beyond the trees, the field stretched before them, and on the far end, their father guided the horse and plow down the furrows. Some distance from him, the older boys were on their hands and knees planting the winter garden. And beyond the boys, Durbin Swamp loomed, crowding the edges of the field the man had carved from its borders.

Hugie put the doll on a stump at the edge of the clearing and followed his brother and sister across the rows of soft black earth toward their father. "Mama's cooking dinner, Papa. When you coming?" the girl asked.

"Right now! I'm getting out of this sun!" her father replied, red-faced beneath the brim of his black felt hat and wringing wet with sweat. He whistled, waving his arm, motioning his sons to follow him. He turned for home.

When Tom reached the cabin, he lowered a bucket into the cypress trunk curbing the well. He heard the bucket splash in the shadowy depths and drew it up. The boys and the little ones trailed up behind him as he splashed his face and beard with water. Suddenly, Hugie grabbed Little Ella's hand and cried, "I left my baby at the field! I gotta get her, she'll be scared." He turned and broke into a run past the main house, down the road, and onto the scrub. The girl ran after the little white-dressed figure heading through the low bushes of the rise, calling to him. Tom watched his young children running in a panic to the north field. Thinking about his youngest son and the rag doll, he cleared his throat, "Uh-hum," and wiped his mouth with his damp hand.

Out on the scrub, Little Ella had caught Hugie by his chubby hand as he screamed to his missing doll, "Don't cry, baby, Mama's coming!" The girl laughed to herself. She would never forget this.

When the children returned to the cabin with the doll, the family had gathered around the table for the noon meal. "I got my doll!" Hugie called brightly. "She was crying 'cause she was afraid an ol' rattlesnake might get her." His sister's warning about snakes was still vivid in his mind.

Tom Oesterreicher had been studying the fried squirrel and grits on his plate, and at the words of his young son, he raised his head and squinted across the table at the boy, who still stood clutching that rag doll with the black button eyes. "Uh-hum." Tom cleared his throat. "Uh-hum." Everyone stopped eating and lifted their eyes to their father. His eyes were glaring at his young son. "What you doin' with a doll, boy? What are you, a sissy?"

The man's words were worse than a slap in the face to the little boy. He stood there, not understanding the derision in his father's voice or his older brothers' laughter. Hugie didn't know the meaning of the word *sissy*, but the cruelty in his father's sneer and his brothers' laughter filled him with shame. He looked at the doll he held in his hand, and suddenly he hated the bits of rag and straw. Salty tears stung his eyes; his cheeks flushed hot and red. The black button eyes stared. Then, with one hand, Hugie jammed the doll through the open door of the stove and into the fire. Through a blur, he saw the flames envelop the rag doll.

Ella watched, hurting for her little boy and aware of her own failure to help her baby differentiate between himself and his sisters in a world where such distinction was of great importance. And Little Ella sat silently, feeling secret reproach for making the doll for Hugie. Only Dora moved. With her large brown peaceful eyes and her firm jaw, she rose from the table, walked to her little brother and scooped him into her round soft arms. "Come on, my little Cotton, let's wash up for dinner," she said carrying him out into the fresh air.

The next morning, Ella would take down a roll of white canvas and begin making Hugie his first pair of trousers, and Tom would take him on the front of his horse for the boy's first trip into Durbin Swamp. In the years to come, Hugie would know that great dark swamp better than any other man—every alligator hole, every bog and creek. And he would be known by hunters as the best shot in Duval and St. Johns counties. But that morning, he burned inside with a sense of shame that he was too young to understand. From a bucket on the back porch, Dora splashed water onto the hot little face and hands of her brother and ran her damp fingers through his mat of blond curls, pulling them away from the pools of his great deep blue eyes, while inside, in the kitchen, the smell of burning rags filled the air.

The Fever

I remember the first piece of ice, official ice, that
I ever saw. When I was a kid, Mama was sick.

—Hugie, 16 February 1984

"IT'S SO HOT," Ella thought as she kicked the thin blanket off her body. The carved mahogany headboard that had belonged to her mother loomed above her and seemed to box her into the small low room of the cypress cabin. "So hot!" She lay deep in the impression of the mattress peering out the open window, longing for some breeze to drift through it and across her. She turned restlessly and, feeling Tom's back against her own, turned again and moaned quietly. "Water. I'll wash my face. That will cool me off," she thought, swinging her feet to the cool cypress floor. A cold shiver shot through her hot body, and she dizzily lunged toward the back porch, where they kept a bucket of freshly drawn water. But just as she reached the low door leading outside, dark swirling clouds seemed to engulf her.

Later, when Tom rose, the eastern sky was only slightly beginning to lighten with the first indication of morning. "Ella's already starting breakfast," he thought, noticing the empty place beside him in the bed. When he reached the back porch, he realized there was no fire going in the kitchen. Then he turned, and in the dim light, he saw Ella in a limp heap by the water bucket. He ran to his wife, hovering over her, gently touching her. Her arms burned in his calloused hands. He placed his right palm on her forehead and his left on the white thigh that extended from beneath the cotton sleeping gown. She had a raging fever. Putting one hand beneath her head and gingerly lifting it, he dampened the other in the bucket beside her body and washed her burning face. But she remained limp and unconscious.

Tom gathered Ella's tiny frame into his arms and carried her to their room, calling frantically to his sleeping children. "Jake! Ella! Clarence! Wake up! Ma's sick! Come on!" They tumbled from their beds and into their parents' small room and stood staring in the shadows of the early morning at their mother's almost lifeless body in the bed.

Little Ella was the oldest girl at home, for Dora had recently married Benny McCormick. The child lit a kerosene lamp and fetched a pan of water from the back porch and began to bathe her mother's face with a rag. The rag would become hot only seconds after it had reached the woman's face, and Little Ella

6

would dip it again in the cool water, wring it out, and place it folded on her mother's forehead. Little Hugie watched, afraid his mama was dying.

Ella took sick in July, when the oppressive heat made the fever even more difficult for her family to fight. They had no way to cool her down. Even the water from the well became tepid in a few minutes. Ella was almost forty years old; she was in the early stages of pregnancy with her tenth child, and her fever raged unchecked for days. The woman's eyes fluttered, and she was only slightly aware of her small daughter's presence and something cool washing over her face and arms and legs. She could not move or raise her eyelids or speak. Periodically, Tom's bearded face peered down at her, and she somehow sensed his anxiety. She heard the voices of her children whispering at the foot of her bed, but she could not turn her head to look at them. She imagined she was dying, and the idea was not frightening to her.

The little girls, Ella and Edwarda, cared for their mother that day, taking turns washing her down and offering her fluids, while Tom and the boys went about their normal chores. But as the fever persisted through that first hot July day and night, Tom's concern increased. The next day, his wife was no better. The fever, if anything, seemed hotter. Her pulse raced and pounded beneath his fingers as he checked it, gripping her wrist in his work-hardened hands. In his heart, without speaking it to his children, he feared for Ella's life and the life of the baby beginning to grow in her belly.

That night, a summer storm poured rain on the Diego Plain. Lightning flashed, and thunder rolled and cracked above the cypress cabin, and winds whipped the nearby trees. Inside, Ella was delirious, mumbling and moaning at the noisome sounds and lights that disturbed her semiconscious state. Tom sat beside her and dozed fitfully.

On the third morning of Ella's fever, Hugie woke from a light sleep to whisperings drifting through the walls from his mother's room. He rose and walked hesitantly, half afraid of what he would find, and stood quietly at the low door, listening. Jake and Clarence stood dressed for riding, talking in low tones to their father. Hugie heard, "Bayard," "fever," "woods under water," and "go 'round Durbin." His older brothers moved out of the house and to the barn. Hugie followed them to the porch and watched them saddle their horses and heave themselves onto the animals' backs.

Last night's storm had passed, and the sun was rising over the eastern tree line. The woods and fields glowed in a soft rosy light as the two young men disappeared down the white sands of Old King's Road. Later that morning, as the sun crept higher and burned in the sky with fury, the soggy ground steamed beneath their horses' feet. Clarence and Jake rode, not fast because they had nearly a thirty-mile trip to make that day and the heat would not allow them to push the animals too hard. They circled the northern head of Durbin Swamp and turned back south across the scrub, making toward the East Coast Railroad tracks and the little settlement of Bayard, which consisted of a railroad stop, a storage barn, Wing's General Store, and an icehouse. The boys rode on, the perspiration streaming from beneath their strawhats and down the sides of their sunburned faces.

At the cabin, Little Ella sat beside her mother in the small room. Her face was hot in the breathless summer air, and her gingham dress stuck to her little body, and her black curls hung wet around her forehead. Her mother moaned, and the girl dipped the cloth once more in the basin and wiped her face. She held a cup of tepid water to her lips, urging, "Drink, Mama, drink." Ella raised her head and sipped and fell again into fevered oblivion.

Late that afternoon, the boys, Jake and Clarence, returned riding side by side, carrying something between them. They reined their horses to the wooden walkway between the main house and the kitchen, dismounted, and heaved an object in a corn sack heavily onto the back porch. Tom appeared quickly with a bowl, and the boys began to chip away at the fifty-pound block of ice they had carried through summer heat across fifteen miles of northeast Florida woods to their sick mother.

Inside, Ella could not of her own volition move, yet she felt she was in the grip of some great hot whirlpool, spinning her round and round and down to greater and greater depths. It was dark and it was light, and it was dark again and it was light again. And Jake's handsome face appeared before her, and he was saying something to her, but his words seemed muffled, and she tried to tell him she didn't understand, but the effort was too great, so she closed her eyes. Something icy slashed through the barriers of her hot and fretful sleep and touched her forehead and trickled down her burning cheeks and into her hair. Her eyes opened, and Jake was there again, smiling and holding something to her lips. It was cold. Cold. Colder than anything she had ever felt. And she drank, and Ella's fever began to break.

When Ella had strengthened, Tom drew a basin of water from the well and brought it to the bedroom for her to bathe. He placed her arms around his neck and raised her to her feet. Her legs quivered weakly beneath her. Carefully, he helped her remove the cotton gown, wet with perspiration in the July heat. Ella bent and dipped the cloth in the tepid water and looked down for the first time in many days at her naked body and was shocked by the appearance of her arms and legs, wasted by her illness. She raised her head and peered into the mirror hanging over the dressing table at her drawn face and graying hair, matted, damp, and clinging to her head. Stepping closer, she looked beneath her breast at her belly, protruding slightly with the baby inside her. "What's this?" she said to Tom when she spied a red rash peppering her abdomen. Holding Tom's arm, she walked precariously to the light of the open window and saw that her entire body was lightly mottled. "What's this all over me?" Fear forced her voice higher than its usual soft, low range. Tom looked at her. "I don't know. . . . I don't know. . . . just that fever and this heat made you break out, I reckon. It ain't nothing. It'll go away in a day or two." They both pushed the thought of the rash into the far corners of their minds, where it remained an unspoken fear.

Ella bathed and dressed in a clean cotton dress and walked to the front porch to sit on the steps of the cypress cabin. The smells of new summer grasses, honeysuckle blooms, and ripening grapes and a myriad of other pungent scents combined to sweeten the warm July air. She breathed deeply, closed her eyes, and sat healing in the sun, gathering her strength.

Seven months later, in February, Ella lay in that bed again with arms extending behind her, gripping the bottom of the carved mahogany headboard and bearing down to bring into the world her tenth child. At her feet, Aunt Jenny, the old mulatto from Zack Hayman's turpentine still at Twenty Mile, sat mumbling comfort and waiting momentarily to catch the baby now crowning. On the other side of the bedroom door, in the parlor, Tom and the children waited, helplessly listening to Ella's groaning and the low mumbling voice of the older woman. The loud ticking of the clock on the mantel marked the minutes, and Tom, in sudden fits of anxiety and impatience, would put his head through the bedroom door and demand report of progress on the other side. The mulatto would nod and smile and shake her head, her yellow skin glowing in the lamplight. "Not yet, Mistah Tom. Not yet." The fire in the fireplace would dwindle, and one of the boys would heave on another log. Little Hugie was crumpled in a corner sleeping, the firelight dancing on his yellow curls.

He awakened to his mother's intensifying groans and Aunt Jenny's voice coming louder from the bedroom. "You push, Miz Ella, that baby's coming. Heyah it is! Heyah it is! You gots another gayal, Miz Ella." The baby screamed, and as Tom opened the door, he saw Ella lying quietly on the bed and Aunt Jenny tying off the bloody naval cord. "You got another baby gayal, Mistah Tom. You better get that warm water here so I can wash this baby off." Tom called for Little Ella, and she came with the pan of warm water that had been warming on the hearth. The baby cried. "All right, little sistah, all right! Aunt Jenny goin' to give you to your mama directly." The old woman deftly handled the tiny baby and wrapped her in a clean flannel blanket.

The baby was crying when Aunt Jenny handed her to Ella. The mother held the infant closely in her arms, but the crying did not cease. Opening the neck of her gown, she put the baby to her breast. Finally, the panicky screams of the baby slowed, and a hush fell on the room. The infant nuzzled and began to suck. Tom sighed as Ella looked at him with relief in her soft brown eyes. The old woman bent over her and smiled, her golden brown color contrasting with Ella's face, drained and even whiter than usual. "She's fine. She's a fine baby gayal."

But then the baby began to cry again and gag. Ella put it to her shoulder, gently patted its tiny back, and then placed it once more at her breast. Again the baby sucked and gagged and cried. Aunt Jenny took the baby and began to walk up and down the room, patting and singing, "Now hush, little baby, don't you cry."

In the parlor, the rest of the family waited for the commotion to settle so that they could see their mother and their new baby sister. After a few minutes, Jenny's soothing, swaying song quieted the tiny girl, and she slept. Jenny placed her gently beside Ella, and one by one, the children came into the room to gaze at the sleeping woman and child.

The sun was painting the sky in rosy hues that early morning when the mulatto left the Oesterreicher place and began to walk down the white sand road to her shack two miles away at the still. Tom fell into the bed beside his sleeping wife and their newborn baby. But as Aunt Jenny's gaunt little figure disappeared around the bend in the road and into the cold shadows of that February morning, the baby jerked in Ella's arms and wailed aloud. Tom reached his hand across his wife to the back of the baby and gently patted it, hoping to rest his heavy eyes for just a few more minutes. But it was useless. The tiny infant continued to cry. And Ella looked at Tom, communicating to him that unspoken fear.

The baby cried, but none of Ella's instincts could fathom its need and give it comfort. She would place it at her breast, and for those first few hours, it only gagged. After a couple of days, though, when Ella's milk came in, the baby would suck and spit the blue-white fluid from its mouth. Tom would cradle the writhing form in his arms and walk her and walk her. Little Ella sat in the chair by the fire and rocked her baby sister. At times, the tiny girl would quiet down and sleep, but over and over, she would jerk and wake and cry, as though in some unseen grip of pain.

Tom sent for Aunt Jenny, but none of the woman's experience with little black babies and little white babies could help solve the Oesterreicher infant's dilemma. The furrows in Tom's forehead deepened with fear for his baby girl, and the circles around Ella's brown eyes turned ashen from sleeplessness and from the nagging knowledge that her daughter's minute frame was diminishing in her arms. Hot tears ran down the woman's cheeks, and she prayed to God for the life of her baby. "Tom, get a doctor! Go get a doctor!" And the dark fear hidden in the secret corners of their hearts since the days of Ella's fever loomed up and engulfed them both. "Get a doctor, Tom! My baby's dying!"

Pulling on a canvas jacket, Tom whispered something softly to Aunt Jenny, rushed to the stable, saddled his horse and mounted, but then paused for a moment looking at the cabin, almost dreading to leave. He turned toward the western field that sloped into the dark thick growth of Durbin Swamp. His oldest son was chopping wood beside the kitchen, and Tom yelled to him, "Jake,

I'm cuttin' across Durbin to Bayard to see if I can get a doctor from Jacksonville out here by tonight. The baby ain't no better."

Jake looked at his father as though he had lost his mind. "Lord, Pa! That horse will bog down in that place!"

"Maybe not. We ain't had rain for several weeks. It might be dry enough. If not, I'll walk the son of a bitch across."

The young man watched until his father had entered the outer edges of the swamp. "God!" he thought, "God!"

Tom pushed into the swamp. He guided the horse carefully, avoiding the lower wet places. Occasionally, he would come upon a small stretch of high open ground, and he would gouge his heels into the sides of his horse and spur him faster, only to be confronted once more by bog and water and thick masses of tangled trees and swamp. Several times, he dismounted the horse and led him through the wet, soft terrain. Finally, as he looked ahead, he saw the ground sloping more deeply and knew the horse could go no farther. Finding the highest ground, he tied the horse and waded on foot into the muddy bogs of Durbin, being careful to keep the sun at his back. "Don't want to get turned around in this place," he thought.

Bayard was only four miles away by this shortcut, yet Tom had never taken this route. Most of the year, it was too wet, with the low areas neck-deep in water and the earth too soft to carry the weight of a horse. He had gambled that the dry spell of the last months had dried out the swamp. If he made it across Durbin to Bayard, he could probably get a doctor from Jacksonville out to his house by nightfall. If he had to turn and go back around Durbin, he would lose time, and the doctor might not get there until the next morning. That could be too late. The bogs steamed in the cold air, and the mist drifted up amid huge languid water oaks and tall slender cabbage palms, seeking their places in the sun in the thick tangle of Durbin Swamp. Tom ran and waded and listened to the pounding of his heart and the sound of his brogans breaking the suction of the thick black mud. His hot panting breath turned to fog and streamed behind him, mingling with the other mists of the place.

Tom reached the general store at Bayard and called a doctor, arranging to meet him that afternoon at Durbin Station, a stop on the East Coast Railroad that was six miles farther south than Bayard and eight miles closer to the Oesterreicher place by horse and buggy. He left the small settlement and trotted on foot down the track toward the place where he had emerged from Durbin. He was almost fifty years old, and his asthmatic lungs felt as though they would cave in from the exertion and from the chilling air he was gasping so deeply. His canvas trousers, still wet and muddy, were rubbing his legs raw, and his sodden brogans were like icy weights on his numbing feet.

As Tom approached the cabin from across the western field, he saw smoke rising from the chimney, but there was no other movement outside. He reined his horse at the kitchen porch, dismounted, walked quietly to the back door, and stood listening. There were no sounds—in a house full of children, there were no sounds. And the baby was not crying. That fear pounded in his chest and brain as he carefully pulled the door open and peered down the narrow hall.

In the parlor sat Aunt Jenny, rocking slowly, eyes closed, humming softly. Hugie, encircled in Jake's arms, broke and ran to Tom, clutching at his father's waist, crying. Tom looked down at his little son's red eyes and wet cheeks and then at his older boys seated on the hand-hewn cypress bench beneath the window, their faces black and pained. Jake shook his head at his father in a wordless communication of tragedy. His three younger daughters huddled in the corner, crying silently. Aunt Jenny just rocked and hummed, never opening her eyes. Tom gently pulled little Hugie from him and walked to the door of his bedroom.

Ella was there, propped against the great carved mahogany headboard of her bed, her head bent over the tiny baby cradled in her arms. Tom couldn't see her face, and the sound of his footsteps didn't move her. He stood beside her, his trousers still damp and cold against his legs from his trek through Durbin Swamp. He reached his hand toward her shoulder and said her name. Slowly, she raised her head and looked full into his face, and the pain in his wife's soft brown eyes pierced him to his heart. Loosening Ella's rigid arms, Tom took the tiny body of his baby girl, still soft and warm, and held her to his face, enfolding her high in his arms. The tears ran down his cheeks as he fell to his knees beside his wife, and the two wept. Hugie stood wordless at the door, and the image of his parents' anguish was etched forever in his mind.

The pale dawn of the next morning was slowly breaking over the cypress cabin when Hugie first opened his eyes in the shadowy light of his room. He rose and followed the low sounds of voices. When he entered the living room, he saw his mother, leaning against the frame of the front door. She was barefoot and wearing her white cotton nightgown. Around her, draping her body, she had pulled a patchwork quilt for warmth. Her long dark hair with its silver strands streamed uncombed about her shoulders and accented the empty, haggard look in her face and eyes. She stood motionless, watching Tom hoist a small narrow wooden box up to Jake and Clarence on horseback. The two young men looked at their mother, nodded, kneed their horses, and began to move slowly down the white sand road toward Samson Cemetery, the narrow wooden box between them.

> I don't know why she died.
> Babies just died in those days.
> Nobody knew why.
> Doctors didn't even know.

—Hugie Oesterreicher, 16 March 1984

Hugie's Education

"Tell me, Papa, if you could change one thing about your life,
what would it be?"
" . . . I'd get an education. I would."

—Hugie, 4 December 1984

On a December morning in 1905, Hugie nestled into the mattress and pulled the quilt over his cold ears. Warmth emanating from George's body beckoned the little boy closer to his older brother. As he crossed the expanse of cold sheets between them, a shudder passed through his little frame. Then, wrapping himself around his brother's wiry body, he dozed warmly against him. Only minutes had passed when, outside the low bedroom door, he heard the soft footsteps of his mother moving toward the kitchen. Raising himself quickly, he jerked a large share of the quilt with him, exposing George's body to the cold air of the room.

"What you doing?" George moaned.

"Time to get up. We got school," Hugie said, reaching for the new canvas britches his mother had made him on her treadle sewing machine. "Let's get going."

In the dark, the seven-year-old boy reached under the bed for his shoes and socks. After finding them, he quickly pulled on the socks and felt with his leathery little hands the shapes of his shoes, deftly pulling them onto his feet and lacing them painfully with his freezing fingers. Hurriedly he pushed through the back door of the cabin, moving through the cold dark morning toward the warmth of the kitchen. He stopped on the outside walkway for a moment; the icy air stung his face and nostrils as he took a deep breath and looked up at the stars paling in the rosy light that was creeping over the sky. Bending over the water bucket on the back porch of the kitchen, he put his hand into it and poked with his finger, trying without success to break the hard covering of ice formed during the previous night. Balling his fist, he crashed through to the freezing water beneath. Then, with the water cupped in one hand, he splashed his face, shuddering as the last remains of sleep fled. Entering the kitchen, he found his mother standing over the stove browning sausage links in the iron frying pan. The sides of the cast-iron stove were glowing red from the fierce little fire inside, and Hugie stepped beside it, slowly turning to warm his entire body.

Shortly after breakfast, Hugie and George ran down Old King's Road toward the little school, which sat in a cleared place beneath a grove of trees a couple of miles from the Oesterreicher cabin. The school was a one-room wooden structure that provided education through the eighth grade. Some of the students were from migrant families that worked at the nearby sawmills, but most were from local families that lived in scattered parts of the Diego Plains area and neighboring Palm Valley.

When Hugie and George arrived at the grove, smoke was billowing from the chimney of the schoolhouse, and several children were outside skidding pinecones across a frozen pond. Hugie liked school. He liked being with children other than his brothers and sisters. But most of all, he liked learning. In this small classroom, he was exposed to math and reading, and his sharp young mind absorbed everything that went on there. The songs and poems Hugie heard made an indelible impression. And in those young years, Hugie began a practice he maintained all the days of his life. If he liked a particular song or poem, he would commit it to memory, and he would keep it always. Years later, when Hugie was an old man, something would trigger his memory, and the words of some nameless song or poem would roll from his mouth—lines by Longfellow or Whitman, a verse of the Bible, or an old folk ballad. So Hugie loved school and always recalled with enthusiasm his brief experience with formal education.

Later that day, after Hugie and George had returned from school, the family gathered around the supper table and listened to Tom tell stories. This too was part of Hugie's education. Tom loved telling tales, such as family histories and Civil War stories, but most of all, Hugie's father enjoyed sharing hunting lore. After a few family stories on that December evening, though, Tom started talking business. "We got a big order for palms. Going to take all of us to fill it," he said, looking at his boys. He caught Hugie's eye.

"Me too?" Hugie asked, excited at the thought of being included with his older brothers.

"Yeah," Tom said, "you too."

Hugie grinned, not understanding that becoming part of the family workforce meant that his formal education had for the most part come to an end. To him, at that time, helping his father and older brothers cut palms meant only that he was gaining their acceptance as an equal.

For the Oesterreichers, cutting palms in the late winter and early spring months added hundreds, sometimes thousands, of dollars a year to the family's income. Each winter, orders came from the nation's churches for fresh-cut palm buds for the celebration of Palm Sunday, one week before Easter Sunday. And each year, the Oesterreichers, along with other families from the area, cut palms by the thousands, packed them in bunches of twenty-five or fifty, and carried them to Durbin Station on the East Coast Railroad, where they were picked up by the train and shipped to churches all over the United States. Later, after the Intracoastal Waterway was finished in 1912, the Oesterreichers carried the stacks of palms to a dock on the canal, where they were picked up by the *Navajo* or the *Alamo,* two packet boats that hauled freight between Miami and Jacksonville over the new waterway.

The year Hugie was seven years old, he spent the Christmas holidays digging sweet potatoes and anticipating his palm-cutting excursions into the woods with his father and brothers. On the days he finished his chores early, he would frolic in the brisk winter air, chasing birds with his bow or slingshot. And when January arrived, it was palm season.

The first morning, Hugie was full of excitement as he climbed with his brothers into his father's cart and began the trek down Old King's Road to Cabbage Swamp, where there were thousands of cabbage palms. As they neared the grove sheltering the schoolhouse, Hugie sat up in the cart listening, intently watching for some of his friends or Mrs. Browning. When they passed the schoolhouse, the young boy peered through the darkness of early morning at the little whitewashed building. No sounds came from the building, no light glowed in the windows, and no smoke streamed from the chimney. "No one here yet," he thought, sinking back into a corner of the wagon, "too early."

The cart creaked beneath the shadows of the cabbage palms and live oaks and past knotted masses of loblollies. It groaned as they passed through the low-lying wet areas. When Tom halted the horse, the boys jumped out and looked around at the swamp in the rosy morning light. They gathered their tools as Tom issued directions. Hugie's job was to gather into bundles the palms cut by his older brothers. The boy followed Jake as he made his way east. Jake carried a long pole with a clip on the end, which was designed to enable a man to move from tree to tree plucking the young tender buds from each palm. Each of the young men worked rapidly, while Hugie trailed behind them, diligently picking up the palm buds, straightening them, and putting them into piles. He didn't want to give his father and older brothers any occasion to tease him for not doing the job right or for lagging behind.

The sun was getting low and the shadows long in Cabbage Swamp before Tom and his sons began to gather the bunches of palms into their arms and carry them to the cart. The joint effort of the day's work had accumulated a cart heaped high with young tender palm buds. The boys and Tom climbed with muddy rubber boots and wet canvas britches into the cart and prodded the horse with his burdensome load forward through the boggy swamp. Whenever the cart bogged down and the horse balked, the boys climbed down and walked alongside, through the mucky terrain. Sometimes they would put their shoulders to the back of the cart and heave, helping the horse propel the load through the lowlands. Eventually, they reached the high dry pine flats, and the boys jumped onto the cart, now moving swiftly toward the white sand of the Old King's Road as the horse entered an anxious trot at the prospect of going home. "It's a funny thing about horses," Hugie mused to himself. "They get so excited about getting back home." He wondered what it would be like to turn a horse from the barn once he had it in his head he was going in that direction.

The sun was sinking behind the trees and dusk was settling over the woods when the cart turned onto the familiar road home. Hugie, lying exhausted on the pile of palms, turned his head and peered over the side of the cart into the shadows of the grove surrounding the schoolhouse. He looked and listened. There were no sounds of laughing children from the schoolyard, no light gleaming from the windows, and no smoke streaming from the chimney. "Too late," he thought, "they all gone home." And a vague twinge in his heart made him feel a little empty. He turned from the dark grove of trees and looked down the road that led to the little cypress cabin resting quietly on the slope at the edge of Durbin Swamp.

Hugie didn't go to school that spring of 1906. In fact, after that he only attended school in the fall sessions. Each year, after Christmas, during the late winter and early spring months, he worked beside his father and brothers deep in the woods and swamps of northeast Florida, cutting palms for the nation's churches, penning cattle, and planting the spring crops.

The Hunt

I went to going in the woods deer hunting with my daddy. I had a little shotgun, and I killed a deer when I was about ten or eleven years old. First deer. I can show you where I killed him today.

—Hugie, 4 February 1984

ABOVE THE BLACK silhouette of the palm trees in Cabbage Swamp, the moon flooded the evening sky with golden light. On the front porch of the Oesterreicher cabin, the men had gathered to share their hunting stories. "That ol' buck, he thought he'd got clear of me, and I ducked back around that tie-tie bay . . . ," Clarence's voice rose above the others and drifted through the open windows of the parlor where Ella mended stockings by lamplight.

And Tom's voice, " . . . and yonder comes that ol' yellow dog. That was the ugliest dog I ever seen, but there wasn't a hog could escape him. And he grabbed that ol' razorback by the ear, and that ol' boar hog swinging his neck, tusks flashing this way and that, and that ol' yellow dog wouldn't let go. And me and Bill Mickler come running up there. . . . "

And Hugie sat there peering through the shadows into the moonlit faces of his father and brothers. He wanted to tell a story too, but he didn't have a story to tell.

Then, one summer evening, Tom brought out a single-barrel shotgun and gave it to Hugie, saying, "Here, son, you take this shotgun. Put away that BB gun." The lamplight shone on the boy's blond curls, and his deep blue eyes gleamed with excitement as he reached for the prize. The wood was smooth in his hard little hands, and the steel was cold beneath his fingertips when he ran them over the barrel of his own gun.

Several weeks later, Hugie lay in bed waiting for the other members of his family to stir. The house was still dark, and although the rains the night before had cooled the August air, it had also raised the mosquitoes. The blackness around him was alive with their droning sounds. A movement from his father's room signaled him to rise, and something in his blood surged so that his heart beat faster. "We're going hunting!" Quickly, he pulled on his canvas britches and cotton shirt and pushed through the back door to retrieve his brogans off the porch.

Almost instantly, the house was alive with young men moving toward the kitchen. Ella was already there, heating coffee and biscuits over the flame in the wood stove. Hugie grabbed a plate from a wooden shelf and took a couple of biscuits and doused them with cane syrup. He poured boiling coffee in a cup and found a place on the bench at the table made of eight-foot planks of lightwood. The light from the kerosene lamp flickered over the faces of the young men gathered for the day's hunt. They never grew tired of it. The excitement never waned. Tom sat at the end of the table, his head tilted back slightly, silently watching his boys eat their breakfast. Clarence, Jake, and Thomas were in their early twenties, George was in his late teens, and Hugie was eleven years old. Anticipation of the hunt charged the air.

After breakfast, Tom and the boys moved to the stables and saddled the horses. Hugie saddled Jenny, the donkey his father had given him the year before. They mounted and moved quietly away from the cabin, heading north across ground sodden from the heavy rains of the night before. The woods would be under water. Jenny trotted briskly behind the large horses as the boy prodded her to keep up. His shotgun lay crosswise in front of him.

They traveled the Old King's Road, skirting the edge of Durbin Swamp to avoid as much water as possible. The rising sun turned the forest's blackness to a dull gray. The birds moved in the trees overhead, squirrels scampered from branch to branch, and small animals scurried across the path before the approaching horses' feet. As morning spread over the Diego Plain, wild animals were beginning to feed, and everywhere there was life.

When the men had reached the head of Durbin, some three and a half miles from the house, they spread out in different directions. Clarence, Jake, and Tom had the dogs with them. Hugie jumped from Jenny, removed her saddle, and tied her to a nearby tree. He was on his own. He stood staring at the gray stillness of Durbin Swamp, looking for a place to make his stand and wait. He was not afraid. He was part of these woods and, from his earliest days, had spent hours riding on the front of his father's horse through the swamps and forests, listening to Tom's comments and observing everything around him as he rode.

He moved quietly into Durbin. The thick black mud oozed over his shoes, and the wet underbrush scraped against his canvas pants. Above him soared the huge gray cypress trees. His father said they were very old. He wondered if they had been there when the Spaniards first came to Florida, or maybe even before the time of Christ. And the stumps—there were stumps seven feet across peering above the black waters—how old had they been when some lumber company had cut them down? As Hugie pressed into the tangle of swamp, the mud grew softer where he approached a run of water he knew must drain into Box Branch and Pablo Creek at the head of Durbin. He waded in, his shotgun still resting with its barrel pointing upward to the skies, now full of light. The water reached the tops of his brogans, and then he felt the cool wetness seep around his toes inside his shoes. He moved on, and the black water curled around his knees. With one more step, he was waist deep. Instinctively he raised his gun shoulder high and pulled his feet through the black water across the muddy bottom of the run and sloshed to the other side. Beyond the bank of the run, a tall cypress rose above a grassy field clear of trees and underbrush. He made his way to the tree and took his stand there and waited, his eyes and ears alert to every sound.

Squirrels chucked overhead, but he was not after squirrels that day. He waited. The mosquitoes droned, and occasionally, the boy brushed one from his face. An osprey glided to its nest high in the cypress, and as the sun climbed in the sky, the wet woods began to steam in the late summer heat.

His britches dried crusty with the mud from the bog through which he had passed, and a little band of sweat formed above his lips and around his forehead, wetting his blond curls and trickling into his eyes as he squinted in the bright noon sun. The field became a blur from the sweat and bright light in his eyes. Scrunching his shoulder upward, he wiped his eyes and mouth with the sleeve of his shirt and pulled the brim of his strawhat lower to shade his eyes from the glare.

More time passed, and the young hunter waited.

Finally, when the sun was high in the sky, he heard a dog baying in a chase. Hugie tensed and then took a deep breath. Utter calm and assurance engulfed the boy. The dogs drew near, approaching from the west toward the field guarded by the tall cypress and the boy. "He will break through any minute," Hugie thought, raising his shotgun and lowering his cheek so that he peered down the gleaming steel of the barrel.

He cocked the hammer. The yelping dogs screamed in his ears. His hands were steady. And then the deer, a young buck in panicked flight before the dogs, leaped and bounded toward the run of water on the far side of the field. Hugie's finger felt the trigger on the shotgun and followed the moving deer with its barrel. He had a place behind its ear in his sights. He squeezed the trigger. The roar of the gun shattered around him. The deer fell.

When the dogs broke into the clearing, they had stopped barking. Hugie stood for a minute. The field was silent. The birds, the squirrels, everything stopped. And then, in the distance, he heard voices calling. He ran to the animal, the dogs whining around him.

He had killed him. He had killed the deer.

With one hand, he wiped the sweat from his face, and with the other, he reached for his knife in the pocket of his britches. He knew what to do. He slipped the sharp instrument deep into one side of the animal's throat and moved the blade through the soft hide. Blood spurted out onto the wet earth beneath him. When the bleeding had slowed to a trickle, Hugie took his knife and skinned the four legs to the knees and tied them with the hide hind to fore, crisscross fashion. Kneeling down, he hoisted the animal, young and small like himself, onto his shoulders. He picked up his gun and headed toward the run of water he had crossed that morning. An osprey soared above him.

Approaching the place he had left Jenny tied on the outer edges of Durbin, he saw his father and brothers galloping toward him on the horses. As they spied Hugie and his buck draped round his shoulders, they let out a tremendous hoot and holler. Their baby brother had killed a deer, and he was not a baby anymore.

Jake jumped from his horse and ran to Hugie, and soon all of the boys were around him, laughing as they lowered the slain deer from the young boy's shoulders, slit its belly, and took out its entrails. And then Jake dipped his hand into the bloody cavern of the animal's body and said, "Hey, Hugie! Look at that!" As Hugie turned toward his brother, Jake's blood-covered hand smeared the boy's face with the thick crimson. Again, all of the young men laughed and hooted at the bloody christening of their youngest brother. Hugie stood there smiling at his acceptance, the blood seeping into his thick brown brows and down the sides of his cheeks.

That night, Ella sat by lamplight tatting a piece of Spanish lace and listening to the menfolk gathered on the front porch recounting the exploits of the day. And Hugie's voice rose above the others, " . . . and I heard those dogs coming—*yap! yap! yap!*—and I knew they had them a deer, and they was heading my way. And I put my gun to shoulder and just waited. And sure enough, out they come from the thicket, and I just put my sights right on that li'l ol' buck. . . . " A smile flickered across her face.

The Woodsman

Since I couldn't get an education, I went to be a woodsman,
so I could go anywhere I wanted to go in the woods and do
anything there was to be done in the woods. . . . I've done it all.

—Hugie, 4 December 1984

HUGER OESTERREICHER WAS eleven years old the day he rode Jenny out
of the woods carrying the first of hundreds of deer he would kill in his
eighty-nine years of life. Under the apprenticeship of his father and older
brothers, he was becoming a woodsman.

What this meant in the early part of this century in northeast Florida was
hunting, not only to put meat on the family table but to track the wild hogs
called razorbacks to be butchered or sold alive at the stockyard. Woodsmen
trapped animals and sold their fur. They caught alligators and rattlesnakes and
sold them alive to zoos. Florida woodsmen spent days in the swamps in the
spring of each year cutting palms. They raised their cattle and hogs off the
area's abundant acorns, berries, and marsh grasses. Hugie had to learn how to
frame a house, build a chimney, and dig a well from the materials available in
the forests. And finally Hugie, like all woodsmen, learned to be a healer, who
used various folk remedies to cure himself, his family, and his livestock.

A woodsman in the early 1900s in northeast Florida could face sudden life-
threatening circumstances any day of his life. Consequently, each of the Oesterreicher boys carried a pistol in a holster at his side. They each always had a rifle
or shotgun close by for hunting, but the instant accessibility of their pistols
saved their lives many times.

One of these times occurred when Hugie was thirteen years old, the year
he and his brothers were hired to assist a crew surveying land for John Pitt,
a neighboring landowner whose holdings stretched into Durbin Swamp. No
other men knew the swamp as well as Tom Oesterreicher and his sons, who
lived on the outer fringes of Durbin and hunted it regularly. In the spring of
1911, Hugie had been in the swamp for days pulling the chain for the surveyors.
In ideal conditions, a man pulled the hundred-foot half-inch steel tape to the
right location and then put down a pin marking the distance before pulling the
chain another hundred feet, gradually measuring and marking off the acres and
miles. But in Durbin, the undergrowth was an annoying hindrance, forcing
Jake and Clarence to move ahead, clearing the way with axes. Often Hugie

wouldn't pull the chain more than five feet before he hit a tree and the surveyors would have to move in with their instruments and take another sighting.

Day after day, the young boy forded neck-deep bogs and felt the mucky earth give way beneath his feet as he stepped into alligator holes. He had seen moccasins slither past him in the water and alligators scramble to the slimy banks, clearing the way for the men invading their place. He had seen his arms black with mosquitoes. And when he wasn't in a bog, watching lest he step directly on an alligator and risk rousing the creature to attack, he was being slapped in the face by branches and briars and all manner of underbrush.

Late one afternoon, just before the sun slipped behind the blue palmetto hammock on the western horizon and just before the first whippoorwill's call echoed across the swamp, Hugie realized he was tired. The surveyors were ready to mark off a corner and go home for the day. Most of the men had fanned into the woods to find heart pine or some other hardwood with which to make a spike that could be expected to last for several years in that wet region. Hugie looked for a dry place to sit down, his muscles aching as he moved toward a tuft of tall marsh grass growing directly in front of him. He had learned that mud collects and builds up around the roots of marsh grass and that those tufts are likely to be drier than the surrounding lower terrain. The sweat streamed into the young boy's eyes, and the rising clouds of mosquitoes droned in his ears as he began to lower his tired body onto the grass. But at the last second, he stopped in midair, hunched in a sitting position. "I don't want to sit here," he thought, "that's where the corner has to be marked. If I sit there, I'll just have to move when Jake and Clarence get back with the marker."

So Hugie didn't sit on that particular tuft, but instead, he moved five feet away to the next protrusion of long green stalks and sank deeply into it, closing his eyes to the red glare of the setting sun. "I could sleep," he thought. And he did, but only briefly. In minutes, his brother Clarence strode past him to the place where the corner of John Pitt's property was to be marked. Hugie raised himself on his elbows watching with heavy eyes while Clarence separated the thick growth of grass on which Hugie had considered resting. And then the boy saw his brother jump back and reach for his pistol. In front of him was a great snake, coiled, his neck and head flared, ready to strike. And in the instant before he heard the pistol fire and saw the head of the snake jerk back and explode from the impact of the bullet, Hugie heard it sing its rattles. Then it was dead.

Hugie felt sick. He had almost sat on that rattlesnake. It would have bitten him for certain. And nothing would have saved him. No dog, no hog, no cow, no human survives a rattlesnake bite. If a man isn't alone in the woods, a companion might cut across the fang marks and suck with his own mouth to draw the venom from the blood of the victim, but the venom moves so quickly through the veins of a man who is already overheated from the exertion of hunting or working in the woods that the most heroic efforts are not likely to extract enough venom to save a person's life. And then the person sucking the venom and blood is risking death if the poison reaches a sore or cut in his own mouth. No, had he sat in that tuft of grass, he would have died, and there wasn't anything anyone could have done.

By the time Hugie was fifteen years old, he was a crack shot with any kind of gun and had used his pistol several times to save his own life. One time, he had been out by himself on horseback checking a line of traps. One of the last traps he checked held a raccoon, its fur full of mud and in need of washing. Hugie climbed back on his horse and rode north toward the cypress cabin carrying several traps, his rifle, and the muddy raccoon. About eight or ten miles south of his home, he came to Snowden's Bay, a swamp with a run of clean water. "A good place to wash the 'coon," he thought. He reined in the horse and climbed down still holding the traps, the rifle, and the raccoon. His eyes were on the water ahead, not on the path in front of him. Suddenly, his feet were tangled in something, and he lurched to one side to keep himself from falling headfirst to the ground. As he did, he saw the thing that had tripped him: a rattlesnake was coiled around his feet and lower legs. Hugie's heart seemed to explode in his chest; yet, almost with one movement, he threw the traps and rifle at the snake, jumped back, reached for his pistol, and fired at the swollen head of the angry rattler. The snake crumpled at the boy's feet.

On another day, Hugie and George were hog hunting. Their dogs had bayed two hogs in a palmetto patch, but the boys rushed in behind, ignoring the sharp saws of the stalks that cut across their bare arms. The boys carried ropes with which to tie the hogs because they wanted to take the animals alive and fatten them for market. Soon each boy had managed to get behind a hog, wrestle it to the ground, and throw a rope around it. The dogs were bounding all over the palmetto patch, barking with excitement. As Hugie crouched over his hog tying its legs, he gave a swipe with his arm to keep the dogs back from the thrashing tusks of the razorback he had pinned to the ground.

Then it happened. *Zip!* That's all he heard. But in the midst of the commotion of hogs squealing and dogs barking, Hugie's ear had picked up on that sound. Without letting go of the hog, he turned his head, and out of the corner of his eye, he saw it bobbing there, swaying, fangs bared, the head of a huge rattlesnake, coiled, singing its rattles, ready to strike at his back. Hugie reached to the scabbard at his side, pulled out the pistol, and shot off the head of the five-and-a-half-foot snake. He never let go of the hog.

Pistols were a necessity in the northeast Florida woods. Rattlesnakes were everywhere in those days, before most of the woods and underbrush had been cleared. There were always rattlesnakes, and Hugie was always hot and miles from home and usually alone.

But rattlesnakes were not the only threat with which men with Hugie's way of life were faced. Hunting the wild razorback hogs that roamed the Florida woods was dangerous for both a man and his dogs. The animals were named for the stiff tuft of hair growing down the backbone and sticking straight up like a razor, and although most of these hogs were not as large as the domestic strains, they could be mean and quite deadly when cornered by a hunter and his dogs.

The dogs were especially vulnerable. A three- or four-year-old boar, with four-inch-long tusks and a powerful neck, wields his natural weapons like knives, slashing anything in his path with the penetration of a rifle bullet. During a hunt, the dog corners the hog, clamps the hog's ear between its teeth, and holds on until the hunter gets there with a rope to tie the hog. Once, Hugie saw a dog's tail cut off with one sweep of a hog's tusks, but generally, the risks were greater than that. One swipe across the dog's belly from the tusks of a big boar could empty the dog's entrails onto the earth at its feet. Several times, Hugie had managed to save the life of a dog by suturing such a wound right there in the woods. He had worked quickly, shoving the entrails back into the injured animal's abdominal cavity, poking holes on the side of the wound with his pocketknife, and stitching the gash closed with a shoestring from one of his brogans. However, just as often the dogs saved Hugie's life.

In the late spring of 1915, when Hugie was about seventeen years old, he had a dog called Ring, a black cur with a white band around his neck. Ring could hunt anything—hog, raccoon, deer, bear. Ring loved the chase and followed Hugie to the woods every time the boy left home. One morning, Hugie saddled his horse and rode north, skirting the edge of Durbin Swamp. He thought he knew where he would find the old razorback barrow, or castrated male hog, that he and George had altered the spring before. Castration settles a wild boar down so that all he cares about is eating and sleeping, and as a result, its meat is more tender and sweeter than that of a regular boar. Local folks would catch razorbacks, mark them, alter them, and either pen them in a patch to root potatoes or set them free to fatten on acorns and berries. Either way, the barrows would be caught again in the early summer and sold at the stockyards. Since this particular hog had been altered and set free to fatten in the woods, Hugie thought he would be fat enough to bring a good price at the stockyard in Jacksonville. He had to take him alive, though; the hog wasn't worth anything to him dead. Catching and tying a big hog was a hard job for one man, but Hugie had done it before.

Ring followed Hugie as he rode toward an acorn-strewn blackjack ridge where he had seen the tracks of the big barrow the day before. Just as they approached the hammock, Ring spied the hog rooting on the ridge for acorns. The sixty-pound dog let out a yelp and lit out for the hog. As the hog turned, running to the shelter of a laurel bay, Hugie spotted him. He was big, over two hundred pounds. Hugie wanted that hog; it would bring him a good price.

With a rope in one hand and a pistol at his side, Hugie slid from the horse and darted toward the sound of Ring, who had cornered the hog in the thick mat of laurels intertwined across the low, sour ground. Normally tie-tie bays, as the locals called them, were impenetrable to anything but bears or hogs, who burrow under their limbs, which seem tied together. But earlier that spring, a fire had burned out most of this bay, leaving big potholes where the mangled roots of laurels had been. Hugie charged into the mass of charred trunks and branches, jumping over boggy holes, running, trying to catch sight of Ring and the razorback barrow. Then he saw them. The dog had the hog by the ear, holding him until Hugie could get there with his rope.

Hugie grabbed the big barrow by his hind legs and with a strong twisting jerk tried to turn the big animal over and throw it to the ground on its back, but Ring still had its ear and the hog couldn't be thrown. Meanwhile, the hog was backing Hugie across the boggy earth toward a burned-out hole. Hugie gave another jerk to throw the hog, and Ring let loose of its ear. But just at that moment, Hugie stepped backward into the hole, losing his balance as his right leg went hip deep into mire. For a second, his grip loosened, and the hog wrenched away from him. Then the barrow turned on the young man and charged. Hugie went down, unable to move. The hog was right in the boy's face slashing with its sharp tusks. It made a powerful pass at Hugie's belly, but Hugie managed to free his left hand and hit the hog on the snout, dislocating its aim. As the big hog moved to strike again, Ring jumped back in the fray, latching onto the hog's ear and disabling him long enough for Hugie to scramble out of the hole. The hog got away that time. But Ring had saved Hugie's life.

Within the year, though, Ring was dead, a victim of razorback tusks, killed when he rushed another hog that Hugie was holding by its hind legs. The hog gave a powerful jerk of his head and stabbed Ring in the heart with its tusk. The dog gave one whimper and fell at Hugie's feet, blood gushing from the mortal wound.

But as deadly as the razorbacks of Durbin Swamp were, the Oesterreichers did not want the bears to eat the hogs. Razorbacks were part of their living, and they couldn't afford to lose one to a bear that was just as happy eating berries, acorns, and wild honey.

One evening when Hugie was nineteen years old, he went to bed with a fever. He spent the night in restless sleep, and in the morning, long before daylight, he lay soaked in sweat as the fever started to break. He was only partly aware of the stillness of the woods outside his window and of George's wiry body next to him relaxed in a deep sleep. Rest and dreams came in great gray billows over him; one moment, he was submerged in slumber, but then the billows would ebb away and he would again surface to consciousness. Out of the rising and falling motion of his fevered sleep, he was startled by George, who bolted up in bed.

"I hear something. A hog's squealin'!" George whispered in a hoarse voice.

"You think so?" Hugie asked, raising himself to a sitting position. The billows fell away.

The two young men jumped from their bed and ran to the front porch to listen. In the distance, somewhere near Durbin, a hog was squealing in fear and pain.

"A bear's got a hog!" George panted. "Come on!"

The two young men pulled on their britches and grabbed their guns. As they broke into a trot toward the sounds in the swamp, George was strapping on a battery-operated headlamp. He turned it on, and the woods before them were flooded with light. Sport, a black and tan cur, followed them. When they reached the place of the commotion, the bear, frightened by the light, released his prey and escaped deeper into the swamp. The poor hog ran in a panic in the opposite direction.

"He got away," George sighed.

But then Hugie heard something. Close by them was a water-filled area where a big steam skidder had dragged out logs. Hugie heard the water sloshing. "Shh!" he whispered. "It's the bear! He's coming back!" And the bear sloshed past so close to the two young men that he almost sprayed water on them. He was after the hog again. "A brazen son of a gun!" Hugie yelled as they took up the chase after the bear.

Again, the forest resounded with the squealing of the hog and the growling of the bear. When he and George found them, the bear had the hog with both forepaws, and the hog was fighting to get away. The two men fired as one. At the blast of the shotguns, the bear roared away through the trees with such a tremendous noise that, to the young men, it sounded as though they had roused every bear in Durbin Swamp.

Hugie whooped to the dog as he took chase. Sport darted ahead, running the bear about a hundred yards before he came to bay. "My God, he's got him stopped!" he shouted to George. As they approached, the sounds indicated that Sport had the bear bayed in a patch of palmettos and briars. The young men cocked their guns and pulled the palmettos apart. When they did, they saw Sport barking ferociously at the fallen hulk of the bear, dead on the muddy earth. When Hugie examined the animal, he saw that both he and George had emptied their guns into the heart of the bear and that the creature had run over a hundred yards through the thick swamp with that kind of wound. The strength of the animal awed the young men.

Hugie cured the meat of the bear and stretched its hide on the smokehouse wall. In the months that followed, Ella carved off slabs to fry, to stew, or to season vegetables. Although the Oesterreichers hunted for sport, they did not kill for sport; they used everything.

In those parts, not only wild hogs but also cattle were mainstays to the woodsmen, and folks couldn't tolerate losing a hog to a bear or a cow to a cattle thief. At that time, there were no fences, so everyone's cattle and hogs freely roamed the woods and marshes of the area. Folks were on the honor system. Neighbors didn't kill each other's cattle or butcher each other's hogs. If a hunter accidently killed a hog with someone else's mark, then the hunter would butcher it and take half to the owner. However, killing another person's cow would forever be a black mark on the offender. Hugie almost did that once.

When a hunter uses a headlamp in the woods at night, and the beam of light falls on an animal, he cannot see the whole animal; he can only see the glow of its eyes. Because the eyes of most animals shine in the dark when struck by a beam of light, even the eyes of a tiny spider emit such a glow that an inexperienced hunter will think he has cornered some large prey. But Hugie always said that nothing looks like the eyes of a deer. When he was just twenty-three years old, this conviction saved him considerable grief and humiliation.

While driving some cattle, Hugie had spotted two old bucks in a blueberry patch that stretched for several acres across a ridge on the north end of Durbin. Several times after that, he saw their tracks and knew those deer fed in that place regularly. Late one night, he decided to go looking for them. He saddled a horse, took his rifle, and strapped on a headlamp. On horseback, he moved almost silently northward along the edge of Durbin to the blueberry patch, where he reined in the horse and turned on the light. Instantly, gleaming back at him above the mist just rising from the ground were two pairs of eyes.

"There they are!" he thought raising his rifle to shoulder. But then he hesitated. He wouldn't fire the gun over the horse's head; the blast could startle the animal. Quietly, Hugie slid to the ground, put the reins over his left arm, and raised the rifle again. He had one pair of eyes between the sights. His finger touched the trigger. But then he lifted his head and peered carefully at the eyes gleaming across the field. Something wasn't right about those eyes. Yet they were the right height, they were the right distance apart, they were in the right place. He knew two old bucks were living out of that blueberry patch. So once more he lowered his eye to the sight and put his finger to the trigger. And then once more he pulled away. He couldn't fire.

He walked softly through the blueberry bushes toward the glow. And then one pair of eyes looked away from the light. Hugie saw the animal. It wasn't an old buck. As he moved closer, he realized that he had almost shot two young calves and that they didn't have the Oesterreicher brand. Had he pulled the trigger that night, folks around Durbin would not have forgotten. They would have proclaimed, "Hugie Oesterreicher's killing cattle." He would have become a man to watch, a man undeserving of trust. But he didn't pull the trigger because he had heeded something that went beyond his own logic and reasoning. Hugie had developed intuition, an instinct of the woods that transcended his five physical senses and enhanced the knowledge gained from his father and from his own experience.

By the time Hugie Oesterreicher was twenty-four years old, he could dig a full-grown cabbage palm and carry it on his back or drag it through the swamp to a waiting wagon. He could track any animal through the densest undergrowth. He could wrestle an alligator or catch rattlesnakes alive and carry them in a sack on his back. He could dig a freshwater well without benefit of machinery and curb it with a cypress trunk. He could build a house and construct a chimney with a fine draw. And even on the darkest moonless night, he would not lose his way in Durbin Swamp.

And finally, like all accomplished woodsmen, Hugie practiced the art of healing, coupling a knowledge of the abundant store of home remedies with his own intuition. He had learned that axle grease kept flies off a dog's wound and that bluestone and sulfur cured the ugly scabs and bald spots on a dog with mange. He knew that white oak ashes from the chimney mixed with boiling water purified cuts and cured ground itch and that soaking a nail puncture in kerosene killed tetanus. Caprice killed worms in dogs, and Professor Field's Antibilious Worm Medicine killed them in people. Hugie knew that the cure for a cold was to stay in the house and take a tablespoon of castor oil with ten drops of turpentine and that the cure for asthma was to breath the smoke from a burning mixture of jimsonweed and saltpeter. He knew that, if a splinter couldn't be dug out of a child's foot with a pocketknife, packing the hole with saltpeter made it fester and come out. He knew that when a person was vomiting, the weakest stomach kept down a tea made from the inside peeling of a chicken gizzard and that sometimes the most healing thing a man could do was keep watch in the dark hours of night beside the bed of a sick child. Hugie had learned all these things by the age of twenty-four from listening, from observing, and from experiencing them himself. Hugie had become a woodsman.

And then when Hugie Oesterreicher was twenty-five years old, he saw Oleta Brown.

The Browns

"Tell me, Mama . . . about your family."
"Well, my great-grandmother was a Gamble, and my grandmother was a
Gunter girl. And my mother was Annie Sadler. . . . "

—Oleta, 10 February 1984

OLETA BROWN WAS born to Tom and Annie Brown in January of 1908. The Browns owned a dairy located on the coastal side of the San Pablo River, twenty miles northeast of the Oesterreicher place and a mile inland from the ocean. Old live oaks surrounded the Brown place, and huge boughs with their smaller branches and myriad green leaves twisted gracefully over the silver-gray sand of the yard and the silver tin roof on the house. Some of those boughs stretched like arms of benevolent giants to the earth. And the little ones raised in that house easily reached them climbing barefoot from one great arm to the next. The bark on some of the oaks had become crusty and almost black with age. One tree had been burned in a fire and had a side with no bark at all, and deep inside that particular tree, hidden beneath the bark that folded back from the scar, lived huge blue lizards with red heads. Occasionally, one could be seen sitting on a gnarled root of that tree, warming itself in the morning sun. And through the Spanish moss that dropped in wisps of gray and through the branches and leaves of those trees sheltering the Brown place, sunshine filtered down and sprinkled the yard with light.

Beneath the massive arms of the oaks, the Browns' white frame house stood, raised three feet from the ground on pilings. The house had three bedrooms, a large dining room, a parlor, a kitchen, and an outhouse that stood some distance from the main house. Probably the most pleasing thing about the Brown home, aside from the oaks surrounding it, was the porch that wrapped all the way around and was lined with rocking chairs and pots of various kinds of flowering plants.

Orange trees were scattered southward beyond the oaks, and although most of the orange groves in northeast Florida had been destroyed by bad freezes in 1898 and 1899, this grove, protected by the Browns' massive oaks, had survived. Among the orange trees, Tom kept beehives for honey. Close behind the house, westward, stretched the arbors with black and white scuppernong grapes. Beyond the arbor, at the outer edge of the oak grove, were cow pens and an outbuilding where the Browns milked their dairy cattle and bottled the milk to sell in Pablo Beach. Also within this livestock area, the Browns raised hogs and chickens, as did most people in this part of Florida. West of the dairy lay fields of white sugarcane. North of the live oaks were situated two large barns where the Browns kept several horses, hay, plows, and other farm equipment. North of the barns rose stands of tall pine trees, and in summer, the blackberry bushes beneath those pines were heavy with fruit. With the hogs, cattle, and chickens, the grape arbors, beehives, orange trees, cane fields, and vegetable gardens, the Brown place was almost self-sustaining. Only flour, grits, rice, and coffee beans were purchased.

Beyond the Brown place were the savannahs, areas of swamps, tall grass, and trees. Here tall pines towered over little ponds and grassy glades and over a little wagon road that wound its way from the Brown house through the savannahs to their south field. West of the savannahs were the marshlands and creeks of the San Pablo River, through which the Florida Coastal Canal and Transportation Company had dug the Intracoastal Waterway. The marshlands and creeks lay one to three miles inland from the ocean, paralleling the coast of Florida. Durbin Swamp drained into these creeks and marshes, which had been there since the sea had slipped back to expose the peninsula and whose waters rose and fell with the tides of the ocean. Probably, in ages past, that low marshland had been the last land to appear above the surface of the ocean, and before that time, the coastal areas had been clearly defined barrier islands, like the ones lining the more northerly sections of the Atlantic coast. To the Pablo Beach people, crossing the marshes meant "coming home." In this place, travelers from the mainland first caught the scent of the sea air and first noticed the change in temperature. Ocean breezes blowing across that narrow spit of land between the Atlantic and the marshes cooled it in the summer and warmed it by several degrees in the winter. On their own place, the Browns could stand on their front porch and gaze eastward across the palmettos, miles of thick silvery green spikes barricading the dunes lining the beach, and see the white sails of clipper ships gliding past.

One cold December day in 1907, Annie Sadler Brown stood beneath the oaks washing clothes in a big iron pot. Steam from the boiling water rose up to drench her dark hair and cause the loose strands to curl about her round flushed face. She was washing with soap made from lye that had been mixed with the fat of slaughtered animals, and as it bubbled to the top, the fumes burned her nostrils. Her chubby hands, chapped and cracked from cold and heat, harsh soap and hard work, gripped the large oak paddle as she stirred Tom's white cotton shirts. Laying the paddle aside, Annie took a corner of the white apron extending over her belly and raised it to wipe the steam and sweat from her deep-set brown eyes. Reaching toward a nearby woodpile for a piece of pine, she moved away from the circle of warmth around the huge iron pot. The splinters of the lightwood knot gouged her moist hands, and the pain was excruciating in her quickly numbing fingers in the cold winter air. With one motion, she shoved the wood beneath the pot and raised herself, placing her hands momentarily over the steaming water to warm them. She watched the flame flare beneath and the bubbles rise more swiftly to the top. Then, with the oak paddle, one by one, she fished the shirts from the boiling water and placed them on a large oak stump beside her, where she pounded them until they gleamed white in the Florida sun. Many other days she had stood over an iron pot washing clothes; many other days, as far back as she could remember, she had done backbreaking work. Wash day was only part of it. "A man's work is from sun to sun, but a woman's work is never done," she thought to herself. "If only he would work from sun to sun."

Tom sat on the front porch, still handsome and lean in his starched white shirt with his sleeves buttoned at the cuff, talking business with the boarder for whom Annie cooked and after whom Annie cleaned. She had to raise the family income. They soon would have another mouth to feed, a fact to which Tom seemed oblivious. She was eight months pregnant, and she was almost barefoot. Because her feet were swollen and spreading from the extra weight she carried, her toes were breaking the seams of her one pair of shoes, and the holes long since worn through the soles of those shoes had been reinforced with pieces of deer hide. Looking at the black stockings protruding from the ends of her shoes, she began with her hands to wring the water out of each piece of clothing and place it in a bucket.

Annie did her laundry the same way her mother and her grandmother had done their laundry. They had made their own soap from animal fat and lye. They had made their own sizing from cornstarch or flour. Clothes had had to be boiled and pounded and hung on the line to dry and starched and pressed with heavy cast irons heated over the fireplace or woodstove. They had wrapped rags around the handles of the searing hot tool to protect their hands from burning. Hours of grueling work had always gone into each step, but the result had always been stiff gleaming white ruffles on girls' dresses and stiff gleaming white collars on men's shirts.

Annie gazed again at Tom in the front porch rocker, gesturing amiably to the boarder, his starched shirt reflecting the brightness of the sun, and something in Annie almost hated her fine, handsome husband. She remembered seeing him for the first time when she was a seventeen-year-old girl in the little town of Perry in north-central Florida. And she remembered the first time she had heard of him two years earlier from the old Cajun woman, whose brown hands had fingered a white porcelain teacup as she muttered strange unintelligible things about the man Annie would marry. That year, in 1887, when Annie was fifteen years old and had first heard of this man, she began to envision him without ever having seen him. Her adventure began, though, one day as she was walking down a white sand road lined with tall pine trees and low scrubby bushes, picking blackberries in the woods near Perry. The silver white sand felt warm beneath her feet, and the air was like velvet on her brown face and arms.

Beside the road in front of her, shaded by an aging live oak tree, squatted the shanty of the Cajun woman, Ol' Reni. Ol' Reni had been old as long as Annie could remember, and stories concerning her had drifted about those parts ever since she had appeared there as a young woman. Folks said she was from the bayous of Louisiana and had killed her young husband there. But other stories said she was a witch who practiced black magic, and young folks whispered that they'd heard her cackling and chanting in the woods at night. Ol' Reni made her way midwifing, practicing folk medicine, and telling fortunes.

That day, Annie saw her seated half-dozing on the front step of her shanty, her head leaning against the post that supported the sagging roof. As the girl approached, the ancient woman produced a snuff-stained smile. "Come 'ere, girl," she said, raising her creaking frame from the boards of the step. "Come 'ere!" Her voice still had the musical quality of the bayou people, and the foreign lilt fascinated Annie. "I have somethin' to tell ya." Annie was mesmerized by the eyes of the old woman and excited by the thought of the secrets she might reveal.

She followed Reni into the musty quarters of her shanty. Inside, the only light came from the open doorway, for the one window was covered with the tattered rag of an old quilt. The walls were lined with rickety shelves full of dusty jars, crocks, and tin pots. The only furniture was an unmade bed, a wood-burning stove, and a table with many layers of peeling lacquer, as though it had sat too long in the sun and rain and had been dragged by the old woman to its present position from someone's trash heap.

Reni reached for a thin white porcelain cup, the only one of its kind in the place. Into it she emptied the contents of a brown paper bag. "Tea leaves," Annie surmised. Her heart raced as Reni began muttering unintelligibly in her strange Cajun tongue and then lifted the cup to the light streaming in the doorway. Ol' Reni stopped and looked the girl in the eye. "There'll be a man," she said, piercing Annie with her small black eyes. " 'E'll come to you in a buggy pulled by a white horse. 'E'll be yer husband, 'e'll take you away from 'ere, Annie. You look for 'im. 'E'll come!"

"Yes, ma'am!" Annie gulped as she grabbed her bucket of blackberries and dashed across the boards of the old porch and onto the white sand of the road.

Her face was flushed and wet when she reached the Sadlers' whitewashed cabin. "Ma! Ma!" she screamed as she pushed open the door and rushed to the thin little woman who leaned over the fireplace stirring the contents of a large iron kettle suspended over the flames. "Ma!" she cried, clutching the narrow shoulders of the woman. "Ol' Reni told me something. She told me about a man coming, driving a buggy pulled by a white horse. Ma, he's gonna be my husband. Reni told me to look for him. Oh, Ma, what do you think? Do you suppose it's so?"

Henrietta looked into the hopeful eyes of her young daughter and said with a sigh "Oh, Annie, there ain't no buggies in these parts, honey, and no man fine enough to drive one. I wouldn't put no stock in Ol' Reni's foolishness. She's just crazy and lonely, that's all."

"But, Ma, she read it in the leaves."

"Don't put no stock in it, Annie."

But Annie did put stock in the mutterings of the old woman. She looked and watched and waited. Though the days stretched into weeks and into months, the local boys still held no charm for Annie; they were shabby compared to the vision she had of a fine gentleman driving a buggy drawn by a white horse.

Annie was seventeen when her mother became pregnant again. Henrietta's small frame sagged beneath the weight of the twins she carried, and her face grew haggard from the pressures of tending the other children. Annie did what she could to ease things for her mother.

One day, she stood by the big iron pot, black from the many fires that had burned beneath it, as her mother stirred the laundry. "Go sit down, Ma, I'll do this." Moving her mother to the stump used for pounding, Annie said, "You sit there, and let's sing, Ma, while I stir." They sang, and Annie's gingham dress became soaked with perspiration and steam; they sang, and she pulled her long dark hair into a knot at the back of her head; they sang, and then they stopped. The sound of approaching horses and wheels and men's voices startled them. Annie stood up, wiping the sweat from her eyes and her hot face. Henrietta didn't move from the stump but straightened her back, lifting her hands to shade her eyes from the sun.

Annie gasped. Moving toward them on the dirt road leading to their cabin was a buggy pulled by a white horse. It stopped, and two men got out. Immediately, Annie recognized one of them as her father's brother, Charlie Sadler, a marshal in the small east coast settlement of Pablo Beach. But the other one, the driver of the buggy, she had never seen before. He had soft dark eyes and a meticulously trimmed mustache: He was dressed in a black suit, a black tie, and a white shirt that was starched and buttoned to the cuffs. His tall lean frame towered over Annie.

"Henrietta, Annie," Charlie spoke, "this here is Tom Brown from Pablo Beach, and he was kind enough to drive me over to see you folks." Tom Brown bowed his head and smiled at Annie.

"Like a real gentleman," she thought. And she gave her heart to him—on the strength of that bow and the words of that old Cajun woman.

But twenty years later, in 1907, part of Annie regretted ever entering the old Cajun woman's shanty. Annie was jolted from her reminiscence by the approach of her oldest child, May, a thin wiry girl whose fragile build masked an uncommonly strong physical constitution. "Let me help you hang out those clothes, Ma," the girl said, picking up the large wooden tub of wet laundry and walking to the clothesline stretched between two live oak trees. The December air chilled them and numbed their fingers as they handled the damp clothes. Annie's raw hands ached, and May drew her sweater tighter over her cotton dress.

Tom Brown did work, but he didn't work with all his strength. He worked cautiously, so as not to soil his hands or his clothes, and even in the most intense heat of summer, his cuffs were buttoned at the wrist because "a gentleman doesn't roll up his sleeves." Tom lacked Annie's hardy determination and physical endurance. May knew this and from an early age had tried to compensate for this weakness in order to help her mother and shield her father from Annie's scorn.

That evening, the family sat at the large round oak table with the light from the kerosene lamps casting a golden glow on the faces of the Browns and their boarder. As they sopped their cornbread in the liquor of the few greens from the winter garden, Tom announced that he was going into Jacksonville on business the following morning and would not be back until the next day.

After supper, Annie went to her chiffonnier drawer and pulled out a thin roll of dollar bills, money she had earned feeding and cleaning after the boarder. She returned to the fireplace where Tom sat smoking a pipe. "Will you get me a pair of shoes?" she asked grudgingly. She hated being in this position of dependence on him, for he had disappointed her too many times. But she was in no condition to make the trip into Jacksonville herself and wouldn't be for months. So, even though she hated it, she asked, placing the money gingerly in his long fingers and raising her black skirt enough to show him the condition of her shoes, as though to convince him of the genuine need.

The next morning, he was gone before the children and Annie had finished the first milking. The sun was glistening silver on the vast expanse of palmettos that stretched from the Browns' live oaks to the coastal sand dunes as Tom drove his horse and buggy two miles north to Pablo Beach, where he would catch the train and ride twenty miles into downtown Jacksonville. From the front porch, Annie watched him disappear down the dirt road winding toward the beach until he was a mere black speck bobbing above the silver-green sea of palmettos. Annie sighed and went into the kitchen to stir the coals in the wood-burning stove and begin cooking breakfast for her family.

As May and Asbury, Annie's only son, left in their wagon to deliver milk to the two or three hotels and stores in that coastal settlement, Annie began the laundry sizing process by mixing a big tub of cornstarch with water and placing the previous day's wash in the solution. Then she stretched the starched clothes on the lines to stiffen in the December sun. The work went on endlessly until she climbed alone into her bed that night, exhausted, and lay looking at the dark ceiling. Her sore hands rested on her belly and felt the baby within her kick and change positions. "Not much longer," she thought and sank into the blackness of deep sleep.

The following day was as the one before it, filled with endless chores. She stood ironing for hours at a board padded with old sheets and supported by the dining table and a chair back. Alternating two irons, she kept one heating on the stove while the other was in use. She had a small one for the delicate ruffles and lace on dresses and shirts and a large heavy one for men's trousers and sheets and pillow cases. Everything had to be ironed. Her pelvic bones ached with the weight of the baby, and her feet swelled, bulging from the sides of her shoes.

The hours wore into late afternoon. Annie finished her last piece of ironing and walked to the front porch. She gazed across the palmettos ablaze in the sun's final fiery burst and sank heavily into a rocker. As the sun slipped behind the pine trees bordering the western fields, dusk settled over the Brown place. The cold air was refreshing to Annie, after she had stood beside the fire all day handling the searing irons. "He's late," she thought. "Stayed off all day." Her baby heaved within her, and she changed the position of her buttocks in the rocker's cane seat, trying to accommodate the aches in her back. Her feet throbbed, but she was too tired to lift them and relieve the pressure of fluid pulsing within them. Her head slumped, and she dozed.

The sound of the buggy approaching woke her, and she watched it enter the shadows of the oaks and move toward the barn, where Tom unharnessed his horse and led him to his stall. He walked toward his wife, nodding to her as he stepped up the wooden plank stairs to the front porch. "You look tired, Annie," he said, patting her arm.

"Yes, Tom, I'm tired. Did you get my shoes?" Tom looked away, out across the palmettos, and hesitated before answering her. "No, Annie, I'm sorry, I couldn't. We'll have to wait 'til next trip."

She looked at him, and hate and revulsion for her husband welled up within her. "Well, give me my money back then!" she demanded, trying to control her indignant rage.

"I don't have it, Annie, I had to use it for something else."

Annie placed her hands on the arms of the rocker and raised herself to a standing position, glaring into Tom's face, her dark eyes full of disgust. "Damn you!" she said in a barely audible voice, and then with all the contempt that had built up during all those disappointing years, she said, "Damn you, Tom Brown, I'll never ask you for anything else again as long as I live." She left him and joined May, who was cooking supper in the kitchen. At that moment, a resolve began to form itself in Annie Sadler Brown.

Two weeks later, she had a baby girl and named her Oleta, after an Indian princess she had read about in the newspaper. She was Annie and Tom's last child. After that, all of Annie's love went to that baby girl, and all of her strength went to making the Brown dairy a success. She had resolved never to ask Tom for anything else again, and she never did. She worked herself and her older children relentlessly. Tom took less and less responsibility. After the incident on the porch that evening, she never encouraged Tom to touch her again. Nor, after that, did he attempt it.

The Kittens

We had these tall palmettos growing out in front of our house, out
beyond the oaks. The hogs tunneled trails beneath those palmettos.
And when I was five years old, I had an old mother cat that went
out there and found kittens. Out there under those palmettos.

—Oleta, 16 February 1984

BECAUSE OLETA WAS eight years younger than the youngest of the other
five children and was part of a family in which all the other members were
either in school or busy with their share of the chores around the dairy, she
was alone much of the time during her early childhood. Her one brother and
four older sisters did what they could in their spare time to compensate the
little girl for the hours spent by herself. Asbury, or Bubba, as Oleta called her
big brother, often took the little girl on his knee and read the funny papers to
her. Oleta loved this time with her brother and longed for the day she herself
could read. At times, her older sisters cradled the child in their arms and sang
to her the old ballads they had learned from Annie.

Only May, the oldest child in the family, had no time for her baby sister.
The young woman was too busy doing the work of a man. At first, May only
worked beside her father and brother. Then, when Tom became sick, she took
on more and more of his chores. Often when Tom went to the field, he had to
rest after plowing only a couple of rows. May saw this and offered to help.
Somehow the young woman found strength to drive the mule and guide the
big iron plow into long straight furrows while forcing it deep into the soil of
the field. She also rose early in the morning to milk the cows and help her
brother load the heavy galvanized containers of milk onto the wagon. Before
the sun was up, May and Bubba had climbed aboard and had driven through
the dark to deliver the milk to their customers. In the winter months, she almost
froze in her cotton dress riding atop that wagon across the open palmetto scrub.

Wherever Tom fell short, and Bubba and Annie were too busy to take up
the slack, May filled in, and at night when she came in for supper, the meal that
signaled the end of the day's chores, every part of her body ached with weariness. Often, she barely spoke, only responding to conversation that was ex-
pressly directed to her. More and more often, she took no interest in the family
recreation and only participated when coaxed by the others. May seemed to
take as her personal responsibility the task of bridging the gap between her
father's growing lethargy and her mother's expectations of him and the other

37

children. Annie drove them all relentlessly, so May had no time for her little sister and no energy left for children's games.

Shortly after Oleta was born, Annie took responsibility for making the trips into Jacksonville for the purchase of provisions not found on the farm or in the surrounding woods. Sometimes Tom went with Annie, but as far back as Oleta could remember, the woman always took her baby girl with her. Oleta loved the ride on the train and the bustle of the city. And sometimes Tom put Oleta in front of him on his horse and took her hunting with him. She especially liked their trips to the savannahs and marshlands west of their land. Perched high on her father's horse, Oleta could see across the marshlands, stretching golden in the sun.

But most of the time she was alone and had to find her own amusement. And so it happened that on a morning in 1913, when she was five years old, Oleta followed a mama cat into the palmettos. She was sitting on the front porch holding an old magazine, turning the pages and mumbling to herself, pretending to read, when, out of the corner of one eye, the child spied her gray cat slipping quickly through the yard toward the palmettos beyond the oaks. Oleta called to the cat, "Come here, White Spot! Come here." The large gray cat with one white spot beneath its chin ignored the little girl. "Come on now," she said again, hoping for some companionship from the cat.

The little girl stood up, and the cat moved on more swiftly, not to be deterred from its destination. Toddling down the stairs, Oleta watched as the cat disappeared into the palmettos. "White Spot! White Spot!" the little girl continued calling as she followed the cat across the yard. She moved from the shade of the oaks into the morning sun. Skirting the green wall of palmetto fans that glistened before her, she lifted one and then another of the prickly fronds, peeking into the dense growth as she called the name of the cat.

Finally, she spied, hidden beneath the fronds and winding out into the mass of green before her, a tunnel or path that had been burrowed by the Brown hogs. Oleta knelt down and crawled on her hands and knees into the cool quiet shade of the secret passages. "White Spot! White Spot!" she repeatedly called her pet as she wound deeper and deeper into the palmettos, staring into the shadows.

When she heard a tiny squeaking noise ahead of her, she paused, listening to determine the location from which it came. She moved slowly, following the sounds until she looked ahead and saw White Spot snuggled into the curve of a palmetto root bulging in the path in front of her. In the sparse light, she could barely see the gray animal or determine the source of the squeaking, but as she reached the animal, she saw five tiny little balls of fur blindly rooting and nuzzling the mother cat. "White Spot!" Oleta cried, "you've found kittens!" To herself, she thought with delight, "Oh! She found kittens in these palmettos. That's why she was in such a big hurry to get out here!"

Oleta lay on the ground beside White Spot and, one by one, picked up the bundles of warm, squirming, squeaking flesh and examined them. The minutes passed, and the little girl was oblivious to anything but her fascination with the mother cat and her kittens.

Presently, the arm on which she was resting began to numb and ache, so she raised herself to a near-sitting position. As she did, her eye casually scanned the path she had used to find the cat. She looked back at the kittens, but something caught her attention, and she turned again to the path.

A pile of something gray had moved, maybe six feet away from her. Another movement caused her to focus on a sinuous mass of gray and black. The child froze. A huge snake coiled before her with its head up and eyes staring at the little girl. The diamondback rattler was not singing its rattles, not yet preparing to strike. He had come there to eat the baby kittens, and the girl presented an obstacle to that intention. At this time, he was only examining that obstacle. Without taking her eyes off the snake, the five-year-old girl shifted slowly to a crawling position and began to move backward down another tunneled path away from the snake. When she rounded a curve in the path, she turned quickly and, scrambling from the palmettos in full terror, ran to the house.

When she reached her mother, who stood at the wood stove stirring the noon meal in a big iron pot, her heart was pounding so fiercely that she couldn't speak. Annie grabbed the child's shoulders crying, "Leta! What's wrong?"

The little girl, white and shaken with fear, finally managed to stammer, "Snake! Snake! He's going to get the baby kittens!"

"Where's a snake, Leta?" Annie demanded frantically.

"Out in the palmettos, Ma. He's going to get the kittens!"

"How do you know that, Leta?"

"I saw him, Ma, right by me. I was with the kittens, and he was right by me, Ma!" The little girl began to sob.

Annie pulled the quivering child tightly to her great breast. "That's all right, honey, we'll get the snake," she said reassuringly, but inside, the woman was horrified at the danger her daughter had escaped.

Minutes later, Bubba came from the fields for his noon meal. When he was told about the snake, the nineteen-year-old boy knew the palmettos would have to be burned to smoke it out. But he determined first to save the kittens for his little sister if possible. The young man loaded his father's pistol, put it in his belt, took a small basket, and walked outside to the place where Oleta had seen the rattlesnake. The little girl directed her big brother to the passage she had used to find White Spot and her kittens. Bubba bowed down and scrambled into the dark passages beneath the thicket, leaving Annie and Oleta to wait in the sunlight. Because the child knew her brother was in great danger, the minutes wore on slowly. Finally, she heard a rustling in the palmettos before her. Bubba emerged on his hands and knees. As he raised himself, he handed her the basket of squeaking, squirming kittens, White Spot close at his heels. At that moment Oleta adored her big brother.

By this time, Tom had come in for his dinner, and Bubba told him of the size of the snake crawl he had seen on the path in the palmettos. The snake had been monstrous, they concluded. Bubba and Tom set fire to the palmettos and watched as the fronds whipped into a raging blaze. The two men stood guard on the outer edges of the thicket, waiting for the snake to show himself. The thick patch of palmettos burned until there were only smoking black stalks poking up from the burnt bulges of their roots, but the snake never appeared; apparently, he had made his getaway.

In the spring, the palmettos in front of the Brown place would send up their prickly green shoots. They would flourish again. Once more, the hogs would tunnel through them, and with the hogs, the rattlesnakes would share those cool dark places of refuge. In the fall, Oleta would start school. She would meet other children her age, and she would learn to read. And after that, she would never be quite so lonely again.

The two men left the heat of the smoldering scrub and returned to the house. Oleta sat in the porch swing, moving gently to and fro, singing quietly, unaware of anything around her except the baby kittens cradled in her lap. Bubba smiled as he and his father sat down on the front steps, relieved from the midday heat by the old live oaks whose great arms stretched overhead, shielding them all from the sun.

Armistice Day

Long about ten o'clock or so in the morning, word came through to
the school that the peace had been signed. And the teacher turned out
school, and we all went out on the porch. . . . We didn't have a flag in those
days, but we all took our sweaters, red sweaters, white sweaters, and blue
sweaters, and put them up there to form the colors of the flag. My brother
came back from delivering milk to pick me up from school, and the whole
town was so overjoyed. And he had the morning paper, the *Times-Union,*
and it had in big letters across the top of the page, "Armistice Signed."

—Oleta, 16 February 1984

THE MILK WAGON, with its burden of galvanized jugs and glass jars, creaked from beneath the covering of the great old oaks. The light wind moved across the palmettos, chilling the two shadowy figures seated on the open wagon. Oleta shuddered and snuggled close to Bubba as she pulled her hands into the sleeves of her red sweater. On that November morning in 1918, several stars still hung in the dark clear air above them. As they headed through the scrub, Oleta watched the sky lighten in the east and the stars melt into the pale pink hue that crept upward in the sky before them. But on that day, Bubba wasn't thinking about what particular colors were filling the sky. His mind was on the war.

One by one, the shapes of the darkened houses near Pablo Beach formed a silhouette against the eastern sky. Oleta was on her way to school, and every morning, she made this trip in all kinds of weather, leaving home long before most of the children in the little coastal settlement had even turned in their beds. Some mornings, the icy winter winds would sweep across the palmettos and through her sweater and cotton dress and chill her until she ached. She had no overcoat, but her mother dressed the little girl in layers of clothing, a flannel slip, a cotton dress, and a sweater. She wore cotton ribbed stockings to her thighs and long underpants reaching to her knees. Yet on many of these cold mornings, by the time the child had reached the wooden schoolhouse and the warmth of its potbellied wood stove, her arms and hands were so stiff from cold that she couldn't hold a pencil.

However, Oleta didn't mind these trips. On most days, the climate in this part of Florida had a magic to its mornings. The orange blossoms, the jasmine, the pine, the palmetto berries, all the smells peculiar to each particular season seemed intensified in the morning dew. On some mornings, the sand road before them reflected the moonlight, as if a silver-white ribbon were banding the dark clumps of shadows that crowded the sides of their wagon. Oleta would watch as the silver ribbon, the dark clumps, the black shadows all around them turned to a gray color and then, according to the particular sunrise, a luminescent golden, silver, or pink. No, Oleta didn't mind the hardship of these early morning rides. They were a small price to pay for a day in the classroom.

School had been a wondrous experience for her. Not only because of the many answers it provided her voraciously curious young mind, but because of the companionship of friends her own age and the acceptance she gained from her teachers.

On this morning in 1918, when she and Bubba reached the dunes lining the unpopulated sections of First Street, the tall thin young man pulled the milk wagon to a stop. Oleta and her brother jumped off the wagon, pulled their sweaters tighter, and walked a worn path through patches of palmettos, sandspurs, and sea oats across the dunes to the beach. Tracking through the soft white sand, the first thing the little girl noticed was the salty air in her nostrils, and as she reached the crest of the dunes, the wind picked up, chilling her face. But before her stretched the wide expanse of white sandy beaches and, beyond the beach, the dark rippling waters of the Atlantic. Everything sparkled with bits of orange fire as the sun, like some waking giant, raised its burning eye above the horizon. Even the backs of the sandpipers darting in and out along the edges of the waves and the moist sand beneath their tiny feet reflected the blazing color. Oleta gasped. The beach in the morning, this was the greatest magic of all.

She remembered the other times she had seen the coast in the half-light of dawn or twilight. Often Tom and Annie, after finishing their chores at the dairy, would bring their children to the beach for an evening of fishing and games. Tom would wade out with his casting net, and the children would run free across the wide white sand and dunes. On cold evenings, Tom would make a fire, and the children, having played until they could stand the cold no longer, would return and warm themselves by the fire. Sometimes, Annie would throw sweet potatoes in the coals, and when they were soft and hot, she would scoop them out and give them to the children to put in their pockets to warm their freezing hands. And often, when Tom drove the milk wagon, he would stop in the early morning to analyze the fishing conditions, decide whether the mullet were running. On many of those mornings, if the sun was in just the right place above the horizon, the water, its foamy waves, the sand, all would be a gleaming silver, and the little girl would have to shield her eyes from the blinding light mirrored a million times before her.

But that morning, as Bubba stood for only a few minutes gazing at the spectacle before him, his mind traveled across those waters to the conflict in which America and all those distant nations had been entangled these last years, and he wondered what news this day would bring. They should have news that day, he thought. He turned and walked to the milk wagon. Oleta followed.

In the milk wagon, Bubba and Oleta traveled slowly down the shell surface of First Street. Lamps had been lighted now in most of the windows, and smoke was streaming from kitchen chimneys. Presently, they arrived at the Gonzales house, where Oleta would wait the hour and a half before it was time for her and the Gonzales girls to walk the half-mile to school. By a few minutes after eight, when Oleta and her friends stood on the long porch of the white frame schoolhouse, leaning over its banisters and waving to approaching children, the sun was well up in the sky and had chased most of the morning chill from the air. The sky above them was a bright blue, and the day promised to exhibit the best of Florida's winter weather.

The principal and only teacher, Mrs. Newcomb, had not found it necessary to put a fire in the stove, and as the children entered the classroom, they found her walking from desk to desk, filling the wells from one of the large jugs of ink Duval County furnished its schools. While each child stood erect waiting for the ritual with which they opened each school day, the woman walked quietly to her desk in the front of the room. She stood for a moment without speaking and then raised her eyes to the children. Oleta thought she saw in them a moist glaze. "Children," she said softly, "children, the word has come that the war might end today." The woman swallowed, trying to control her shaky voice. "Let us bow our heads and pray to God for peace for our nation and all the nations."

The children bowed their heads and prayed, but the truth was that this war had little changed the lives of the children in Pablo Beach—only in that it had been the main topic of conversation of the adults around their dinner tables, and that some fear had been engendered in them by the talk they heard of the devastation of this war involving so many nations of the world. Few of the young men from that area had been called into the war, but more, it seemed of late, had been receiving draft notices. The people of Pablo Beach feared for their sons and brothers. So their children prayed earnestly for peace to come on that November morning in 1918.

The morning seemed to wear on for Mrs. Newcomb. She paced the floor a bit while the children took their turns reading and then reciting multiplication tables. The children noticed her tension. Oleta and her classmates began their writing exercises. Except for an occasional scratching noise from the pens moving across paper, the room was quiet. The minutes seemed to drag by for Mrs. Newcomb.

Then suddenly, the little frame building shuddered with an explosion of noise. Wild peals issued from the bell in the Episcopal church across the street, where the schoolchildren often ate their lunches and warmed themselves on its sunny steps. Mrs. Newcomb ran to the door and threw it open to meet a man shouting joyously. The children dropped their pens and crowded to the door and windows. "It's over! It's over! We've signed the armistice!" the man was screaming.

Mrs. Newcomb, with tears streaming down her cheeks, turned to the children and cried, "Praise the Lord! Praise the Lord! The war is over!"

The settlement seemed to burst open with life. Everywhere, people were spilling out of houses and stores into the unpaved roads. The churches that had bells were ringing them. Whistles were blowing, and the owners of the few automobiles were blasting their horns. The little school had no flag, but the children draped their red, blue, and white sweaters proudly across the banisters. Mrs. Newcomb was beside herself, and for that day, the children in her charge ran freely in and out of the building and around the yard.

The day before this, twenty miles from this schoolyard, a questionnaire from the draft board had found its way to Hugie Oesterreicher in the cypress cabin on the edge of Durbin Swamp. And on the morning of 11 November 1918, he was tracking a deer through the quiet woods near his home when he heard from twenty miles away in Jacksonville the steam whistles blowing. He left the deer and ran home. He didn't know whether the whistles signaled tragedy or joy. His family stood on the front porch listening to the noise resounding across the northeast Florida woods. At that moment, one of the Mickler boys came bounding in on horseback shouting that the war was over. Hugie never returned the questionnaire he had received the day before.

From the porch of the schoolhouse, Oleta saw Bubba in the milk wagon rolling down the dirt road toward her. When he reached the place she was standing, he stopped and jumped out holding a *Florida Times-Union* newspaper. In huge black letters, it proclaimed, "Armistice Signed." With that, Mrs. Newcomb dismissed school. Bubba and Oleta climbed into the milk wagon and drove to the beach, where people from all over town were arriving on foot, in cars, and in wagons. And there on the wide sandy strand beneath fair blue skies, Pablo Beach celebrated the end of World War I.

The Donkey

In the mornings she would wake up before daylight, wanting her breakfast. You
would hear this most gosh awful sound out there, "Hee-haw! hee-haw!
hee-haw!" Wanting her breakfast, she would holler 'til she got it.

—Oleta, 18 February 1984

OLETA PRESSED HER nose into the thin feather pillow beneath her head, pulled the patchwork quilt over her shoulder, turned, and drew her legs up and into the flannel gown. Again she tossed herself and hid her head beneath the pillow. From outside her window, a noise was piercing her early morning slumber, and the little girl was desperately trying to hold onto that slumber lest it slip from her and she be forced to leave the warmth of the bed and start her day. But the noise did not stop. Finally, the child lifted her head and peered out the northerly window into the blackness from which that noise came. "Jenny!" she thought. "That donkey sure lets you know when she wants her breakfast."

Jenny was the same donkey Hugie Oesterreicher had ridden to the woods when he killed his first deer. After he had outgrown his need for the little animal, the Oesterreichers had sold her to Tom Brown's sister for her grandchildren. As the years passed, her grandchildren lost interest, and she had mentioned to Tom that Oleta might like the donkey to ride to school.

When Tom told the eleven-year-old girl about the donkey, she was ecstatic at the thought of having her own transportation. Because the Browns always kept a few horses, Oleta had become a good rider. But what was more important, she was all too aware of the hardship her trips to school were posing to the family, especially with her father's poor health and her older brother and sisters marrying and leaving. She imagined herself riding to school in the morning and being totally independent. What fun she would have with her donkey; the donkey would be her friend; she would talk to her donkey all the way to school. And in the spring, she could even use Jenny to help pen the cattle. Having Jenny would be wonderful. So Tom bought Jenny for Oleta and built a pen at the home of Oleta's older sister Ada, who had recently married Garland Strickland. The young couple lived in a little house on Seventh Avenue South, only a short distance from the Pablo Beach school. The plan was for Oleta to ride to Ada's every morning, leave the donkey in the pen, and walk the half-mile to school with the Gonzales girls. In the afternoon, Oleta could walk to the post office on Mundy Drive, only one block from school, and pick up the mail for the family. The donkey was going to make life easier for everyone.

45

However, Jenny had aged considerably since the day ten years before when Hugie had ridden her into the woods and killed his first deer. Horses and donkeys tend to become cantankerous with age, and so it was with Jenny. Oleta buried her ears deeper into the mass of mattress, pillows, and quilts, but there was no escaping the sound of Jenny's insistent braying from the barn, echoing beneath the silent oaks and through the open window of the girl's room. *Hee-haw! hee-haw! hee-haw!* Oleta knew there would be no quiet until she ventured out into that cold dark morning and fed the donkey, her donkey.

The little girl raised herself to the edge of her bed and dangled her feet above the floor for a moment, hesitating because, sometimes in winter months, the cold winds swept through the open space beneath the Brown house making the floors as cold as ice. Her feet touched the bare wood. Shuddering, she reached for the doorknob and pulled it slightly open to allow light from the kitchen into her room. There where Annie was starting breakfast, a lamp burned on the table, and a fire roared in the wood stove. In that dim light, Oleta saw her school clothes draped across a straight-backed chair in the corner of her room.

She grabbed them and rushed to the kitchen, where she stood shivering by the stove, whose sides glowed red from the blazing fire inside. Oleta slipped her black ribbed-cotton stockings up her long thin legs and secured them at her thighs with elastic garters. Then she pulled her white cotton knee pants to mid-leg. Almost in one movement, she pulled the flannel slip over her head and let the flannel gown fall around her ankles. With another quick movement, she was in her cotton dress with its skirt hanging loosely from her narrow waist to below her calves. Picking up her wool sweater, she took a step over to her mother, who was frying sausage, and put her arms around the ample little woman.

Annie kissed her little daughter on the forehead and smiled. "She's sure kicking up a terrible fuss out there, isn't she, baby?" Annie said.

Oleta nodded.

"Ma, I've never heard such a racket as that donkey makes."

"No," Annie replied, "I don't think I have either."

With that, Oleta found a long kitchen match on the cabinet beside the stove, walked out onto the back porch, and took a lantern hanging from a nail on the outside wall. Raising the glass shade slightly, she struck the match on the wooden floor and lit the wick. As she pulled her sweater close around her, the girl walked outside.

From her position on the back porch, she could see a glowing light from the dairy and knew May was already there milking the cows. And a place in the eleven-year-old-girl's heart hurt for her older sister with a pain she didn't understand. "May," she thought. "She must be cold out there."

Of her brother and sisters, only May was left. Ada had married. Jean had married Arthur Kelly. Ida had married Clarence Oesterreicher and moved to Jacksonville. And recently, Bubba had married and found work in Pablo Beach. He probably would have stayed and worked the dairy for them, but he and his parents had different ideas about how the dairy should be run. All kinds of modern equipment had been invented, and Bubba wanted to invest in it. He was convinced the Brown dairy could support all of them if it were modernized, but Tom and Annie were against those new ideas. So when Bubba married, he had had to leave and find another way to make a living for himself and his wife, Lovey. Bubba had built a little house at the corner of Tom's forty acres. From the front porch of the Brown home, Oleta could see the new tin roof of Bubba's house glistening like a big mirror out there on the palmetto scrub.

Oleta missed him terribly. She missed having him come for dinner and take her on his lap and talk to her. She missed their early morning rides on the milk wagon. But maybe more than anything, she missed him because of what his absence meant for her oldest sister. May had always had her own work to do, and for many years, she had done part of her father's, but now she had Bubba's work to do as well.

With the lantern in one hand, Oleta skipped out into the strange shadows cast by the setting moon, which dappled the ground beneath the oaks. And as she moved around the house and toward the barn, the light from the lantern threw an eerie luminescence into the tangle of moss and twisting boughs above her head. Jenny screeched. *Hee-haw! hee-haw!* And the sound seemed to reverberate within the cave created by the shelter of the old oaks.

Jenny had an obstinate nature; she did not like taking the little girl to school and seemed determined to make the trip a kind of obstacle course for Oleta. The donkey's irritable disposition before breakfast was only part of it. Later that morning, when it was time to leave for school, Oleta eased the saddle from the board it straddled in the barn, took the bridle from a nail on the wall, and walked gently up to Jenny, talking softly to her all the while. Carefully, the girl placed the bit in the donkey's mouth and buckled the harness. Oleta threw the saddle over the animal's back, and Jenny took a deep breath, expanding her abdomen. The girl reached under the donkey for the strap and began to pull and tighten. Jenny held her breath, her belly fully distended, while Oleta, pulling with all of her strength, fastened the girth.

The sun had climbed fully over the rim of the horizon above the palmettos when Oleta, with her lunch and schoolbooks in one hand, pulled herself onto Jenny's back. The donkey's belly was still fully expanded, so Oleta rode cautiously, expectantly, waiting for the donkey to exhale and the saddle to slip to one side. Jenny wanted to dump the girl to the ground and head back for the barn, and Oleta knew it, for the cranky donkey tried the same thing every morning.

One damp morning after a heavy rain, before Oleta knew Jenny's ways, she had prodded the reluctant animal out onto the palmetto scrub on her way to school. The earth was muddy, and puddles of water pooled in the deeper wagon ruts of the road. The little girl carefully guided her beast to higher ground, trying to avoid the inevitable splashes. She was barely fifty yards beyond the oaks when Jenny exhaled, the strap around her stomach loosened, and the saddle slipped to one side, spilling Oleta with her clean clothes, her books, and her lunch into a big mud puddle. Then, wet and muddy, the little girl had to go home and change. "Never again!" she thought. "That donkey won't catch me off-guard again."

So today Oleta rode carefully, and when Jenny blew out and the saddle began to tilt, the girl jumped quickly to the ground, tossed down her books, and tightened the girth until Jenny was hard put to take a deep breath.

Although the temperature had been near freezing when Oleta went out that morning to feed Jenny, the day was warming quickly as the sun rose higher, and she pushed the donkey beyond the unpopulated palmetto scrub and onto the sand roads of the beach town, sprinkled here and there with wooden bungalows. After she had penned Jenny at Ada's and pitched a bit of hay to her, she walked out onto the road leading to the Gonzales house and to school. Down the sandy avenues, beyond the low dunes, the ocean danced with reflections of the morning light and the impenetrable reaches of the vast blue sky above it. The green of the leaves, the green of the palm fronds, and the green of the little grassy yards lining the road seemed a translucent gold in the light of the winter sun. Oleta stood still for a moment; she closed her eyes and raised her face to the light, taking a deep breath of the clear cool air. Like a brush of velvet against her cheek, the sun patted her face with its warmth. "Oh!" she thought, "it's going to be a golden day."

Oleta often felt awkward at school because of her height. She was taller than any of the other children, even those who were older. But also because of her height and some of her particular abilities, she had privileges that made her the envy of the other students. She was sometimes given the lead in school plays, and because she was artistic, the teacher gave her the day off from regular tasks occasionally to decorate the classroom before holidays. She was an excellent reader, and she was often asked to entertain the other students by reading to them; something of the actress lived in the shy little girl, and she expressed that in every nuance of the literature she recited. Reading aloud always remained a great pleasure to Oleta, and in years to come, she would gather her husband and children around her and entertain them, reading with a twinkle in her eye as she acted out the passages.

Before Oleta had the donkey and before the responsibility for fetching the mail had fallen to her, the Browns always made a stop at the post office when they picked up the little girl from school. But there was a time during World War I when May made a point of making that trip every day to fetch her young sister and to pick up the mail herself. May had never given much attention to the young men around Pablo Beach, or perhaps they had never given much attention to her. She was pretty enough, but there was something in her manner that made her unapproachable, maybe even unnoticeable. May was of medium height, with a light olive complexion and small dark piercing eyes that seemed to hide an inner heaviness. Like all of the Brown women, she possessed two outstanding features. She had a beautiful figure, perhaps the best of all the Brown girls, slender, small-waisted, and long-legged. She also had a thick mane of wavy brown hair. But in spite of these assets to her appearance, there was a plainness about her, probably a result of her own indifference to whether she was attractive or not. She seemed to have weightier matters on her mind.

May had watched all her younger sisters marry except, of course, Oleta. Yet she had remained without any attachments to the young men in the area. However, for a time in her early twenties, May began a correspondence with a young trooper in World War I. The family never knew exactly how this came about. She had never met the young man in person, but he wrote her often. They exchanged pictures, and May exhibited a breathlessness that her family had never seen in her. After hours of work in the fields, May came in at night and, by lamplight, wrote the young man long letters. She used the bit of money she had to send him cigarettes. Every day she rushed to the post office to check for letters from him. When one came, the young woman sat in the milk wagon and fervently read each line. She said that when the war was over, he would come to see her. Something had sparked in the young woman; although she had never seen this man in person, May had fallen in love with him.

But one day, the letters stopped coming. For weeks, May journeyed to the post office daily to check for mail, but after awhile, she left the task to other members of the family. And the youthful breathlessness left May, and she became once more the sober young woman who always had work to do.

May never could bring herself to check on the young man's whereabouts. He could have been killed in the war, but then perhaps he could have just lost interest, and May could not bear to face that. So she chose never to know for sure. Years later, when May came to live with Oleta and Hugie and became a member of their family, she brought with her a shoe box of her most precious possessions. In it were the letters and the photograph of that young man. Oleta put them in the old trunk where she kept her own rare treasures. When May had become very old and her thick mane of brown hair had become a thick mass of silvery white, Oleta knelt on the floor before that trunk with her youngest daughter and pulled out the letters, parched with age, and the yellowed photograph. Handing the photograph to her daughter, Oleta said, "See, he was very handsome. He looked just like James Drury. That's why she will never miss *The Virginian* on Wednesday night."

May remained thin and limber all of her life, but no man ever held that strong slender young figure, and no man ever put his hands in that thick brown mane. During those early years of the 1900s, the Brown girls would take their older sister to dances with them. They encouraged May to shake her serious nature and enter into the pleasure of the evening with some of the young men. And she would try, but something within restrained her and made her feel ill at ease. She did not think she was pretty, and she knew she didn't have the quick wit and outgoing nature of her younger sisters. Besides, those slender arms she extended to the young men as they danced, plowed fields and put up fences and heaved jugs of milk. She was no delicate flower, and she knew it.

What's more, how could any of them understand the burden for her parents that she carried in her heart. No one could grasp the sense of responsibility she seemed unable to escape; not even her own sisters could fathom the depth to which she bore her parents' care. So certainly, these young men with their light-hearted ways could not comprehend or appreciate just what character shaped the actions of this young thin woman with her dark piercing eyes.

Oleta remembered some of those dances. Often they were attended by the whole family, especially the ones held at the pavilion, a large open-air wooden structure standing on the beach at the end of Mundy Drive. On Sunday afternoons, bands played their music for the residents of Pablo Beach who gathered there. Many brought picnic lunches, and with the ocean breezes blowing through, they spent the afternoon visiting, eating, and dancing with friends, while the children played on the white stretches of beaches in front of that place. Oleta loved it. With the rhythms of the music all around her, she could barely stand still, and sometimes, the boyfriends of her older sisters would humor the little girl and take her onto the floor for a dance.

In the spring of 1920, when Oleta was twelve years old, she had ridden the donkey, Jenny, to school for almost nine months. Every morning, she pushed and prodded the stubborn animal across the scrub to school and away from home; every afternoon, she fought to keep the animal from its headlong charge back across the scrub to the barn at the Brown place. One afternoon in May, Oleta had picked up the mail and walked to the pen at Ada's. After saddling Jenny, she climbed on the animal's back. As usual, she had the reins in one hand, and with the other, she held her books, her lunch box, and the letters from the post office. As she guided Jenny out onto the soft sand road leading from Pablo Beach to the scrub, the donkey started trotting. Jenny wanted to go home. Oleta bounced awkwardly, trying to control the stubborn animal with one hand and hang onto her books with the other. The donkey picked up speed, so that the little girl tightened her knees into the sides of the donkey. The mail was slipping from under her arm. One letter floated away from her. Oleta turned her head and saw it behind her in the ruts of the road and tried to yank the donkey to a halt. Her efforts were to no avail. Jenny was heading home, and no slip of a girl would slow her down. The animal started to gallop.

Another letter slipped from under Oleta's arm and onto the road, which had now become a bouncing blur behind her. The palmettos bobbled swiftly past her, and in spite of Oleta's efforts to keep a firm seat in the saddle, she rose and fell with every stride of the determined donkey. And every time Oleta came down, she expected to keep going and hit the dirt. One by one, the letters slipped from Oleta's hand, strewing the road to Pablo Beach with the Brown mail. By the time the donkey had jerked to a halt in front of the barn, Oleta was bent over with one arm around the animal's neck, grasping anything to keep from being spilled to the ground. When Oleta walked into the house, she announced to her parents she never wanted to ride that animal to school again. She was finished.

So Tom found a buyer for Jenny—Aunt Rodie Martin, a black woman who lived on the Hill, or Colored Town, the black section of Pablo Beach. Tom tied Jenny to his wagon, and he and Oleta rode down the white sand road, past Small's Hammock, to Aunt Rodie's house. Colored Town consisted of a few gleaming whitewashed shanties beside the sandy streets. In the summer months, it seemed to Oleta, all of the yards in this part of town were banked with bright yellow sunflowers, purple and pink petunias, and various containers of geraniums and periwinkles. Aunt Rodie had purchased the donkey for her grandchildren, and Tom knew the gentle old lady would give Jenny a good home. But in spite of the donkey's poor behavior toward Oleta, Jenny had come to love the little girl and the Brown place, and she often broke away from Aunt Rodie's and came back for visits. On some mornings, Oleta was wakened again by the donkey's loud braying, and the girl would peek out her window into the early light of dawn at Jenny standing there next to the barn screeching. *"Hee-haw! hee-haw! hee-haw!"* And on those mornings, Aunt Rodie's grandsons would come timidly down the white sand road to the Brown place to fetch Jenny back home.

The days of Oleta's independence were over. Once more, she rode to school with the milk wagon. But after Jenny, the girl appreciated those early morning rides in a way she never had before.

Tom's Death

I remember going in there and looking at him. He looked
so white, he did, like wax laying there in that casket. And that
feeling came over me that he was dead. I reached over in that casket
and kissed him there, that icy, cold skin. I kissed him on his forehead,
and that icy, cold skin. It really hit then that my father was dead.

—Oleta, 3 March 1984

BY THE FALL of 1921, when Oleta was thirteen years old, she had been given more responsibilities around the dairy. Her father had grown weaker with each passing year, and often, he was little more than an onlooker to the family business.

Since that day over thirteen years before when Tom had returned from Jacksonville without her shoes, Annie Sadler Brown had taken over more and more of the family's financial affairs. But this is not to say that during those years Tom contributed nothing to the family workforce or to the family decisions. He did, and this fact became suddenly and painfully apparent in the fall of 1921.

One day in October of that year, May picked up Oleta early from school so that the girl could get started on her share of the work. The family had planned to attend a dance that night in Mayport, and in order for all the chores to be finished in time to leave for the dance, everyone had to put forth extra effort. At about two o'clock, Oleta was in the dairy washing bottles and stacking them to dry in the afternoon sun. Tom and Annie sat on the back steps taking a break from the rushed chores. Tom's white shirt with its buttoned cuffs gleamed in the fullness of the afternoon light. Excited about the dance in Mayport, Oleta looked across the yard and smiled brightly at her parents. Then suddenly, from the back steps, she heard her mother screaming, "Tom! Tom!"

Oleta raised herself from the pot of boiling water and saw Tom leaning limply over on Annie. The girl rushed to her parents. Her father was unconscious, his eyes rolled back in his head. "Go get Lovey!" Annie ordered the girl, and as she broke into a run, she heard her mother wailing loudly for her sister to come from the fields: *"May! May!"*

Annie's voice resounded beneath the oaks, and from the Brown place, it echoed across the woodlands of the savannahs to the south field where May was plowing. The young woman heard the call, unhitched the plow from her horse, climbed onto his bare back, and pounded her heels into his sides until he broke into a gallop. May could hardly breathe, fear gripped her heart so tightly. She had just seen her mother an hour before. Annie wouldn't summon her home except for something desperate.

When Oleta returned home with her sister-in-law, May and Annie had managed to move Tom to his bed.

"Make him a toddy," Lovey suggested. "Maybe that will revive him."

So Oleta made her father a toddy, but when Annie tried to spoon the syrupy liquid into her husband's mouth, it just drained out the corner onto his chin. Then May and Annie noticed Tom's face pulling to one side.

"I'll go get a doctor," May cried with urgency, as she turned and headed for the barn. After quickly hitching the horse to the buggy, she climbed aboard and headed across the palmetto scrub to Pablo Beach, wildly cracking the long buggy whip above the horse's head. "Hurry! Hurry! Hurry!" a voice screamed in her head. "Pa's dying. Hurry! Hurry! Hurry!" Pablo Beach had no doctor; May would have to call one from Jacksonville. So the object of her headlong drive down the white sand road and across the high palmetto scrub was the only public telephone in town. She whipped the horse until he was racing past the houses and dunes on First Street, past Ada's house, past the school, and past the pavilion. Finally, she reached Jones's Grocery on Pablo Avenue and yanked the long reins to halt the horse and buggy. She was almost in tears as she shouted into the mouthpiece of the telephone, "Get me Dr. Alford in Jacksonville!"

When May returned to the Brown house, she saw that Tom was still unconscious. Annie sat beside him holding his long slender hand in hers and talking softly to him. But there was no response, and when May looked full into her father's face, she saw that it was completely distorted. "He's had a stroke," May thought to herself. She walked over, put her strong thin arm around her mother's shoulder, and said, "You can go, Ma. I'll sit with him for awhile." But Annie said she wouldn't leave him now. Annie knew Tom was dying, and as she sat beside him, she thought of their time together. She remembered those first years of their marriage and the way she had loved him so totally and how that love had turned to ashes in her own mouth.

All this time, Oleta was standing in a corner of her parents' room, staring with her great brown eyes, silently trying to grasp the meaning of her father's limp body on the bed in front of her. The way Annie had fastened herself to that chair beside him and the look of dark fear on May's face was indication of something Oleta couldn't quite make herself understand.

Bubba slipped into the shadowy room and saw his father with his mother bent beside him. "Pa!" he called forcefully. "Pa! It's Bubba! Pa, wake up!" And the young man took his father by the shoulders and stared full into his face.

Oleta watched Bubba as the full realization of his father's condition dawned on the young man. She saw him sink to his knees beside the bed and cry, "No, Pa, don't do it. Don't, Pa!"

"Don't do what?" the thirteen-year-old girl thought to herself, but as soon as she asked herself the question, she knew the answer. "They think he is dying. They believe Pa is dying." And suddenly, she felt very cold, and she left her corner in the room. Lamps burned in the living room, and someone had put a fire in the grate. Oleta walked to the circle of warmth before the fireplace and stood trying to comprehend what his dying meant. But death was beyond the realm of her experience, and she couldn't fathom its nature or its consequences.

At that moment, the sound of lowing cattle broke into her reverie and brought her to the awareness of present demands. Even though a terrible heaviness had descended on the young girl, she quickly made her way to the dairy.

After milking the cows, Oleta returned to her father's bedside, where Annie was pacing restlessly. Dr. Alford was supposed to come to Pablo Beach on the six o'clock train, but at seven, he still hadn't arrived, and Tom seemed to be sinking into deeper oblivion. "Well," Annie thought finally, "he knows the way to our house. Maybe he had another call to make."

Around nine that night, they heard a wagon creak beneath the oaks. When Bubba walked out with a raised lantern to light the doctor's way to the steps, he saw a thin young man timidly approaching. He told them he was Dr. Alford's assistant and that he had lost his way and gone to Palm Valley. After the young doctor had examined Tom, he announced, "I'll have to bleed him, but I don't have what I need to do it tonight. I'll have to come back in the morning." Bleeding was a method used to relieve patients of the high blood pressure that often caused strokes.

"Bleed him!" Oleta thought. "What's he talking about?" And then she said to her mother, "Ma, what's he going to do to Pa?" Annie shook her head, not willing to give an answer to her daughter.

The next morning was unusually warm for October, and a strange stillness had settled over the Brown place. Not a tree was moving, not a bird made a sound, and even the cattle seemed held by an uncanny quiet. But the Browns hadn't noticed; they were completely absorbed with Tom's condition.

Oleta had taken up her post near the foot of her father's bed, but when the young doctor returned, she rushed from the room. But May stayed with Annie and Tom, and as the doctor began his procedure, she pushed the bedroom door closed. Oleta agonized as the minutes dragged by, "How could they do that to him. He's dying, and they're taking his life's blood." She thought it was like some barbaric ritual she had read about in a book. "And May's still in there. I don't know how she can stand it. Why doesn't she come out?" the young girl asked herself. "But she won't. She would never leave Ma and Pa in there alone."

After awhile, the bedroom door creaked open, and the thin young woman did come out. Her color, usually sun-bronzed from working in the fields, was ashen white. Only briefly, she leaned against the wall beside the door, and in her hand, she held a milk jar full of thick red liquid. Oleta turned and buried her face in her arms resting on the mantel. May tightened her jaw and walked outside. Looking down at the jar, May thought, "I can't just pour it out. It's like part of him." So she walked to the barn and found a shovel, and there behind the barn, the young woman buried her father's blood.

As Oleta watched May coming back from the barn, she wanted to run to her and say, "I'm so sorry you had to do that. I'm so sorry." But she couldn't, because at that moment, she was just thankful that she had not had to handle that grim task. "I couldn't have done it," Oleta thought to herself, "I could not have done that." But the young girl didn't know that in the months and years just ahead, she would ultimately have to reach into herself and find that same kind of fiber of which May was made.

Meanwhile, Aunt Jane Floyd, Tom's sister, had arrived from Mayport. Oleta remembered later that, as she entered the door, the tall gentle woman brought with her a peace that transcended the circumstances around her. The woman leaned over her brother, took him in her long arms, and held him next to her heart for a moment. When she raised herself, she looked at Annie and said, "We better get a priest for him." So they sent for a priest from Immaculate Conception in Jacksonville, for in those days, there was not a regular priest at the Beach, and one came only during the summer months to say Mass on Sundays.

After the bleeding, Tom seemed to rouse momentarily. When May returned to his bedside, she noticed a flickering movement of his eyelids. "He looks like he's trying to come to," she cried excitedly. Oleta rushed to the room in time to see Tom's eyes open wide and see him raise one arm slightly toward May. When the young woman bent closer to her father, his hand brushed her face, and he whispered, "May . . . May!" And he closed his eyes and slept.

That night, the second night after Tom had collapsed, Bubba stood on the front porch and looked up into the branches overhead. "Nothing moving," he thought, "not a breath stirring. Funny feeling in the air. Not one bit like October weather. Warm and still." Again that night, the family took turns sitting with Tom. They spent a restless night, and before daylight the next morning, Oleta awakened to rain pelting the tin roof. "Odd! Yesterday was like a summer day, not a cloud in the sky," she thought as she turned in her bed.

Aunt Jane had spent the night, and the old woman had curled next to Oleta in the bed, holding the frightened young girl close during those long dark hours. So when Oleta moved, it roused Aunt Jane, who said, "I had an idea last night just before I fell asleep. I think we need to find some jimsonweed and make Tom some tea with it. I have seen that work like a miracle at times. You never know, it might help." If there were something that could be done, the girl thought they should at least try. After she and May had finished tending to the cattle, they went to their mother, and Annie agreed they needed to find some jimsonweed in the fields.

By the time they had stepped out onto the back porch, it was daylight. Outside, it was still pouring down rain, and when Oleta looked through the openings between the branches, she saw the clouds tearing across the sky. The light wind that moved above her seemed to lift the higher branches of the tall oak trees, tugging upward at them, as though trying to catch them and send them away with the clouds dashing across the heavens. The oaks, the cabbage palms, the orange trees, the pine trees were not bending in the wind—it wasn't that kind of wind—but their upper fronds and limbs all seemed to be caught in the wind's lifting motion.

May and Oleta stepped into the rain and headed to the fields in search of the jimsonweed. They had no raincoats or umbrellas. Besides, trying to cover themselves in that driving rain would have been pointless. Walking to and fro, they skirted the edges of the fields as the rain pelted their faces. Even though they could barely see, May finally spotted a weed growing nearby. "There!" she said, tugging at Oleta's arm. "By the fence!" After running through the driving rain, they huddled over the low weed and picked several of its leaves. With these in their hands, the two sisters held on to each other, leaned into the wind, and headed back to the house.

When they reached the covering of the back porch, their dresses, stockings, and slips were clinging to them, water was spilling over the tops and out the seams of their brogan work shoes, and the force of the wind and rain had so loosened their hair that it streamed around their faces and shoulders. Overhead, the wind whistled through the great oaken boughs, making a thrashing noise as it whipped their waxen leaves together. May put her head in the back door, calling for someone to bring a towel. Finally, Ada came hurrying with two blankets and urged, "Come on, Pa's not good." May and Oleta kicked off their brogans, wrapped themselves in the blankets, and stepped inside.

The noise of the storm seemed intensified as the rain pelted the roof and the wind whistled beneath the floor. Nevertheless, when Oleta entered the hall leading to her father's room, one sound caught her attention and made her stop and listen. It seemed to fill the house and overpower the howl of the storm. "What is that?" she asked herself. "What is that?" She thought, as she stood there, that the sound could have been the rattle of rain surging through a pipe, or the rattle of wind buffeting the tin roof, or the timbers of the house itself shaking in the fury of the increasing storm. It could have been, but as the frightened girl stood there, shivering and soaked, she realized that the sound wasn't any of those things.

As she entered Tom Brown's room, she saw him there with his eyes wide open and his head back. Every breath seemed to rack his long thin body. And in all of her life, the girl had never heard anything like the sounds of that breath, gurgling and fighting its way through the fluids that were rapidly filling his heart and lungs. And then she knew. The rattling noise was the sound of her father dying.

Aunt Jane said, "It won't be long now."

And for those next few minutes, for the Browns, all the world, all of life, all of care seemed to converge on the man who lay on that bed before their eyes, hovering over the bridge of death. They were all huddled there in that room, each desiring in some way to reach out to Tom Brown, to pull him back, to assist him through, to communicate all the unsayable things, but ultimately, none of them could do anything.

Annie Sadler Brown sat on the edge of her husband's deathbed, proud and determined to the end. She was a woman accustomed to her own sorrow, and previous experience had taught her that she could survive anything. She would survive this, and she knew it. So she took her poor husband's slender hands into her own strong hands and bowed her head forward. As her daughters had leaned into the winds of the storm that morning, so she leaned into this circumstance, holding onto Tom with all her strength, helping him to press through to that place of rest and tranquillity she knew would be on the other side.

May and Oleta stood close beside her, soaked and wrapped in blankets, the water of the storm still wet on their faces and hair. Oleta's salty tears slipped down to mingle with the fresh rain on her cheeks, while in her soul, she wrestled with the unnameable fears of youth and inexperience.

But no tears fell from May's eyes. Her own eyes had been fixed on those of her father from the moment she had entered the room. She saw fear darting there in those dark orbs, and she wished with everything in her nature that she could face this moment for him, that she could somehow make up the difference for him. For one brief moment, she glanced down at the jimsonweed she was still clutching in her hands, and it seemed to represent all her futile attempts to be what her parents needed when they needed it. She put the soggy leaves on the table beside Tom Brown's bed, and as she lifted her eyes once more to his face and heaving frame, something lifted from her thin shoulders. In that moment, she resigned herself to her father's death and to her own helplessness. Unlike Annie, she did not lean into the wind of this circumstance but, rather, lay back on it, let it buoy her up, let it take her where it would. She could not fight it.

So May stood there watching her father's passing. She had never seen anyone die before, but it occurred to her that it was not unlike seeing a birth. A struggle was taking place between those forces that would hold him in this place and the forces that were pulling him into the next. Within the universe of that room, this struggle was the focus of all energy and all attention. His eyes were wide open, staring into the faces of his wife and children yet not seeing, for they were fixed on a point beyond them to which he was fast approaching.

And then there was a hush. The rattling stopped. The struggle stopped.

He was at the very portals. His eyes stopped darting, and a great peace fell upon him. And May heard someone say, "He's going now! He's going now!"

May said in a voice that perhaps only the soul of Tom Brown heard, "Bye, Pa . . . bye." He breathed out slowly . . . and then again, without inhaling, Tom Brown breathed out the last of his life. At that moment, May was aware that the person she had known as her father had just slipped quietly out and away, and that the figure before her on the bed was only an empty physical representation of that person . . . empty . . . vacant . . . or vacated.

"He's gone." Annie sighed, and slowly loosening her hands from those hands, she raised one to his open eyes and softly closed them. "He's gone."

Even though Oleta saw the sudden stillness fall on her father and heard her mother's words, the thirteen-year-old girl could not grasp what those things meant. After a few minutes, the other members of the family left Tom's side and began to tend to the grisly business of planning his burial, yet she stood fixed to the place beside his bed. And even though she watched his lips become a grayish color and saw that color spread slowly over his whole face, she did not believe he was really dead. "They've made a mistake," she thought. "In a minute, his eyes will flutter, he will move his hand, he will sigh and breathe again." The finality of what had just happened was incomprehensible to her.

Finally, Aunt Jane noticed that the young girl was still caught there in the moment of her father's death and came to put her long arms around her shoulders, turning her away from Tom and saying, "Come on, baby, he's out of our hands now." A tremendous shudder convulsed her thin frame, and she suddenly felt very cold. As she left her father's room, she became aware once more of the wind and rain outside.

Shortly, two of Tom Brown's lifelong friends arrived. Mr. Rodenizer and Mr. Oehler washed the body of their friend and dressed him in his best black suit. Mr. Oehler took his own gold cuff links and put them in Tom's white starched shirt. They placed an ironing board across the backs of two straight chairs and lifted him to it. They laid him there and crossed his long slender hands over his chest.

When Oleta saw her father stretched straight and lifeless on the ironing board, she did not experience grief, but, rather, a morbid gloom descended on the young girl. She didn't know how to rid herself of it.

Later, a casket arrived on the six o'clock train from W. C. Cooper Funeral Home in Jacksonville. The men placed Tom Brown in it and set him in the middle of the living room with a lamp burning at each end of the casket. Arrangements had been made for a priest to come the next morning and meet the family at the cemetery. But that night, a vigil was kept on the body of Tom

Brown. A few friends and relatives came in the early evening, but the storm kept most away. And as night fell, the family members started, one by one, taking their turns keeping watch with their father.

Oleta had avoided the living room. She knew she would be expected to take her turn sitting in there, not so much to relieve other family members of this task but to show respect to her father. This was her final duty to him. But in that room, in that narrow wooden box, was a dreaded reality the girl couldn't bring herself to face. Finally, at about half past ten that night, she gathered her resolve and walked to the living room door. No one was in there, which seemed to make it easier for Oleta to do what she knew she must. The girl stood for a moment at the door and through the dim lamplight looked at the open casket elevated on a table at the other end of the room. Slowly she moved forward with her eyes on the floor. Then she raised her head and looked full into her dead father's face. She was not prepared for what she saw.

The lamplight glistened on his starched white shirt and on the gold cuff links in his cuffs and in the black pools of Oleta's eyes. Tom Brown lay there like a carved figure, white as wax. As she looked at that white face, Oleta thought that face was not her father's face. When she looked at his hands crossed there on his chest, she thought those waxen white hands were not her father's hands. She raised her hand to touch him, to hold his hand in her hand, but as her fingers touched his fingers, she pulled them back.

The morbid gloom, the dreaded reality crowded at her heart. Yet, still, there was something in the girl that half-expected him to look up and smile in response to her. She bent over and kissed him, and the iciness of his skin made her shudder. She put her lips to his forehead, and with the touch of that icy cold skin, the reality of his death cut her. "Pa's dead," Oleta whispered to herself. "He's dead." The girl turned and walked from the room.

Outside, the wind and rain gathered strength. By morning, the wind was such that at times the gusts seemed almost to lift the Brown house off its pilings, and the great boughs moaned and creaked overhead, as though they might be torn from the massive trunks of the old oaks. Darkness was slowly dispelled, but when Oleta looked out her window through the gray light, she saw those limbs, usually immoveable, writhing in the grip of the storm.

But in spite of the storm, the Browns went on with the funeral. Mr. Charlie Jones, the owner of the grocery store on Pablo Avenue and one of the few people in the area with an automobile, came with his car to take the family to the cemetery. Mr. Rodenizer and Mr. Oehler came in a wagon to take the casket with Tom's body. When Oleta stepped outside to the front porch, the wind almost swept her against the wall. She feared leaving the protection of the porch; the limbs overhead were in such a commotion that she imagined them crashing to the ground at any moment. But she dashed to the automobile and crowded herself in with the other family members.

The wagon and car inched through the driving rain. As always, when they left the barrier formed by the oaks, the wind hit with greater force. The rain, like white wet sheets, curtained the car so that the travelers could not see beyond its hood. They did not take the usual road to Pablo Beach but went north on the road that the family called the "white road," a ribbon of powdery white sand. Through the storm, the little procession made its way along the white road, skirting the edge of Small's Hammock. Oleta knew that to her right lay miles of palmettos and twisted low-lying scrub oaks and that to her left lay the hammock, but they were both invisible to her. In the road ahead, through the shroud of wind and rain, she could see only the faint gray outline of the wagon containing her father's casket.

When they arrived at the cemetery, the priest from Jacksonville was there waiting in a car. After the casket had been unloaded and the family had huddled in a small circle, he came, said a few prayers for Tom Brown and ran back to the car. As the family stood and watched the body being lowered into the ground and covered with earth, there might have been tears streaming down their cheeks and loud cries rending the air, but no one would have known, because the rain had soaked each of them, and the wind roared louder than a freight train overhead. But they stood banded together, Oleta, Annie, and May with the other members of their family, bidding Tom Brown farewell and watching his casket disappear beneath the piles of muddy earth. Afterward, Annie placed a wreath on the soft dirt mound of her husband's grave. Turning to Mr. Jones's waiting automobile, Oleta bent and picked a flower from the wreath. She would keep it for years, pressed in the pages of her Bible. In the car, Annie, May, and Oleta, with the flower cradled in her open palm, huddled wet and exhausted. And for the three women, life began without Tom Brown.

As the family made its way home from the graveyard, the wind and rain that had persisted for two days stopped. The clouds parted, revealing a blue sky and bright sun. When they reached the Brown place, they were surprised to see huge limbs scattered across the yard. Bubba looked at Annie and May and said, "I'll be damned! I'll be damned if we haven't buried Pa in the middle of a hurricane!" Annie nodded in agreement. Only hurricane-force winds had ever broken those limbs before.

That night, Annie and May and Oleta were alone. The three women sat by themselves at the big oaken dinner table eating their supper. Annie gazed across the table at her youngest daughter. Oleta looked so frail, she thought, and so grave. The family had never expected much help from the girl. She was the baby, and by each of them, she had been accorded some special treatment and privileges. That would have to change now, Annie knew. If the three women were to survive, if the dairy were to survive, Oleta would have to do her share of the work. And yet somehow this idea bothered Annie. She had never minded exacting labor from those of her household, but Oleta was different from her other children. The young girl had developed in other ways. She was artistic and musical. She loved to read. She could amuse herself for hours in her own fantasy world, furnished with books and music and her own vivid imagination. And when Oleta walked, Annie thought it was with the same bearing one would expect from a young princess.

But Oleta was no princess. She was a member of a family that had managed, only by endless hard work, to stave off the poverty that was common to this area. No, Annie thought, Oleta could not be spared. And she was very sorry for that.

There had been no conversation at the table that night, only the quiet sounds of evening beyond their doors and the crackling of the dying fire in the wood stove. Annie broke the silence. "Tomorrow morning, Leta, you will have to get up and help me get the cows milked before I take you to school. May needs to go back and finish the south field." The girl nodded, but somewhere beyond that small circle of light, the morbid gloom crowded at her.

That night, she climbed into her bed, and in the dark, in her exhaustion, it claimed her. And as she slept, she dreamed of her father. In her dream, he was alive and walking back down the white sand road from the cemetery, and in her dream, she was crying, "Oh, no! Pa's alive again. We'll have to go through his dying again and burying him again." And she awoke, strangling in sorrow and gloom.

Over and over in the weeks ahead, the young girl had the same dream, and over and over she would awaken shivering in the darkness alone. Every morning, far earlier than she had ever risen before, she was awakened by May or Annie. She would milk the cows and pour the liquid into large galvanized jugs and quart jars, which she and Annie would load onto the wagon. The horses had to be fed and then hitched to the wagon. And long before sunrise, May would be off alone to the fields. For now, Oleta would continue her schooling. Annie couldn't bear to take that from the girl. But in the afternoon, when she returned home, she would begin her chores immediately and would work until long after dark. Every night, the three women sat silently eating, exhausted and indifferent to the milk and bread before them.

One evening several weeks after her father's death, Oleta finished her chores early. The sun had just dipped behind the western trees, and May was not yet in from the fields. The thirteen-year-old girl had helped Annie move a section of fence that afternoon and had sterilized the milk containers, fed the animals, and milked the cows. Every part of her body ached from doing labor to which she was not accustomed, labor for which she was not physically suited. She walked to the front porch and sat down on the top step. Looking up into the branches above and to the twilight skies beyond them, tears welled in her eyes, and her throat hurt with choking them back. "The work," she thought, "the work! It never ends."

And there, sitting on that step in the cool December twilight, she understood exactly what her father's death meant. "Pa's gone! He's gone, and he's
never coming back!" And the young girl drew her knees to her chest, burying her face in them as she began to sob. She cried the tears one cries when
confronted with truth. She cried the tears that wash and cleanse and set free,
and with every sob that convulsed her thin young body, the morbid gloom
dissipated. Deep within her, something of Annie's stubborn determination and
May's quiet strength began to well up in the young girl.

She looked out beyond the shadows of the oaks and saw in the gray light
May approaching from the south field; she was walking, leading the horse. Her
feet were dragging, and her shoulders were hunched. Oleta stood, and through
her tears, she perceived May's weariness. With tears still streaming down her
cheeks, she leapt to the ground and ran to her sister, throwing her arms around
her and crying, "I love you, May. I love you." The two stood for a moment
enfolded in each other's arms, and May found comfort there in the arms of her
young sister. Then holding May's calloused hands in her own, Oleta urged,
"Now, you go on in the house, May, I'll take care of the horse."

"Oh, no," the woman responded, "I'll do it."

But Oleta insisted, "May, go in."

The young woman handed the reins to the girl and turned toward the
house.

The Dance

We worked all the same amount of fields with some hired help we would get
sometimes. We worked! I remember one New Year's Eve, there was going to be a
dance at the Beach, and I was looking forward to going to that dance so much.
And my mother, she took that day to move some fence. She was always changing
fences around. We worked out there in the cold that day until almost dark.

—Oleta, 3 March 1984

IN THE EARLY morning quiet, while all the coast of Florida lay still and black
and before the sun had sent its first light shooting upward in the eastern sky,
the Browns' rooster climbed onto his perch, puffed out his chest, stretched out
his neck, and began to sing with all his strength. The sound of his song pierced
through the darkness of Oleta's room, and the fifteen-year-old girl jerked to a
sitting position in her bed.

"It's late!" she thought. "We've got to get started." The rooster crowed
again, and the girl reached for a match on the table beside her bed. When she
found one, she struck it on the undersurface of the table and lit a kerosene
lamp. Rising to her feet, she picked up the lamp and hurried quietly to May's room.
She leaned over and gently shook the woman's shoulder. "Come on, May! We
have a lot to do today." May turned sleepily, peering into Oleta's anxious face.

"You afraid we gonna miss the dance tonight?" May whispered in amusement.

"Well, you don't want to miss it, do you? And you know Ma won't let us
go before every lick of work is done."

May climbed from her bed, and both young women slipped into their cotton dresses and brogan shoes. And because it was winter and there was a chill
in the air, they pulled on their sweaters. In the darkness, they lit the lantern on
the back porch and made their way to the dairy. Quickly, Oleta tended cow
after cow and poured buckets of their milk into the five-gallon galvanized jugs.
Then she and May loaded the containers onto the wagon and hurried inside for
breakfast.

It was New Year's Eve, 1923, and there was a big dance that night at Plummer's Pavilion on the oceanfront in Pablo Beach. People from Palm Valley to
Mayport would be there this evening. And Oleta had set her mind to finish the
day's chores in time to dance every dance.

After a hasty breakfast, Oleta led the horses from the barn and hitched
them to the wagon, and she and May left to deliver the milk. In the two years

since her father's death, many changes had taken place in Oleta's life. Some of these changes were hard adjustments for the young girl. The three days of her father's illness and his sudden death had transformed her from a child of whom little was expected to a young woman who must shoulder an adult's share of the work.

In spite of Oleta's increased workload and Annie's renewed efforts, May still did the bulk of the hard labor. Several months after Tom's death, Annie noticed that May's gingham dresses were hanging off her. Often, the young woman came in after a day in the fields and scarcely ate her supper because she was so tired. Annie was concerned for her older daughter. Something had to be done.

Then, one day, a transient appeared in the front yard beneath the oaks. He called to the Browns, "Anybody home?" Transients, black and white, were not uncommon on roads near the Brown place. And they often approached the white frame house seeking work from its owner. Jobs were scarce in those days, and some men would work all day for a meal or two. But this was the first time since Tom's death that a strange man had been near the place, and when Annie peered from the front door at the man in the yard, for the first time, she became aware that she and her daughters were in a vulnerable position. They were totally unprotected out in those woods, with no man in the house and no close neighbors.

The presence of any stranger would have alarmed Annie, but this stranger was a black man, and Annie Brown was scared to death of black men. So on that day, Annie walked to the closet and picked up Tom Brown's rifle before going to the door and opening it.

"What do you want?" she demanded in her meanest voice, as she cracked the door open and pointed the gun straight at the man. Now, even though Annie was barely five feet tall, she now weighed close to two hundred pounds and was a formidable woman. And when that man saw the stout little woman step out on to the front porch with her rifle aimed right at him, he was frightened. "I don't want nothin'. I'm goin' now, ma'm!" he stammered.

"You going!" Annie yelled. "Where you going?"

"I'm leaving, ma'm! I'm gettin' off your land right now!" The man turned and headed briskly for the road in front of the Brown place, glancing back over his shoulder at Annie to make sure she wasn't chasing him.

But as Annie stood there watching the man leave, an idea came to her. Even though she didn't like having a strange man around her daughters, maybe she should hire him for a few days and give May a break from the more demanding tasks. She yelled, "Hey! Hey, you, come back here! Come back here!" Well, she still had a gun on the man, and he figured he'd better listen to her, so he turned around and stepped carefully back up to the front porch. "You want to work for a few days?" Annie asked.

The man responded somewhat hesitantly, weighing silently in his mind the prospect of going hungry with that of working for someone like Annie Brown. But he was as desperate for work as Annie, May, and Oleta were for help, so he said, "Yes, ma'm."

"Then be here at sun-up," Annie said. "Now, get on outa here! Now!"

That night at the supper table, Annie told the girls, "I've got a hired hand coming tomorrow morning. He can help with the plowing, May, but I'll go to the fields with him." Annie wasn't about to send her daughter off to those distant fields with a man about whom she knew nothing.

The next morning, after the girls had finished milking the cows, they went in for breakfast. Annie was standing at the wood stove. Around her large hips and over her long skirt was a big leather belt, and on the belt was a holster, and in the holster was Tom's long six-shooter pistol—an arresting sight. That morning, the stranger and Annie, with Tom's six-shooter at her side, climbed into the wagon and headed to the south field. From that time, she periodically found chores for men who came looking for work, and after that day, whether there was a hired man around or not, Annie Sadler Brown always wore a gun. To Oleta, seeing her mother daily with a six-shooter strapped over her ankle-length blue-checked apron was a hard adjustment.

On the morning of New Year's Eve in 1923, as May and Oleta made their way down the sandy streets of Pablo Beach delivering milk, they passed the white frame schoolhouse, and the fifteen-year-old girl was reminded of another hard adjustment she made after her father's death. Oleta had been graduated from eighth grade the year before. For months before that, she had listened to her friends talk of the tremendous adventure they would have attending high school in the city. The Beach had no high school, so the young people would have to take the train to Jacksonville, get off at Union Station, and walk downtown to the big Duval County High School. Every day, the Beach students would catch the morning train at seven o'clock and not be home until after six that evening. Oleta had listened and kept quiet because she knew without asking that her mother and May could not spare her all day everyday, not to mention the continued hardship of taking her and picking her up at the train. But her teacher, Mrs. Newcomb, had urged the young girl to at least discuss it with her mother. So Oleta did. But Annie had only confirmed what the girl already knew: she and May could not manage without her anymore.

But Annie tried to compensate her youngest daughter. She bought Oleta a piano and gave a music teacher free room and board in exchange for lessons for the girl. Another time, Annie made similar arrangements with an art teacher. And visits to the library to borrow books for Oleta became part of Annie's routine on her trips to Jacksonville.

Even so, on that New Year's Eve in 1923, the sight of the school, dark and empty for the holidays, reminded Oleta that her formal education was over.

May jerked the milk wagon to a halt in front of Jones's Grocery, and the girl was jerked from her reminiscing. After unloading milk for Mr. Jones, the two women turned their wagon north to their biggest customer, the Continental Hotel in Atlantic Beach, a small community north of Pablo Beach. Finally, after all of their stops, they turned south again, driving the wagon quickly down First Street. The horses picked up speed, renewed in vigor by the lightened load and the prospect of going home to their stable. May and Oleta whisked across the palmetto scrub in the milk wagon and slipped beneath the oaks. By the time they had tended the horses, it was well after midmorning, and they hurried on with their chores.

Always with the thought of the New Year's Eve dance in the back of her mind, Oleta moved with determined speed as she fed the chickens and gathered eggs and washed and sterilized the bottles and jugs for the next day's milk delivery. May tossed hay to the animals in the stable and picked collards from the winter garden. Then she chopped a fresh stack of wood. Except for the tending of the cattle later, the girls had finished their chores by early afternoon. And then Annie came to them and declared, "Since you girls have finished early, I think we ought to go ahead and move that fence by the north field, so the cows can go in there and get that grass."

"Now, Ma?" the girl asked. "You know we have the dance tonight, Ma. We could do it tomorrow."

"No, I think we need to do it while we have time. Let's go ahead and get started. It'll be getting dark before you know it."

Oleta did not argue with her mother. At this particular time, Annie did not have a hired man to help them, so May and Oleta went to the barn and picked up the necessary tools, a shovel, a posthole digger, a hammer, some nails, and a pair of wire clippers. The three women strode to the north field, and Annie, plump and packing her six-gun, explained, "You see this section from where we're standing to those little pine saplings over there across the field?" The girls nodded. "Well, I want to move that so that all that grass over there is fenced and the cattle can get to it."

Moving the fence was not an insurmountable task for the three women, but to Oleta, it appeared nearly impossible to finish in time for the dance that night. And for a moment, her spirits flagged. But only for a moment. The girl had learned in the last two years that great amounts of work could be done, if a person only starts and doesn't stop. So the three women began moving the fence on that New Year's Eve afternoon.

Pulling down the fence, digging up the poles, rolling up the wiring, carrying the supports to their new positions, digging new holes, stretching and attaching the fence, and on and on, the three women worked as the sun sank lower over the western tree line. Fortunately, it had been a clear afternoon with a brisk temperature that tended to invigorate the three women. As the sun dipped behind the trees, they looked up and saw only one more small section to move in the fading light.

"Let's go!" Oleta urged her sister. "We're almost finished!" The girl moved to the last poles, loosened the nails holding the fence and began to pull it away and roll it up. Annie worked with the shovel, digging up the poles, while May went over and started digging the new holes. Then Oleta went and helped her mother free the poles, lifting them from the bed of soil. Two or three at a time, she dragged them to the holes May had prepared for them and positioned them into the earth. Then she shoveled the dirt around each pole, closing the hole. With one last piece of fence to stretch, the shadows reached across the field and engulfed Annie, May, and Oleta. In the dim light, Oleta tapped in the nails holding the last section of fence. "We're finished!" she cried brightly. "It can't be past six o'clock. Let's go take care of the cattle."

Whoosh, whoosh, whoosh, whoosh. The milk sprayed into the bucket as Oleta's hands rhythmically pulled the udders of the cows, first one hand and then the other, one hand and then the other. *Whoosh, whoosh, whoosh, whoosh.* She filled bucket after bucket with milk. "We're going to make it," she thought to herself as she finished stripping the last cow.

"Now," the girl said, "I'll heat a bucket of water, take my bath, and get ready to go to the dance." She almost ran to the house, and as she bounced onto the back porch, she grabbed a bucket and quickly began to pump water into it. Just then, Annie stuck her head out the door and said, "Come on, baby, I've got your bathwater hot." Inside, a pot of water steamed on the wood stove, and toasted biscuits warmed in the frying pan for their supper. With the early winter darkness, the air chilled, so Oleta stood beside the wood stove bathing herself, the weariness of her long day forgotten in anticipation of the evening ahead of her.

After the three women had eaten a quick supper, Oleta and May went to their rooms and dressed for the dance. The young girl finished first and called, "May! I'm ready. You ready?"

"Just a minute," the older sister answered.

At that moment, Annie walked out of her room, cleaned, combed, and dressed—without her gun. "Well, I'm ready!" she said, smiling, satisfied with herself.

"Ma, are you going?" Oleta asked with surprise.

"Yes," Annie answered, "I believe I will. I'm not going to let you girls have all the fun."

The girl laughed and said, "I'm glad, Ma." Her mother had not been to a dance since Tom Brown's death.

Annie, May, and Oleta climbed into their new car and drove to Pablo Beach. When they pulled up to Plummer's, it was a few minutes before eight o'clock. The place was already filling with people, but as Oleta sat in the car listening, she could hear that they had not started the first dance. "We made it! We got here for the first dance!" she called to Annie and May as she jumped from the car and ran ahead of them into the pavilion.

At that moment, young Howard Mickler picked up his fiddle and struck his bow to it. He made it sing. Oleta's great brown eyes flashed with excitement. Glancing around the room, she caught the eye of one of the Floyd boys, and he walked up to her and said, "You want to dance, Leta?"

"Yes!" she said, and he swung the young girl out onto the floor, and they danced.

And May danced.

And even Annie Sadler Brown danced that night.

The Onion Poultice

Jean was sick. She had plasters on her chest, mustard
plasters for pneumonia. That was all before penicillin.

—Oleta, 23 July 1984

OLETA'S SISTER Jean was married to Arthur Kelly. The couple lived in Jacksonville and operated a neighborhood grocery store out of their home on Tallyrand Avenue.

In the spring that Oleta was sixteen, when she and May made a routine stop at Jones's Grocery delivering milk, Mr. Jones told the young women that Arthur had left word to call him. So May put a call through. When Arthur answered the phone, May could hear his children crying in the background. "Jean's awful sick," her brother-in-law said. "With her being sick and the store and the babies, I've got more than I can handle. I've got to have some help. Do you suppose one of you could come up here and give me a hand?"

"What's wrong with Jean?" May asked with concern.

"I don't know. She took a cold last week, and now she's running a fever. She just keeps coughing and vomiting, can't keep nothin' down."

"Have you called Dr. Alford?" May asked.

"Yes. He's got me putting mustard plasters on her. But I've got my hands full with the babies and running the store and changing those plasters. I need help," Arthur pleaded.

"How long has she been like this, Arthur?" May asked.

"Three days! I didn't get Dr. Alford out here 'til yesterday. She kept saying she would be okay. And I can't see Alford's done her any good. She seems worse to me."

"Well, somebody will be there by this evening. You just hold on 'til we get there," May reassured him. May turned to Oleta and explained to the young girl what she knew of her sister's condition.

After finishing the milk delivery, the two hurried home, where they found Annie bent over a large black pot of boiling soap and water washing clothes. Annie raised her eyes and saw the worry in their faces. "What's the matter?" she asked.

"It's Jean again," May said in a voice full of pain and compassion for her sister.

Normally, Ida or Ada could have helped Jean and Arthur. Ida and Clarence lived in Jacksonville, but they were visiting Clarence's sister Edwarda in Valdosta, Georgia, and would not be back for several days. And Ada was expecting a baby any day. So after talking it over, the women agreed that Oleta would go to Jean's, while Annie and May stayed to tend the dairy.

Later that day, when the three women entered the Kellys' little grocery store, Arthur met them with a toddler on his hip. Annie looked at his flushed face and glassy eyes. "You been drinking, Arthur?" the blunt little woman asked.

"No, no, I've just been trying to keep everything together with Jean being sick," the man answered, looking away from Annie's direct stare. Then he added, "I ain't had no sleep in two days."

"Well, you look terrible," Annie said and put her hand to his cheek. "You got a fever too. Watch you don't come down with it."

The women passed through the little store and into the small living quarters. Beyond the parlor was the Kellys' bedroom. They entered that room and saw Jean in the bed. She turned and smiled weakly at her mother and sisters. Annie examined her daughter, using her years of experience in tending family members to judge the young woman's condition. Every breath seemed an effort. Her skin was gray from lack of oxygen, and her arms and face felt feverish under Annie's hands. She hacked a dry cough and moaned with the pain in her ribs.

"I think you have pneumonia, Jean. We better take you to the hospital," Annie declared.

"No, Ma. No, I can't leave the babies. I'll be all right in a day or two," the woman answered in shallow grunting breaths.

"Listen to me, Jean; you need to be where you can get full-time care. We'll take the babies home with us. We won't leave 'em here for Arthur to tend to."

"No! Ma, please."

Annie understood. Jean's oldest child had died when Jean was in the hospital with diphtheria. Oleta too understood her sister's fears and stepped closer, putting her hand on her arm. "It's all right, Jean. I'll take care of you."

Annie looked around. Jean had not been bathed in days. Her hair was matted, her cotton gown was stained, and her sheets were wrinkled and dirty. The rest of the living quarters was strewn with unwashed clothing. The unfinished white pine floors, which Jean usually kept glistening, were ground with dirt, and nothing had been prepared for Jean or her family to eat. The women rolled up their sleeves. Annie heated a pan of water on the stove and then started bathing her sick daughter. May put a fire under the wash pot outside and started gathering soiled sheets and clothes. Oleta found a broom and began sweeping the floors; then, on her hands and knees with a bucket of water, the girl scrubbed the pine floors with a brush. By the time Annie and May were ready to leave, Jean was bathed, in a clean gown, and in a clean bed. Clean clothes were stretched to dry on a line in the late afternoon sun, the house was in order, and a pot of soup was on the stove. The two left Oleta in charge, with instructions to leave word at Mr. Jones's grocery store if she needed them.

That night, Oleta stayed up with Jean, while Arthur spent the night on the daybed in the parlor. He had not slept for several days and looked as though he could not go on another hour. Through the dark hours, the girl tended her ailing sister. She heated mustard plasters and placed them on the woman's chest. Over and over, she offered Jean liquids, but drinking only brought on more spasms of coughing and vomiting, yet Oleta knew the woman must have fluids. Sometimes, though, Jean's coughing was so severe that she cried out in pain.

The next day, Oleta tended the children while nursing Jean. Arthur, who seemed to be better after a night's sleep, managed to tend the store. Again that night, Oleta stayed with Jean, while Arthur slept in the other room. With caring for Jean and comforting restless, fearful young children, once more the sixteen-year-old girl went without sleep.

The next morning, Oleta agreed to mind the store while Arthur ran an errand. By this time, the girl was almost numb with exhaustion, and she knew nothing about running a grocery store. It all seemed so confusing to her. Everything had to be weighed. She had never counted out change. And sometimes when customers asked for things, she wasn't even sure what they wanted.

After several hours had passed, Arthur hadn't returned. Back and forth, Oleta went between the customers in the store, Jean's sickbed, and crying little children. Late that afternoon, when Arthur returned, he looked pathetically at Oleta and Jean. "I'm sorry," he said, "I'm sorry." He started coughing, a dry hacking cough that convulsed his muscular body, and Oleta realized he would be no help to her; he had contracted Jean's sickness. Oleta walked to the storefront and locked the door. The Kelly Grocery on Tallyrand Avenue would have to stay closed for a day or two. She walked back into the parlor and looked at her brother-in-law. "You better go to bed, Arthur," the girl insisted. "You sound terrible."

On the third night, Oleta slept only spasmodically. If she wasn't up tending Jean, Arthur, and the children, then she was awakened from her fitful sleep with their painful coughing. The next day was also a blur to her. She changed babies' diapers, washed clothes outside in the big black pot, stirring and pounding them, scrubbed the pine floors, changed mustard plasters, spoon-fed her ailing sister and brother-in-law, and then held a bucket as they coughed and vomited up the few fluids she had managed to get down them. That night, she bathed the children and put them to bed on the cot next to Jean's bed. Every part of her body ached as she stood washing the dishes. If she could just hold out one more day, she thought, Clarence and Ida should be back from Valdosta, and Ida could help her.

She walked to Jean's bed and gently laid herself beside the dozing woman.

As she lay there drifting into an exhausted sleep, she listened to her sister's shallow grunting breaths. "She's no better. I have to get help. Who can I call? Oh God, who can I call?" And the girl buried her face in the pillow trying to hide the sound of her sobs. At that moment, she heard a pounding noise from the grocery store. She raised herself from the bed and walked quietly into the parlor, past the daybed where Arthur lay. He lifted his hand and whispered, "Someone's at the front door of the store, knocking. You better see who it is." The girl picked up the lamp and walked through the store. She couldn't imagine who could be out there, certainly not a customer at ten o'clock at night.

"Who is it? Who's there?" she asked.

"Leta, is that you? Open up, it's Clarence!"

"Clarence! Oh, thank God! Clarence!"

Oleta quickly unlocked the door for Clarence Oesterreicher, her sister Ida's husband. "What are you doing here tonight? I didn't think y'all were due back until tomorrow night."

"I had to get back for work, but Ida and the kids aren't coming until tomorrow. When I got home, someone had left word with a neighbor that we needed to check on you and Jean."

"They are all sick, Clarence. Jean's terrible. I think she needs to be in the hospital. Clarence, there was no one I could call."

"Well, let me see her." Oleta knew the Oesterreichers doctored themselves with home remedies. Clarence might be able to help Jean. The young man walked softly into Jean's house, bending first over Arthur to ask, "You down, ol' man?"

"Yeah! I'm down, but never mind me. See about Jean!"

With Oleta holding the lamp, Clarence leaned over and listened to Jean's chest. He held the woman's wrist in his hand checking her pulse and touched his palms to her cheeks. He put his hands on her sides and felt her exposed ribs as she lifted her shoulders gasping for breath.

"She vomit any blood?" he asked Oleta.

"Rust," the girl replied.

"She probably pulled all her insides loose, vomiting and coughing. They got any onions out there in that store?"

"Yes."

"Well, get as many as they got and bring them in here and start peeling and slicing them. We'll get her chest opened up right now."

The girl did as he instructed, while Clarence went to the back yard and started chopping wood. When he had several armloads, he brought them in, stuffed some in the wood stove, and stacked the rest in the corner. He started a blazing fire. "Now find me some clean flannel, while I cook up these onions," he directed. "We'll make up a plaster that will get that poison out of her."

"An onion plaster?" the girl said. "I've never heard of such a thing."

"Well, course you haven't! That's one my Grandpa Jake used to use on the slaves when they was sick back at Spring Island."

The onions cooked and filled the air of the two-room house. Clarence laid out strips of flannel and spread a layer of the hot moist onions on them. "Now, Leta, unbutton her gown and put this directly on her chest." And so they started. All night they worked. As soon as one plaster cooled, Clarence had another one ready for Oleta to put on her sister. With Clarence's help and encouragement, the girl had found new hope and strength. All night, Jean moaned and coughed. But finally, just before dawn, color crept back into her cheeks, and the woman no longer seemed to be stretching up and out of herself for every breath. Clarence stopped the procedure, removed the last plaster, and listened to her chest. "You better, aren't you?" he asked, and the woman nodded her head. Oleta stood over them holding the lamp, swallowing hard to keep from crying tears of relief and exhaustion.

Clarence walked to the daybed and listened to Arthur's labored breathing, saying, "Jean's going to be all right."

Arthur smiled, "Thank the Lord! God Almighty, Clarence, she's been sick, and there ain't no talking her into the hospital. God Almighty, that is a stubborn woman." And his frame shook with a stream of hacking coughs.

After the coughing had subsided, Clarence said, "You can't blame her for not wanting to leave the babies after the last time, Arthur."

"Oh God, no! I know it. That was so terrible. I don't know if she will ever get over losing that baby."

Then Clarence turned to Oleta. "I've got to get to work. You hold on here today, honey. Keep those plasters on Jean and better start them on Arthur too. Can you manage that?"

"Yes! Yes, I can manage if I'm doing some good. Nothing I did helped before you came, but Jean seems better and I'll be fine."

Though the girl had not slept for several days, she ran on renewed hope that day. Jean was getting better, and Ida, she knew, would be there that night. All day she cooked onions over the hot wood stove and made plasters for Jean and Arthur, so that the two-room frame house was like an oven from the blazing fire. Strands of Oleta's hair, wet with perspiration, stuck to her face and neck, and beneath her cotton dress, she could feel the beads of sweat forming across her midriff.

Night came, and it was time to ready the children for bed. Oleta's exhaustion began to take its toll. She moved as though she were in a dream. Her eyes burned, and every part of her body was heavy. "Where's Ida?" the sixteen-year-old girl asked herself. "She should be here by now." After putting the children in their bed, she went to Jean and began to wash her face, rousing the sick woman to give her a sip of tepid tea. "Come on, Jean, you need this."

Jean opened her eyes. "My poor little sister. We are putting you through it, aren't we?"

And as she had done many times in the last days, the girl bit her lip to keep from crying. The girl lowered her body to a sitting position on the bed beside her sister. Too tired to move another step, she just sat there watching Jean drift in and out of sleep. And then she heard voices at the storefront. "They're here! Ida's here, Jean. She'll help us!" Oleta cried, running to the door to open it for Clarence and Ida and almost falling into the big arms of her older sister.

"Oh, baby, Clarence tells me you've had your hands full. What a mess for you to have to handle all by yourself. We didn't know anything until Clarence got home last night. And my train was late today, wouldn't you know?" And then to Clarence, "My God, Clarence, look at her! She looks like she's going to drop on the spot. We better get her to bed. How long's it been since you slept?"

"I think, days," the young girl murmured.

Ida spread a clean sheet on a sofa in the corner of the parlor and gently put the girl to bed there, covering her with a thin blanket, but Oleta couldn't sleep. Her feelings of responsibility could not be relinquished so easily. Every movement, every sound urged her to wakefulness; the body she had driven for days did not know to relax. And when she tried to force herself to be still and sleep, she began to tremble.

Finally, Clarence noticed the young girl there, curled and shaking beneath the blanket. The young man pulled a chair beside her, putting his hand on her shoulder as one would pat a restless infant, gently comforting her. And softly he spoke to the weary young girl, soothing her. "Go to sleep now, baby. Go to sleep. You've been a good girl. We're here to take care of things now. Go to sleep." Hot tears welled in her eyes. "It's all right, now, go to sleep. We're here. You've been a good girl. You can sleep now, Leta." And Oleta drifted into sleep.

Hugie and Oleta

I asked your mother for you, little girl.
She said you were too young.
I wish I never saw you, little girl.
I wish I had never been born.

Darling, though storms may rule this ocean
And heaven may cease to be
All this wide world may lose its motion
If I prove false to thee.

HUGIE OESTERREICHER HAD known Oleta Brown's family for as long as he could remember; the Browns' plot of land was twenty miles north of the Oesterreicher place but closer to the coast. The Oesterreicher cattle often roamed onto the Brown property and had to be rounded up from there in the spring. And his brother Clarence had married Ida Brown, one of Oleta's older sisters. However, Hugie had never noticed Oleta because she was just a little girl.

But in 1924, Hugie took a job for several weeks tending the Palm Valley Bridge over the Intracoastal Waterway. That year he was twenty-five years old. He had a muscular build that in later years became bearlike in appearance. His blond wavy hair tumbled over heavy dark brown eyebrows and thick black curling lashes, and his deep blue eyes were the color of a Florida sky on a clear autumn afternoon.

Tending the Palm Valley Bridge was an exciting change for the young man, who spent most of his days doing backbreaking work in the isolated woods. During this brief period of his life, he would stand on the bridge and greet with open gaze and broad smile the locals who were plying peacefully over the glistening waters of the Coastline Canal or passing by in automobiles or wagons. Occasionally, Hugie had to open the bridge for the big white yachting vessels of wealthy northerners on their way to south Florida or for the dredge that inched its way along pumping sand from the main channel.

A fishing camp with docks nestled beside the Palm Valley Bridge, and people from miles around used those docks for fishing. One Sunday afternoon, Hugie's brother Clarence and his family pulled up to the camp in a car. They honked the horn and waved to Hugie standing on the bridge. As he watched them pile from the car, he saw Ida and her sister Ada and Ada's husband, Garland Strickland. And one other young girl was with them, but he didn't recognize her from that distance. The bridge-tending business was quiet that afternoon, so Hugie decided to join the group on the docks. As he walked closer, he realized the girl with Clarence and Ida was Ida's youngest sister, Oleta. Hugie hadn't seen her for several years.

Oleta had become a pretty little girl, Hugie thought. She was tall for a girl in those days, as tall as Hugie, over five-feet seven-inches, and uncommonly thin, with a thick mass of long brown hair worn in large loose buns over her ears. Her huge brown eyes seemed like dark moons in her pale face. When Oleta first saw Hugie walking down from the bridge to join them, she noticed that he was a ruggedly handsome young man. But that didn't impress her; she was far too level-headed to be won by either a handsome face or a flattering tongue. Besides, she was wary of the Oesterreicher men. They were known to be wild and headstrong woodsmen, and she didn't want to spend her life trying to tame one of them. So she went over to the edge of the dock and fished by herself.

All the while that Hugie laughed and joked with Clarence and his family, something about the young girl with them drew his attention. Her quiet grace was rare in one her age and in that place. Oleta was sitting on the edge of the dock with her bare feet dangling into the water below her. She had an air of gravity about her, but when Hugie approached and offered to help bait her hook, she smiled with genuine appreciation.

Hugie stayed with her that afternoon. They laughed and talked, and he noticed that the quiet, serious attitude of the young girl quickly dissipated. With a song, a funny story, or a kind gesture, she would lighten and sparkle like the sunlit waters around her. And by the time Oleta had waved good-bye to Hugie from the car pulling onto the dirt road that wound fifteen miles from the bridge to Pablo Beach, she knew this man possessed a simple strength and genuine kindness that surpassed that of any man she had ever known.

Hugie and Oleta didn't see each other again for a year.

But on a March morning in 1925, Hugie and George set out from the Oesterreicher place on spring roundup. During the past winter months, their five or six hundred head of cattle had ranged from their place on the edge of Durbin Swamp fifteen or twenty miles north to Pablo Beach, feeding in the grassy swamps and marshlands.

As the two young men headed north on Old King's Road past the black waters of the cypress swamps, the only sounds in the early morning darkness were the sounds they made themselves: the sound of the horses' hooves breaking fresh into the crust of the sand road, the sound of a horse occasionally rattling his bridle with a snorting shake of his head, and the sound of the leather saddles squashing from side to side as the weight of the men shifted back and forth with each of the horses' movements. When they crossed Box Branch and Pablo Creek, the woods were still black. But as they drew near the Intracoastal Waterway, the first signals of dawn were highlighting the eastern sky. Around them, gray shapes of trees and brush were becoming apparent, and somewhere in the distance, a rooster was crowing.

When the men reached the waterway, the tide was low, so they guided the horses onto the mucky black banks looking for a narrow place to cross. Fiddler crabs scurried beneath the feet of their animals. The young men pushed their horses into the brackish water and saw it quickly rise to the flanks of the animals, swirling about them as they moved forward. Wading onto the opposite shore, they began to traverse the marshlands that lined the eastern side of this part of the coastal canal. The waking birds were singing, and looking up, the men saw the first tinges of pink in the early morning sky.

They moved onto the Brown land, passed their south field, and followed the wagon ruts through the tall pines of the savannahs and around the outer edges of their cattle pens. Ahead of them loomed the oak grove, and on the fringe, they saw a light gleaming from the milk house. The two men guided their horses to the lantern light.

That morning, Oleta had risen before daylight, dressed for work, and found the lantern on the back porch. After splashing her face with water from the pump, she had hurried to the milk house. And though the day had started as every day had started in the four years since her father's death, this would be a singular morning that she would remember the rest of her life. As Oleta sat milking the cows by lantern light, she heard voices coming toward her on the quiet morning air. She raised herself from her stool and walked to the edge of the shed, looking to see from whence these voices came. Two men on horseback were riding toward her, skirting the edges of the cow pen. Standing in the shadows of the shed, she watched to see if the riders were heading for the Brown place or if they were only passing by.

At first, the seventeen-year-old girl, peering through the dim light, didn't recognize the men. But as they drew nearer, she was mortified. "It's Hugie!" she thought and looked down at herself in dismay. Her worn cotton dress hung loosely on her. She had barely taken pains to pin her hair out of her eyes that morning, and she felt her face seemed too scrawny and pale without rouge or lipstick and her legs too naked and skinny without stockings. But her shoes were the most embarrassing to the sensitive young girl, as she looked down at the thick clumsy brogans caked with months of mud from the cow pens and fields.

"Maybe I can hide and they won't see me," she thought as she ducked back into the shadows of the milk house, but it was too late. "Hello, there!" one of the men called. Oleta stood back for a moment. They called again, "Hey, Leta!"

"Too late," she thought as she stepped from beneath the shed and gave a faint smile. Hot embarrassment at her appearance welled in her, and she blushed as she waved her hand in greeting.

"Hello!" she said, "What you two doing this far away from home so early this morning?" And for the first time since the day they had spent fishing together over a year before, she looked into Hugie Oesterreicher's clear blue eyes. He smiled, "We just trying to get our cattle together for penning. How you folks gettin' on here?"

He didn't say, "How are you three women doing here all by yourselves?" but she knew that was his real inquiry. Were they managing to hold together? Everyone knew Annie had determined to keep the dairy running, though many had thought she should sell it and move into Pablo Beach to find work for herself and her daughters there. Oleta answered because she knew Hugie's question had been in sincere concern. "We're doing fine. We had to sell off some of the cattle and hogs, and this fall, we didn't plant the south field, but we've managed to hold on to most of our dairy customers, so we're making out fine."

At that moment, the aroma of breakfast floated across the morning air from the Browns' kitchen, and Hugie looked up and questioned Oleta with a grin, "What's that I smell?"

The girl laughed and said, "Ma's cooking sausage."

That morning, the Oesterreicher men stayed for breakfast with the three Brown women. During the whole meal, Hugie talked to Annie, but he watched Oleta. And as he watched her, he became aware of a dull empty place inside himself that he had never realized was there. And when Oleta looked at him with her dark oversized eyes and gave a shy smile, deep inside that empty place, something moved, came to life, and began to grow. Hugie never noticed that Oleta's gingham dress was too big for her or that her ankles were dwarfed in the high loose tops of the dirty brogans, because on that March morning in 1925, to Hugie Oesterreicher, Oleta Brown became forever beautiful. And before he rode his horse from beneath the quiet shade of the live oaks, he had determined in his heart to marry her.

Now, in Oleta, as she sat across the table from Hugie, something stirred, responded to this man's openness, his warmth, the comfort of his strength. However, she would not have called this stirring love or even the beginnings of love. And although Oleta knew she would see this burly little woodsman again, she did not wait with impatience or anxiety for that day, because without anything being said between them, Hugie had transmitted that quiet confidence to the young girl.

Two months later, on a Sunday afternoon, the Brown women were taking a rare afternoon away from chores. They sat quietly on the front porch gazing across the stretches of palmettos. After awhile, Annie saw a black speck bobbing across the silvery green fronds toward them. "Someone's coming," she said, and within minutes, George Oesterreicher had galloped in beneath the oaks on horseback.

"Howdy," he said as he climbed down from his horse at their front porch. George untied something from his saddle horn. When he started up the steps, they could see it was a small basket. He walked straight to Oleta and handed it to her. "Got something for you," he said. "Hugie sent them." The girl smiled with delight. She had received few presents in her life, so she took the basket heartily. At first glance, all she saw were the remnants of an old flannel baby blanket. She looked puzzled for a moment, and George said, "Go on, look under there." So she carefully pulled back the flannel and there, snuggled in the folds, were two baby squirrels, no bigger than her own little finger and still without any hair. Oleta gently took the squirming little things into the palm of her hand. She named them Romeo and Juliet.

Two weeks later, Hugie came to check on the baby squirrels. And thereafter, he drove to see Oleta every Sunday. Shortly after she turned eighteen, he asked her to marry him, and she agreed, not because she loved him, but because he loved her. Somehow the young woman had enough understanding to know that the love Hugie Oesterreicher bore her was an uncommon privilege—one she might go her whole life without ever experiencing again.

On many Sundays, Hugie would drive Oleta to see members of his family. They would visit Clarence and Ida Oesterreicher in Jacksonville, or they would drive the twenty miles of dirt roads to the cypress cabin and spend the afternoon with his parents. Often the dirt roads would become almost impassable: if there had been heavy rains, they would turn to a bog of thick mud; if there had been a prolonged dry spell, the surfaces became soft sand in which the wheels of a Model T Ford might only spin and bury themselves. When the roads were in these conditions, Hugie and Oleta would try to catch a low tide and use the beach as a highway south. If the tide was right, they could travel most of the distance on a surface that was harder and smoother than many of the roads in this part of the state. They could get on the beach in Pablo Beach and drive the ten miles to Mickler's Pier, the only access across the high dunes that lined the coast between Pablo Beach and St. Augustine. After crossing the dunes, Hugie and Oleta could take Mickler's Road to the Palm Valley Road, which took them to the Palm Valley Bridge. From there, it was only a few more miles through the woods to the cypress cabin.

Oleta and Hugie were to be married in a few months. One Sunday afternoon, they sat on the front porch of the cypress cabin, and Hugie said, "Well, I went to town yesterday and bought the material to start building our house. It'll be delivered at Durbin Station on Tuesday afternoon. I'll be able to start building on it in my spare time. I thought I would put it right over there on that little rise." He pointed to a place about a hundred yards from the Oesterreicher cabin.

"What?" Oleta wasn't sure she had understood exactly what he was saying. "You're building it over there?" She pointed to the place in front of them. "You want to live out here?"

Hugie nodded and smiled.

"But I thought we would live closer to Pablo Beach, closer to my mother," Oleta said.

"I've got to live out here. I can't leave the folks. I'm the last one home. There's no one else to take care of them."

The girl looked at the man she was to marry, trying to hide her disbelief. But Hugie saw it in her eyes and stated with a conviction that left no room for argument, "I've got to, Oleta."

She didn't say anything. She just sat there trying to grasp what he was saying to her, trying to reconcile herself to this new development. For the first time, the girl considered the place Hugie called home. To the west and north of the rustic cabin was the great dark swamp and to the east and south were miles of uninhabited woods. The only link with the outside world was an endless succession of bad roads. If she were to live in these woods, there would be no quick dashes to Pablo Beach or quiet visits with her mother on the summer evenings when she and Hugie wanted to get out of the house for an hour or two. Her only neighbors would be Hugie's parents.

As Hugie drove Oleta home late that afternoon, every mile of the trip seemed magnified in the girl's mind. "Every time I want to go some place, I'll have to pass through these woods," she thought, "and across these pine flats and through that cabbage tree swamp and across that bridge and down that winding road through those deep Palm Valley woods." And by the time Hugie and Oleta had pulled beneath the oaks at the Brown place, she was having doubts about her decision to marry him. But she said nothing to him at that time.

But as the days and weeks passed, her doubts increased, and she tried to talk to Hugie. To have been forthright would have been cruel, to have said, "I don't want to live down there, cut off from the rest of the world. I don't want to live next to your parents. The idea of it makes me feel choked. I can't bear the thought of it." So she dropped hints to the young man, but he seemed not to hear them.

The weeks passed. Hugie filled his visits with talk of the house he was building for them. Each Sunday afternoon, he would report with excitement the progress he had made. "It's framed." "The walls are up." "I got the roof on last Thursday." "I found a nice little wood stove for us in St. Augustine last week." However, the truth was, in his heart, Hugie knew Oleta was having doubts. But his love for her and his own fear of losing her were such that he could not bring himself to discuss her doubts openly. So with all of his love, he built the little house on the rise in front of his parents' house, believing, hoping that when the tall quiet girl saw the home he had prepared for her, her doubts would vanish. In his mind, he had no choice but to stay and take care of his aging parents. Although other men would have walked away from that situation, he could not. And also, Hugie knew his place. He knew the woods.

In that element, he was peerless, superb, self-confident. To put him in another environment would have been to put him at extreme disadvantage. And in that spring of 1926, he thought that the northeast Florida woods would always be there and that he would always be able to provide for Oleta and their children out of those woods, so rich in game and grazing land for cattle and hogs. So in choosing to make his home out there on the edge of the great Durbin Swamp, he was not being entirely stubborn and selfish. He knew that, at what he did, he was the best, but that, in trying to make a living any other way, he would become less than other men.

And through all of this time, Oleta too began to realize this about the man she had agreed to marry. He was a woodsman, and if she did indeed marry him, then she must go to the woods with him. Possibly, she knew, she could be insistent and demand that they make their home elsewhere, but to take Hugie Oesterreicher out of those forests and swamps would be to take from him part of his essence, his substance. She could not do that. She would marry him on his terms or not at all. And with this realization, the young girl felt more and more trapped by her decision. She loved Hugie, but it was not that quality of love and passion that demanded satisfaction. Therefore, she was not driven to overcome obstacles and fears in order to meet some unquenchable need within herself. However, her respect for the man had only grown in the weeks since their engagement. She knew he was a man in whom she could place absolute trust and because of this assurance, she hated herself for being less than honest with him. She was in a dilemma.

She had made a commitment that, with each passing day, seemed too great to keep, yet she only knew to be faithful in keeping commitments. She had never wanted to hurt Hugie Oesterreicher, yet to marry him with these ambiguous feelings would be totally unfair to a man who deserved much more. If she could not go out there and be a wife to him with all her heart, she should not do it at all. So the young girl made her decision. Sunday afternoon, when Hugie came for his usual visit, he announced that next Sunday, he would take her to see their home, finished and completely furnished. The girl swallowed to keep from crying. They walked beneath the oaks, and the girl called the squirrels he had given her. At the sound of her voice, Romeo and Juliet leapt from the branches overhead to the shoulders of the girl and scampered around her neck in a frenzy of tag with each other's tails. Oleta laughed, and Hugie loved her.

But she could delay no longer. So she took his rough hand in her own slender fingers and led him to the steps on the back porch. As she sat there holding his hand, it occurred to her that she had never seen a hand like Hugie Oesterreicher's hand. His hand was short and broad, like a bear's paw. The palms were more thickly calloused than any hands she had ever felt, more like leather that had been exposed too long to sun and rain than like human skin.

And though she knew Hugie Oesterreicher was a very handsome man, it was his hands she loved. They revealed at once all facets of his character, his bearlike strength, his endurance, his gentleness.

"I'm not going to marry you," she declared. She hated saying it. And in her hand, his hand made a fist, squeezing her fingers until they hurt. He looked enraged. She pulled her hand away. "I can't, Hugie. I can't marry you." She stood up and moved away. She had never feared Hugie, but in that moment, he looked as though he might kill her.

And only briefly, his own instinct for self-preservation wanted to cause her physical suffering, because she had just ripped his heart out by its roots and he was standing there before this slender brown-eyed girl with a gaping wound, bleeding and dying. But he didn't hit her or accuse her. He just said, "If that's what you want," and he turned and walked to his Model T.

She watched his car leave the shadow of the oaks and move onto the palmetto scrub. The girl sank to the back steps and sobbed.

Hugie rode across the scrub. His heart was gone. In its place was a huge throbbing hole. He knew he would not die, but he wasn't sure he wanted to live. His wheels whirred across the dunes and hit the wide white beach. Overhead, a great thundercloud blackened the early summer sky, and beneath it, the ocean reflecting its dark color stirred and chopped, a wind whipping the waves as they rose and peaked in white foam. A song ran through Hugie Oesterreicher's mind:

> I asked your mother for you, little girl.
> She said you were too young.
> I wish I never saw you, little girl.
> I wish I had never been born.

The Decision

Going back down the beach that afternoon, I still didn't know what I was going to answer. I still hadn't made up my mind. He said, "Have you decided what you want to do?" I knew in my heart then, whatever I said, I was going to stand by it.

—Oleta, 9 March 1984

MONTHS PASSED, and every day of that time, whenever Hugie saw the little house he had built for Oleta there on the rise in front of the cypress cabin, he remembered the gaping hole he carried everywhere, hidden beneath his clothes. He tried to fill the place with backbreaking work in the woods and headlong hunting forays into the swamps. He went to dances with his brothers and cousins only to come home more empty than before. Girls other than Oleta were willing to help him through, but none of them compared to the one he had lost. And every night during that time, he climbed into bed and stared up into the darkness and believed God was there. Hugie talked to God in the lonely stillness, "God, if it's for the best for Oleta, if it's for the best for me, let us get back together. God, if it be your will." And every night, Hugie fell asleep with that prayer on his lips.

And after a year, he had healed sufficiently that he was willing to risk another rejection by putting himself on the line once more with the girl he loved. And when Clarence said to him one day, "You know the Brown women go to those dances at Ivanoski's every Friday night. You ought to go," Hugie looked at him and said, "I believe I will." So on a Friday night in early September of 1927, Hugie went to the dance in Pablo Beach with purpose. No confusion clouded his mind; he knew exactly what he wanted.

But when Oleta heard that Hugie would be at Ivanoski's Pavilion on Friday night, all of her confusion returned. The young woman knew that if Hugie came to the dance at Ivanoski's, it was only to see her. She knew too that he would propose to her again, and she had no idea how she would answer. So the turmoil began again within her mind, the voices shouting from all directions within her head. To Oleta, a year had only increased the soberness with which she faced the choice before her. But she composed herself and, with Annie and May, went to the dance. Ida and Clarence, Ada and Garland, Bubba and Lovey were there. And as she whirled about the floor, her eyes were always on the door, expecting any minute to see Hugie appear there. She was filled at once with dread and expectation, a lightheaded giddiness, and an almost overwhelming soberness.

And then, at a few minutes after nine o'clock, he was there in the doorway, his deep blue eyes scanning the room for Oleta. When he found her, they rested until he caught her eye, and she stopped for just a moment on the dance floor. In those brief seconds, when his eyes held her eyes, she felt a rip in her own heart as she remembered the pain she had seen in those blue eyes of his on that day a year ago. She whirled on. "Oh, God! What do I do?"

Even though a slight ocean breeze swept through the pavilion, it was a hot September night, and after several more rounds on the dance floor, Oleta's face was flushed with heat. She excused herself from her partner and walked to the front porch. A full moon rising in the east formed a pool of yellow light that glowed in the blue-black skies, and straight from her place on the porch, it created a path of silver and gold, broad and bright, eastward across the nighttime seas. She remembered that, as a child, she had wanted to climb upon that path and run to the face of the moon. Legend said the great sea turtles traveled atop those moon paths to these shores, where they buried their tiny soft-shelled eggs. The girl wanted to run across that path, touch that yellow moon. "What do I do? What do I do?"

She turned, took a deep breath, straightened her shoulders, and walked back into the dance. At the edge of the room, she looked across the floor and saw Hugie moving through the crowd toward her. He was standing before her with that broad gentle smile. "Would you like to dance?" he asked. He took the risk.

"All right!" The girl smiled. She would take the risk.

He closed his strong arms around her slender waist and whirled her onto the floor.

The hours passed, and Hugie danced several more dances with Oleta. As the band announced the last number for the evening, Hugie said to her: "Will you let me drive you home?"

She paused for a moment. "Yes," she said.

Beneath the moon swimming full in the sky, they were quiet, as Hugie's Model T Ford skidded down the white ribbon road, slicing through the silver and black palmetto sea surrounding them. And then, as he pulled the car under the great live oaks and turned off the engine, once more, he risked breaking the silence between them, "Have you thought anymore about us, Leta? Have you thought anymore about marrying me?"

She didn't know what to say, but she said, "Yes, I've thought about it, Hugie. I believe we're finished." She hated herself for saying that, but she couldn't give him hope, she was so unsure of her feelings. She got out of the car.

And right then and there, Hugie Oesterreicher decided this woman was worth all the rejection she wanted to serve up to him. She could plow right over him, she could twist his heart out again. He didn't care. She was worth the price and worth the pain. For her, he would risk it. He smiled broadly, his blue eyes twinkling in the darkness. "Leta!" he called. She stopped and stood beside the car, facing him. "How would you like to see the house I built for you? I could come pick you up Sunday afternoon, and we could ride out and have dinner with the folks, and I'll show you the house."

"All right," Oleta agreed, but she thought to herself, "Why did I say that?" The full moon dappled the silver sand beneath the oaks as she turned toward her front door. "What do I do? What do I do?"

And like a great loggerhead turtle crawling along the moon path stretching across the ocean, the Model T slipped down the ribbon, cutting through the waves that sparkled in the palmetto sea. He would risk it. She was worth it.

On Sunday afternoon, as Hugie and Oleta approached the cypress cabin in his Model T Ford and turned the last bend in the road, Oleta saw his whole family on the front porch. As she and Hugie climbed from the automobile, all the Oesterreicher eyes were upon her, and in their faces, she saw the same question that taunted her: "What will you do? What will you do?"

Hugie and Oleta spent the afternoon with the folks, and then the two of them strolled over to the little house Hugie had built for her the year before. The house sat on a rise in the full sun, with trees banking on the southwest side. To the northeast was a grassy clearing. From where she stood, the cypress cabin was not in view, but hidden behind a bend in the road. Hugie had built the twenty-four-foot-square house of pine siding and painted the outside with three or four coats of oak-colored varnish, so that it seemed to blend with the surrounding forest and swamps. The house stood about three feet off the ground on pilings. A covered front porch was lined with cane-seated rockers, and as Oleta slowly stepped onto it, a breeze swept through from across the open field.

Inside, the house was partitioned into four twelve-by-twelve rooms. The white pine floors were unfinished, but the sheetrock and wood-paneled walls were painted white. And Hugie had furnished the parlor with a sofa, chair, high tea table, and a fireplace and mantel constructed by his own hands. In the kitchen stood a sink and drain board. Shelves lined one wall, and a wood stove sat in the corner. In another corner waited a square oak table and four chairs. Outside, beside the kitchen door, was a hand pump for water.

She turned and walked to the bedrooms. The first one was empty, but when she entered the room at the front of the house, she saw a mahogany four-poster bed. On one wall stood the matching dressing table and chiffonnier. She ran her hands along the spindles of the bed posts as she admired the wood with its blond and brown tones gleaming in the afternoon sun that streamed in the open window. Suddenly, there was an intimacy in the room that made the girl want to run. But she didn't.

And even though the question still taunted the girl as they made their way down the winding road toward Pablo Beach, one thing had been settled in her mind. Whatever answer she gave Hugie that day would be her final answer. "What do I do?"

And across the dunes at Mickler's Pier, the Model T raced onto the broad white beach, and there beneath the purple-blue of the early autumn sky, the ocean stretched sparkling azure and white and gold in the late afternoon sun. They skimmed the glistening sands skirting the water's edge. Sandpipers darted before them, and flocks of seagulls mounted to the air, their white wings reflecting the brilliance of the afternoon light.

Hugie stopped the car, and they began to walk. An ocean breeze blew her thick brown hair away from her face as she stood gazing at the depths of blue in the sky and sea before her, and Hugie looked at her and asked, "Leta, will you marry me?"

Oleta didn't move. Voices like the wailing of banshees careened through her mind. "What do I do? What do I do?" She turned and looked into the depths of blue in Hugie Oesterreicher's eyes. The voices howled. "Yes!" she said. She was shocked at her own answer.

The voices stopped. The confusion ceased. "Yes," she said aloud again, "I will marry you, Hugie."

Hugie laughed. "You will? You mean you will marry me?"

"I mean I will marry you." Oleta laughed.

And Hugie put his strong bearlike arms around the slender young woman and felt her soft brown hair blow across his face as he held her. From deep within him something welled, filling the dark cavern that had been his soul these last months. And there in Hugie Oesterreicher's arms, Oleta Brown found a place of security, a place of rest that she had never known in her life.

On a crisp November day two months later, Hugie and Oleta were married. He arrived at the Brown place that morning to take Oleta away with him. In the last two months, she and Ida had made several trips to Jacksonville shopping for her trousseau. Oleta bought several pairs of shoes, nightgowns, lingerie, and a black evening coat trimmed in white fur. Except for the clothes she needed for her honeymoon, she had packed all her things in a fine new trunk she had purchased from a leather shop in town. Hugie had already transported that trunk and Oleta's piano to her new home at the edge of Durbin Swamp.

On the day of her wedding, she had risen full of the kinds of complex feelings one experiences on a day that marks everlasting changes in one's life. Even though she knew she was doing the right thing in marrying Hugie, she hated leaving May and Annie. How would they manage without her? So much of Annie's fight had left her in the last year or two. And what of May? What would May do with her life now? In recent weeks, the girl had realized, "Ma and May went to dances because I like dances; they went to church because I go to church; they made those trips into town because I love shopping in the

Without me around encouraging May, will she just sit and molder in this house beneath the oaks?" And what about this life she had picked for herself in choosing to marry Hugie Oesterreicher? Could she stand being so far from her mother? Could she stand being isolated from the rest of the world out there in those woods? "Too late to worry about all that," Oleta thought.

She slipped into her wedding dress, a silk chemise in shades of cocoa, cream, and cinnamon. Several creamy silk ribbons fell from beneath her breast. Her thick brown hair, cut in a bob, accented the size of her eyes and the whiteness of her skin. She powdered her nose, rouged her cheeks lightly, and reddened her lips. As she slipped her slender feet into her shoes of cocoa-colored satin, she heard Hugie's Model T drive into their yard. She pulled a velvet cloche over her hair, picked up her satin purse, and stood back looking in the mirror at herself for just a moment. And when she walked into the parlor, elegant, stately, beautiful on her wedding day, Hugie knew God had smiled on him, and the light of that smile lit the young man's countenance.

George was waiting in the car to drive them to the depot at Pablo Beach. From there, they would go to Jacksonville, where they would be married. Annie and May followed the young couple to the front porch. Hugie shook Annie's hand and said looking into her dark little eyes, "Don't worry about Leta. I'll take care of her."

"I know. I know," the little woman said and threw her big arms open to her youngest child. Oleta nestled into them, reluctant to let go of the woman, Annie Brown.

And then the girl turned to May, taking the thirty-five-year-old woman in her arms, "Bye, May, take care of yourself. I'll miss you. I'll be back next week." Again she pulled away . . . hard to do . . . hard to let go . . . hard to leave them standing there on that porch.

Oleta turned to Hugie. They climbed into the car, and George started the engine. As the car pulled onto the road leading away from the Brown house, Oleta stuck her head and arm out of the window, waving to Annie and May on the front porch, calling farewell to them.

Annie and May stood watching the Model T slip from beneath the oak trees and out onto the white sand road. They saw it become a tiny black speck bobbing above the green palmetto scrub. They watched, and finally, when they couldn't see it anymore, Annie said, "He'll be good to her," and May agreed, "Yes, he will be." The two women turned and walked into the house.

The train from Pablo Beach deposited them at the new Union Station, and from there, the young couple walked to the county courthouse to buy a marriage license. From the courthouse, they went to Greenleaf and Crosby's, where Hugie bought Oleta a slender white gold wedding band to match the engagement ring he had given her a few weeks before.

After this, they walked to Holy Rosary Catholic Church on Laura Street. Inside, Ida and Clarence, Hugie's mother, Ella, and his brother Thomas waited for them. The smell of warm wax and incense permeated the air. Two candles burned in the sanctuary, while several votive lights flickered at the side altars. A few rays of sun slanted downward, finding their way through the stained-glass windows to shed a dim light on the center aisle leading to the altar. A priest stepped to the communion rail.

Oleta felt almost outside of her own body as she and Hugie walked down the center aisle of the church. Her legs trembled. She grabbed Hugie's arm to steady herself. Standing before the priest, Oleta managed a faint smile. He began to speak, but his voice came to Oleta muffled, as though her head were wrapped in cotton. The altar, the faces of the family, the face of the priest, everything seemed obscured by some dark cloud pressing into her. Through that cloud, she saw the priest looking at Hugie, talking to him, but his voice was not registering in Oleta's mind. Then she heard Hugie saying, "I will!" The sound of his voice jolted her. She tightened her grip on his arm, and somehow that boundless physical strength of his flowed into her, fixing her own determination.

The priest turned to Oleta. "Oleta, wilt thou take Huger here present, for thy lawful husband . . . to have and to hold from this day forward . . . for better, for worse . . . for richer, for poorer . . . in sickness and in health, till death do you part?"

For just a moment, she saw herself as she had been that night two months before, standing on the porch at Ivanoski's, looking out at the ocean with its bright moon path swimming before her; for just a moment, she heard the question that had tormented her, "What do I do? What do I do?"

She looked at Hugie. He waited.

"I will!" she said, smiling at Hugie. Oleta had made her decision.

The Klan

At that time, back along about '26 or '27, they sprang up at the Beach. And I
understand that the whole city council and all belonged to the KKK. And they
used to hold meetings up in Georgia somewhere, Waycross or somewhere. I knew
of people that went up there to the meetings. It was pretty open about it then.

—Oleta, 9 March 1984

BEFORE SHE OPENED her eyes, Oleta sensed the dim light of a kerosene
lamp beside her bed. Even the thought of stirring from that still position sent waves of nausea sweeping over her. She moaned. Hugie's rough hand
gently touched her face, brushing the hair from her damp forehead.

"You leaving?" Oleta whispered, her eyes still closed.

"Pretty soon. I've got to get Pa's cattle moved today, but I want to make
sure you're all right before I go."

"Oh, I'll be fine. It's the same every morning. It passes."

"I know, but it's gettin' close to your time now, and I hate to leave you
sick."

Oleta slowly opened her eyes, and in the soft lamplight, she saw Hugie
kneeling beside the bed, his deep blue eyes and golden curls reflecting the glow
around them. Oleta rolled to her side and carefully raised herself to a sitting
position on the side of the bed, her belly ballooning beneath the cotton gown.
She rose to her feet holding Hugie's arm. "Let me wash my face and try to
drink a cup of coffee. I've never known anyone who stayed sick the entire time
they were pregnant like I have. None of my sisters were like this. I can't do
anything. If I eat, I get sick; if I don't eat, I get sick. If I get too hot, I get sick.
If I ride over those bumpy roads, I get sick. Everything I do makes me sick."

"Yes, I know!" Hugie sympathized, considering the ashen color of her thin
face, so pale it was almost blue. He sat with her as she sipped her coffee. "Go
to the folks after it gets light," he said. "You shouldn't be here by yourself all
day. I'll be back before dark." And he bent and kissed her, the heavy stubble
on his face scraping her cheeks.

She smiled. "Go to the folks," she thought, "isn't that what I do every
day? Go keep company with the old folks. If I'm thirty minutes late, they start
worrying."

Hugie and Oleta had been married eight and a half months, and she was
eight full months into her pregnancy in that early August of 1928. The days
were long and hot. Folks called them dog days. She didn't know why, but she

guessed it was because they weren't fit for a dog. She agreed, they weren't. Not a breath had stirred for days. The cooling winds off the Atlantic that often blew over the stretches of palmettos to the front porch of the Brown place could not find their way across the Intracoastal Waterway and through those thick woods on the Diego Plain.

During these last eight months, Oleta had come to realize that many of her fears about marrying Hugie had not been groundless. She had feared being isolated in those woods. She was. She had feared Hugie's aging parents would be her only companions. They were. She had feared Tom Oesterreicher's backward ways would somehow stifle her. They did. She had feared being cut off from her mother would be too painful. It was. At times, standing on the front porch of the little house Hugie had built for her and looking northeast across the field, across the thick wet cabbage tree swamps, she would think, "If only that intracoastal canal wasn't there, I could cut straight across those woods and be at Ma's in no time."

Every morning, the young man left before daylight and did not return until almost dark. Oleta had never seen a man work the way Hugie Oesterreicher worked. His endurance seemed unlimited to her. Even in the oppressive heat of summer, he did not allow himself the luxury of slowing his pace. To him, the summertime only meant more daylight in which he could labor. Every night, he came home drenched with sweat, face and hair dripping, clothes soaking as though he had been working in a rainstorm instead of in the dry heat of the Diego Plain. And clinging to his wet face and hair and clothes was the dust and muck encountered in his toils that day. Sometimes, the young wife would tell her husband that he was working too hard, that she was worried for him, and he would just laugh and say, "This is nothing to me. I'm strong. And besides, I'm making lots of money." And Hugie did make good money. And because their needs were simple, most of it went into the bank.

So on that morning in August of 1928, she sat at her kitchen table slowly sipping the strong black coffee that Hugie had boiled earlier on the wood stove. Because intense heat still emanated from the dwindling fire in the stove, she stepped to the back door and opened it wide, hoping the early morning air would cool the room. Staring into the shadowy grayness of dawn, she felt that the deep dark woods of northeast Florida crowded at her from all sides. She felt stifled and gasped for air, but there was none, none beneath the heavy blanket of heat that settled over the Diego Plain, suffocating every breath at its inception.

Later that morning, just as Oleta finished her chores, she heard an engine approaching. She walked to the front door. A car turned into her place. "Bubba!" she cried excitedly as she stepped carefully down the front steps and across the front yard to greet her brother. "Bubba! What you doing all the way out here?" she asked as he turned off the engine.

"I just wanted to see my baby sister."

"Why aren't you working today?"

"Well, I am working. I'll go in later." Bubba stepped from the car dressed in his blue uniform, for he was now chief of police at Pablo Beach. But the small settlement was no longer called by that name. A few ambitious politicians had successfully promoted a name change for the little seaside community, from Pablo Beach to Jacksonville Beach, the logic of which had been based on the prosperity of Miami Beach and its close association with its big sister, Miami. The small-town businessmen figured Pablo Beach needed to align itself with the booming city of Jacksonville, even though it was twenty miles away. However, the locals never really accepted that association and didn't call their town anything except Pablo Beach for almost twenty years after that. Sometime in the early forties, though, the name Jacksonville Beach began to stick.

Bubba put his arm around his sister as they entered the house. "You want a cup of coffee? I'll heat it for you," she asked the young man. He nodded yes. "You look so handsome in that uniform. Every time I see you in it, I think you were made to wear a uniform." Poking another lightwood knot in the stove and stirring the coals, she set the pot of coffee on top. "How are Lovey and the children? Y'all doing all right, Bubba?"

Bubba didn't answer but stepped to the back door and looked out at the porch and back yard of his baby sister's place. "You and Hugie got the place looking real good. You doing all right out here, Oleta? You get lonely?"

"Oh, yes. I get lonely. But I'm doing fine. Hugie works all the time, Bubba. But we're making out fine. I knew what I was gettin' myself into when I married him."

"I know, Leta, but he's a good man. God, I don't know any better. He'd fight the devil himself for you." He sat down at the kitchen table.

"I know that, Bubba." She tilted the coffee pot and let its contents boil out into her brother's cup.

"I brought you a book and a couple of magazines. They in the automobile. Don't let me leave with them."

"Oh, I won't. But you haven't answered my question. Is everyone all right?"

Bubba shook his head, watching the morning sunlight that danced on the white pine floors.

"We're fine, but they're out to get me, Leta. They not going to stop 'til they finished me in this town."

"Who's out to get you, Bubba? What are you talking about?"

"Some of the folks in town. Some of my friends."

"But, Bubba, you're the best chief of police that town ever had. Everyone knows that. Everyone says that. You're the most fair, and you can't be bought."

"That's what they did say, but that isn't what they're saying now. They're accusing me of drinking on the job. Leta, you know I drink, but I don't drink on the job. They just cooking up any lie they can think of to get me out of there."

"Bubba, these people are our friends. They were Pa's friends. The Browns have done business with them all of our lives."

"Leta, this Al Smith thing has got the Klan all stirred up. When I come out for him, I just wrote myself out of a job in that town. They don't mind having a Catholic chief of police chasin' their niggers off the street and roundin' up their drunks, but they don't want him to have any opinions of his own. The Klan."

"The Klan, Bubba? All my life I've heard rumors about it, but I never knew anyone to own up to being in it."

"We never knew anyone to own up to it because we're Catholic. They just kept their mouths shut about it in front of us. But let me tell you, the Beach is full of them. And they want me out. They as much as told me they would lay off if I switched my support to Hoover. Well, I'm not doing it. Al Smith would make a fine president. Not just because he's a Catholic. I'd vote for him if he was a damn nigger. He's for the little man. That Hoover isn't going to do anything for us. He's for big money."

"Bubba, I never knew folks hated Catholics so much. I've always been so proud of my church. No one's ever said anything to me until this election, and now all of a sudden, Hugie and I go in a store, and folks stand over on the side and whisper."

"I tell you it's the Klan that's behind it. They have everyone stirred up. They are saying terrible things about Catholics. Saying there's a papist plot to take over the United States, and telling lies about what we believe and what we do in church. Leta, to the Klan, Catholics, Jews, and niggers are all children of the devil and need to be kept in control. Up 'til now, they left Catholics alone in this part of the country. But with Smith running for president, it's got them worried. I believe they would like to crucify him. I ain't never heard such hate as I hear around that town these days. And Lovey, she says some of the folks around town hardly speak to her, and here she is the wife of the chief of police. I tell you, Leta, I'm scared. I don't want my name ruined. I don't want to lose my job. I don't want my wife and kids harassed."

"This just seems impossible. Not here. For years, I've heard about the Ku Klux Klan and the terrible things they do to Negroes and Jews and even Catholics in other parts of the South, but I never thought I would see it here."

"Oh, they've been here. We just never been faced with 'em. Those niggers out there on the Hill, they know about the Klan, let me tell you. I've seen it in their eyes since I've been chief of police. You see the fear in their eyes. You see it in their bowing and scraping and in their 'yes, sir'-ing and 'no, sir'-ing. They have always known they better keep their place—be off the streets after dark and walk a wide path around the white folks. And the Klan has always been big in St. Augustine, but they always left the Catholics alone down there because so many of the folks in St. Augustine are Catholics."

"Well, Bubba, I guess I don't really know much about the Klan. Like I said, I've heard things, but that's the kind of thing nobody talks openly about. Kind of everyone's deep dark secret."

"You bet, Leta, the Klan has been here all along. Secret, but here. Spreading their lies. They hate anybody that isn't white and Protestant and poor. They do it all in the name of God, quoting the Bible at you. They going to keep our town back, Leta. And I'm afraid they won't rest until they have me out on the street."

"How did this happen, Bubba?"

"Well, Pa always said, and he remembered 'cause he was in his early teens, that it got started after the war, the Civil War."

"Well, Bubba, someone needs to tell the Klan that the war is over and that they lost. Bunch of grown men going around threatening innocent people. Bubba, what are you going to do?"

"I don't know. God, Leta, I don't know! I know one thing, I'm not backing down. I won't switch my vote to Hoover. He's the devil if you ask me. I'm standing behind Al Smith. He was good enough for the Democratic Party, he's good enough for me. What are the Oesterreichers doing?"

"They're all going for Al Smith."

"Nobody's threatened any of them?"

"No. No, they couldn't hurt any of the Oesterreichers. They don't need anyone."

Bubba laughed for the first time.

"I suppose the Klan stays out of Palm Valley. All the Micklers and the Oesterreichers are Catholic. Probably wouldn't want to tangle with that bunch."

"I suppose not!" the young woman agreed. "And even though Tom Oesterreicher has no love for the Catholic Church, he's a Democrat, and his party is more important to him than any religion. But besides that, he's so stubborn, nobody could tell him how to cast his vote."

"God! I'd hate to be the man that tried."

"I tell you, Bubba, he thinks he's dying, but he's still a deadly shot and would think nothing of pulling out a shotgun on anyone that threatened him or his family."

"I know that, and I think most of Duval and St. Johns counties knows that too."

"Well, Bubba, as far as I know, all the Oesterreichers and Micklers are supporting Al Smith."

"Thank God for that. At least I'm not alone. I think half of the Democrats in Duval County are crossing over and voting for Hoover come November. They're in a panic at the thought of having a Catholic president."

Bubba crossed again to the back door. The August sun flooded the morning, drenching in light the wooden planks of the porch, the bright colors of Oleta's flowers, the garden, the white and red chickens scratching in their pen, and the fields and woods pressing around them all. "God. Another scorcher. We need a good rain. Maybe it would cool things off." The young man pulled his sister to his side and winked at her. "Guess I better get back and face the Klan."

"Oh, Bubba, I hate them for doing that to you."

"I'm going to be all right, Leta. I suppose I just wanted you to know. If you hear anything about me drinking on the job, it's not true. I've never done it. I know you know I've done my share of running and drinking, still do, but not when I'm on duty. Hell, most of the fellas I've run with are the ones that are ready to fire me from my job 'cause I've made a stand for Smith, and they say it's 'cause Asbury Brown's drinking! And it's nothing of the kind. I guess I just wanted you and Hugie to know that. The rest of 'em can go to hell, for all I care."

"Bubba, I know that. But don't let them get you down. You know sometimes you drink more when you're upset about something, and that worries me more than what folks say. And Lovey hates it when you drink."

"Yeah, she does, Leta. Come on, walk me out to the car, and I'll give you those books. How much longer you got before the baby, do you think?"

"Not long. I'm going next week to stay with a midwife in St. Augustine."

"Why? Why not have it at home or go to St. Vincent's in Jacksonville?"

"Well, Hugie's sister Ella has used this woman. I don't want to go all the way into Jacksonville. Besides, we're not sure I would have time to get all the way up there after I go into labor. If I go to this woman, it will be real easy for one of the St. Augustine doctors to get to me when I get ready to have the baby. And besides, Hugie can come down and spend the night with me and still get home and do his work."

"Well, I guess if Ella has used this woman, she's safe. You look mighty poor though, honey." He reached into the car for several magazines, a newspaper, and a novel.

"Here, read all the trash about Al Smith. The magazines and papers are full of it."

He drove away. Oleta watched as the dry dust rose in clouds behind his automobile, disappearing around the curve of the road. She stepped into her house, gathered her sewing, and walked to the old folks waiting for her on the porch of the cypress cabin.

The Birth

I didn't know anything about taking care of a pregnant woman. Neither
did she. First baby was awful hard. She wasn't in the . . . I didn't have . . .
sense enough, I guess you would call it, to put her in the hospital. She
had a terrible time having the baby. . . . It's a wonder I hadn't a lost her.

—Hugie, 3 March 1984

ONE WEEK AFTER Bubba's visit, Oleta stood at her front door looking
inward at the rooms of her home. Beside her on the floor sat a small suitcase packed for her stay with the midwife in St. Augustine. As Hugie picked
up her suitcase and walked to the car, he tried not to think about the emptiness
of that house without Oleta.

He helped her into the automobile, pulled the stick shift into low gear,
and drove away. As they rounded the curve of Old King's Road, Oleta looked
back through the white dust stirring behind them for one last glimpse of the
little frame house standing in the clearing that edged the tangle of swamp and
forests. The August sun blistered the black top of the Model T as it whirred
through the hot white sand of the road. Every leaf, every blade of grass, every
grain of sand reflected the merciless heat and light of that late summer morning. Oleta squinted in the glare and held one slender hand above her brow to
shade her eyes.

A month would pass before she returned to her home near Durbin Swamp.
She was with the midwife and her family two weeks before she had her baby.
The midwife, a married woman with children who was known to most folks as
Miss Hedy, lived with her family on one of St. Augustine's sandy streets in a
bungalow with a yard full of chinaberry trees and cabbage palms. Being with
a strange family was not pleasant for Oleta. She was far too private a person to
like the presence of strangers twenty-four hours a day. Fortunately, she had her
own room, a small back porch that Miss Hedy's husband had enclosed to accommodate his wife's live-in patients. And every other night after work, Hugie
would drive the twenty miles to spend the night with her.

Except for the nights Miss Hedy knew Hugie would be there for dinner,
she cooked the same thing for every meal, stewed green peppers. She had a
garden full of that vegetable and did not want any of them go to waste. After
a few days of green pepper stew, Oleta had to force herself to eat.

Also, the bungalow had sulfur water. Every time the pregnant woman drank
it, she became sick to her stomach. So Hugie bought bottled water for her and

brought it to her when he came to visit every other night. As it turned out, Miss Hedy and her family didn't like sulfur water either, and whenever Hugie brought bottled water for Oleta, they would drink it themselves. Oleta said nothing. She felt she was captive there in a strange house with strange people.

The days wore on, and Oleta's face and arms grew thinner. Hugie's concern for his young wife increased. He started bringing pints of ice cream to her, and night after night, he would sit on the front porch of the little bungalow coaxing her to eat.

Oleta began to wonder if she had miscalculated the time for her baby's birth. But then one evening she lay in bed unable to sleep because of a dull ache in her back. She rose and paced around her room, rolling her shoulders for relief. The pain intensified. "Whew!" she thought. "I wonder if this is it. I wish Hugie were here." But Hugie wasn't due until the next evening. The hours seemed to drag by. Several times during the night, she was able to fall asleep, only to be awakened in the grip of some great force that was contracting the muscles in her lower back. Finally, toward dawn, she heard Miss Hedy stirring, so the young woman dressed herself and entered the kitchen, where the midwife was making coffee. "I'm having cramps in my lower back," Oleta announced.

"Yeah?" Miss Hedy asked. "How often?"

"Every ten minutes or so."

"Well, that's about right. I was looking at you yesterday. You look like a grapefruit that's about ready to fall off the tree. That baby of yours has dropped in the last day or two."

"Yes, I can feel it. I can barely walk, it's so low."

"Well, you better not eat anything if you think you getting ready to start into labor."

"One's coming on right now," the young woman exclaimed.

"Here," the leathery old midwife said, "let me feel your stomach."

Oleta stepped forward, grimacing a bit with the discomfort in her lower back.

"Oh, yes, that's what it is. You going to have back labor. That's the worst kind. Ain't going to be like your sister-in-law. She just pops those young'uns right out, like it ain't nothing to her. No, it won't be like that for you. I've seen you big tall skinny women have the worst time. But you'll make it. You gonna think you won't. But anyhow, you still got a wait. Here, have some coffee. Hugie going to be here tonight, I reckon?"

"He's suppose to . . . I hope."

"I guess I'll walk over to Dr. Walkup's after awhile and let him know he needs to be available tonight."

"Tonight?"

"Yeah, I imagine you'll have you a baby before midnight."

Oleta smiled.

The dull aching cramps continued in Oleta's lower back, and as the hours inched by, they intensified and increased in frequency. Late that afternoon, she moved outside, and selecting a wooden chair beneath a chinaberry tree, she turned it so she could watch the road in the direction from which she expected Hugie. The sun went down, and just at twilight, she heard the engine of his Model T. Peering down the dim road for a first glimpse, she sighed, "Thank God!" She rose to meet him as he drove up. Radiating smiles, she said, "I think it's going to be tonight. Miss Hedy thinks so too."

"You think so?" Hugie asked enthusiastically. "What's happening?"

"I've been having these pains in my back all day. They're getting harder."

Hugie put his arm around his wife as they turned toward the house.

"Are you all right?" he asked. "You're not hurtin' too bad are you?"

"I'm fine. Just anxious, that's all." Oleta tried to reassure him, but just at that moment, she grabbed Hugie's arm, and he saw her cheeks blanch as she bent over with the constriction in her lower back and abdomen.

"My God, Leta! Shouldn't you be in bed?" the young man asked as he helped her into the house, and then, inside, he questioned Miss Hedy, "Don't you think we ought to get the doctor over here for Oleta?"

"Aw pshaw, not yet. When it's time, I'll get him. I hadn't said anything to her, but she's dillydallying. She ain't done much today. She might not have it until tomorrow, at the rate she's going."

"I don't know, she's hurting pretty bad."

"She ain't hurting yet. She just thinks she's hurting. She ain't going to be like Ella, now. You need to know that."

"What do you mean?" Hugie asked.

"I mean, having a baby isn't going to be easy for her. Now, you go to bed. Both of you try to get some sleep. You're going to have a big day tomorrow."

There beside Oleta, in Miss Hedy's guest room with its low ceiling, in the hot dark stillness of the late August evening, a tremendous uneasiness gripped Hugie. What did he know about this woman with whom he had entrusted his wife? Maybe he should have insisted she go to the hospital. Was it too late for that? Beside him, Oleta dozed, moaning. Resting his hand on her stomach, he felt the muscles of her body contracting over and over again.

And as Oleta relaxed in sleep, some mechanism deep within her brain set in motion the last stages of birth. Her body began in earnest the process of expelling the baby it had nurtured all these last months. Oleta jerked awake. "Ohhh! Ohhh!" She was caught. There was no escape. "Ohhh! Hugie, you better get the doctor."

"What's the matter?" Hugie jumped from the bed and with one motion pulled on his trousers.

"This baby is coming, Hugie! Go tell Miss Hedy to get the doctor."

In a moment, Miss Hedy's sun-dried face was bent over the young woman. "Let me see . . . oh, yes! I'll send my husband for Dr. Walkup right now! Yes, sir. Looks like you might have this baby tonight after all."

After about thirty minutes, the man poked his head in the room beckoning his wife to one side. He whispered, "The doctor is out on another call. His wife said keep the girl as comfortable as possible, and she will send him over as soon as he gets back."

Miss Hedy came back into the room. "The doctor will be along after awhile. Just hold off pushing 'til he gets here."

Oleta moaned. In the intense heat, she was already soaked with perspiration. Hugie sat beside her, wiping her forehead with a cloth dipped in tepid water from a bowl beside the bed. Suddenly, she grabbed his shoulder and pulled herself to a sitting position. Wild fear flashed in her eyes. "Something's happening, Hugie! Look!" And throwing back the thin sheet that covered her, she saw the mattress, the sheets all flecked with blood and soaked with a warm clear liquid.

"What in the world's happened?" Hugie yelled at the midwife.

"Her water's gone and broke. It happens. Nothing to be alarmed about." And to herself she muttered, "Dry birth. Just makes the birthin' a little harder. We better get ready to deliver this baby. The doctor might not make it."

Hugie helped Oleta from the bed to a chair so that he and the midwife could change the sheets, while she washed herself and put on a clean gown. With Oleta back in bed, Hugie sat beside her, wiping her brow, his gentle bear-like hands pushing her damp hair from her hot face. The hours dragged by, and Miss Hedy mumbled to herself, "Should have had it by now. Something ain't right here."

By four o'clock that morning on 22 August 1928, Oleta's body was in one long contraction. Every muscle in her body was pushing the child through the birth canal, and she felt as though some giant foot was inside her kicking its way out. In the midst of this frenzy, Oleta started seeing things flash before her. Images appeared in her mind's eye . . . a cow, its head laying over in the sand . . . a bloody hand and arm. "What hand is that?" she wondered. And with the pain, she dug her nails into Hugie's arms.

"My God," he thought, "I've never been so helpless," and to the midwife, trying to maintain control, trying not to give himself over to fear, "Isn't there anything you can do? She should have had this baby by now. What's the matter?"

Miss Hedy didn't answer.

Over and over, she examined the young woman, looking for a sign that the head was crowning. And without saying anything to the couple, she became afraid. She walked to her sleeping husband and woke him saying, "I don't care where Dr. Walkup is, you find him and get him over here. Something ain't right with that girl in there. She should have had that baby by now. There ain't a sign of it yet. Find him!"

Finally, just before five o'clock that morning, Dr. Walkup arrived. As he examined Oleta, small beads of sweat formed on his brow and across his upper lip, and after a few minutes, he strode from the room, motioning for Hugie to follow him.

Hugie watched the doctor, waiting. Shaking his head, the man began to speak, "She's in for a time of it, I'm afraid. The baby's in breach position. Caught up there in the birth canal, can't move any more. If your wife can push it down a little more, I might be able to get a hold and pull the baby on down." The man hesitated before he went on, "But, Mr. Oesterreicher, that girl in there don't look strong enough to do much more than she's already done. What do you think?"

Hugie looked at Dr. Walkup in unbelief, "What are you saying, Doctor? Are you saying Leta might not be able to have this baby? Are you saying she might die?"

Dr. Walkup looked at the floor for a moment and then reached for the handkerchief in his pocket and wiped his brow. "I'm saying we might not be able to save the mother and the baby, maybe one of them, but not both."

Hugie wanted to hit the man who had made that evil pronouncement, wanted to curse him. But he said, looking Dr. Walkup in the eye, "You're wrong about Leta. She might look like she doesn't have any strength, but she's still got plenty of fight left in her. You just get back in there and tell her what to do, and she'll do it. She'll have that baby. And she'll make it too."

The two men returned to the room with the low ceiling, where Oleta labored to bring into the world her first child. At the moment they entered, she was caught in the grip of a hard contraction. Her great dark eyes were wide with fear, and something in her young husband broke as he saw her. To Hugie, it seemed that every cell of her body, every tendon, every muscle was joined in concentrated effort to birth the baby within her. As the contraction mounted in strength, her body automatically curled into a near-sitting position, knees up. With white knuckles, she clutched the sides of the bed. A sound emitted from deep in her belly, not a cry, or a moan, but the long low groan the human spirit utters when a body has exerted itself beyond its limitations. She groaned again, sweat pouring from her brow and hairline, mixing with the hot tears that streaked her face. The seconds seemed interminable to her husband, standing paralyzed and helpless in the face of what he knew to be a mortal struggle for his wife and unborn child.

The contraction ended, and she fell back exhausted, sobbing. "Hugie, Hugie! I'm not doing any good. I'm not doing any good. What's wrong?" And in her mind, she kept seeing something, images that wouldn't quite come together and make any sense to her . . . a cow with its head laying over in the sand, its eyes rolled back in its head, and a hand covered with blood. "What hand is that?" The question plagued the woman in her struggle. And there was fear. Oleta remembered a feeling of fear, but in the trauma of her circumstance, the image was all but unintelligible to her. At her side, Hugie was calling her name, "Leta! Leta!" She opened her eyes, but before she could speak, she was caught once more in the momentum of that great force mounting within her. "Hugie! Hugie!" she screamed. "I'm having another one! Doctor, can't you help me? Please, help me."

Hugie turned to the doctor in full consternation. "Are you going to help her, or do I need to put her in the car and take her to a hospital. Goddamn it, man, do something!" Hugie bent over Oleta, "Leta, listen, honeybunch, the baby's breach. You have to push it down a little more, before he can help you. Can you do that? Leta, can you do that?"

She didn't answer. She just groaned. Every fiber of her being agonized with the intensity of exertion. "Can I do that?" In her mind, she saw that cow and that bloody hand. "What hand is that . . . can I do that . . . can I do that? Can I have this baby?" She fell back again exhausted.

"Leta, can you do that? It's too late to take the baby. Do you understand what that means?" Hugie was asking, tears burning his eyes, searing a path down his cheeks. "Do you understand, honeybunch? If you can't, we'll take our chances trying to get to a hospital."

Hugie was losing control. He could feel himself slipping into an absolute state of panic. He had to hold on, he knew. Clenching his jaw and swallowing back the tears, he called again to the woman being sucked away from him into the depths of some invisible vortex, "Leta! Leta!"

Fleeting images surfaced in her mind. The eyes were rolled back in its head. The cow's eyes were rolled back in its head, lying there on the ground. And there was sand on its tongue, hanging swollen and bloody from the side of its mouth.

Doctor Walkup stepped closer. "Oleta, I can help you if you can get the baby down. Just a little more. Can you do that?"

Hugie was bent over her. "Leta! For God's sake, answer me! Can you push the baby down? Can you do that?"

And again her body raised itself involuntarily, caught in the wringing motion of the muscles of her own body. And suddenly, in her mind, the images came together. She remembered. The bloody hand was her own hand. Grabbing Hugie's arm, she nodded wildly, gasping, "Yes! Yes! It can be done! I've done that with a cow. I can do that! I'll push! Help me, Hugie! Oh God, help me push!"

Oleta remembered. The bloody hand and arm were her own. The cow had been near death, calving, no strength left. And from the birth canal, amid bleeding bulges, the girl had spotted one little hoof protruding. The calf was coming out wrong. It could never be born that way. Fear had swept over the sixteen-year-old girl. She was home alone. "Can I do that?" she had asked herself, "Can I do that?"

"I've got to do it!" she had decided. There was no one else. And she plunged her hand deep into the open bleeding orifice of the cow and found the body of the little calf caught helplessly between the forces pushing it into life and the forces holding it back, the flesh and bones of its own mother's body. Probing to her elbow into the abdomen of the animal, she found one little leg cramped and jamming the calf's descent. Taking hold, she slowly straightened the leg and moved it downward. "The head! The head!" Groping with her hand, she found the head and maneuvered it into birthing position. Oleta remembered that the cow was barely breathing; yet every muscle in the animal's body still labored to push the little calf through the birth canal. No matter if it killed the mother, no matter if it tore the calf to shreds in the process.

Oleta grabbed Hugie's shoulder, pulling his ear close to her mouth, and in the midst of one continuous contraction, she gasped, "I'm going to be all right, Hugie. I saved a calf that way once by pulling it out when the mother couldn't do any more."

"So have I," Hugie said easing her head back onto the pillow. But he thought to himself, "And I've seen it go the other way, the cow and the calf both die."

The minutes eked by. Oleta pushed over and over again, breathing deeply, pushing out and then falling back on the bed in exhaustion. Hugie sat beside her, places on his arms bleeding from where his wife's hands had gripped them wildly, furiously, as he fanned her and washed her face and neck and arms. In the dim light of early morning, he could see her, white as the sheets on which she lay and soaked in the sweat of a battle she waged there in the crowded little room of that bungalow in St. Augustine in the hot still air of late August.

Suddenly, a look of horror filled those great dark eyes of hers, and a scream pierced the still morning air. She fell back unconscious.

"That did it! That one got it down! I see a little rump!" Dr. Walkup shouted. "Here Hugie!" he said, reaching into his black leather bag and pulling out a small bottle. "Put a drop of this on your handkerchief, and if she comes to, put it to her nose. She's done her part. Now I can do mine. She doesn't need to be awake for this. It would only make it harder on her."

Hugie looked at his wife, wrung and white and limp on the bed, her dark hair wet against the wet pillow. Automatically, he reached for her wrist, feeling for her pulse. Finding it, he was reassured and uncapped the bottle Dr. Walkup had given him. The smell of chloroform filled the air.

And in Oleta's mind, she sank deeper and deeper into some dark tunnel, tumbling over and over, upside down, turning, slipping into obscurity. She reached, flailing, trying to halt her headlong descent. In her hand, she felt something in the darkness, and clutching it, she began to crawl back to some far point of light. She was the calf; she was her own baby climbing, fighting its way through the tunnel of her body, struggling to come into the light. She heard voices. The light was full in her face. "Oh God! I hurt!" Something white covered her face, and she was falling again, flailing, reaching. Over and over, she saw the calf, she saw her baby, she saw that bloody hand. Over and over, she would struggle back up to the light and the pain, only to slip away into that silent darkness.

"She's flailing again, Hugie. She's coming to. Give her one more dose. We're almost through here," Dr. Walkup called. Behind him, Miss Hedy held the lamp. Once more, Hugie put the handkerchief to his wife's nose and then looked at Dr. Walkup. The sight of blood had never bothered Hugie before, but this was different. This was Oleta's blood, and it was everywhere, on Dr. Walkup, soaking the sheets, and smearing his wife's thin legs. "My God! My God!" he thought. "Get her through this. Get her through it!"

Just at that moment, Dr. Walkup started yelling, "Here it is! Here it is!"

And Hugie saw him pull from Oleta's body a bloody squirming mass. "You got a little girl, and she doesn't look like she is any worse for what she's been through!" Doctor Walkup said, tying off the naval cord. With one hand, he lifted the little girl by her feet to an upside-down position. With the other, he thumped her lightly on the back. And there in the full light of that August morning, the bloody little infant coughed and cried, gasping for air, for life, her harrowing passage finished.

Oleta was still crawling up and out. Light was beyond this darkness; she could feel it. Voices around her grew louder. She opened her eyes, blinking in the brightness of the morning sun that streamed in the window, and through a blur, she recognized Hugie's form standing before her. She tried to move her arm, but it was too heavy; she tried to speak, but she could not form words.

"The baby! The baby! What happened to my baby?" she wanted to ask, but her mouth was dry and seemed full of cotton. Hugie came closer, smiling, holding something in his arms. "My baby?" she managed to whisper, "my baby?"

He bent over her, almost laughing, almost crying as he placed the bundle in her arms.

Oleta lifted her head and gazed into the face of her sleeping child. "Annie," she said looking at her husband. "We'll name her Annie, after Ma, and Mary, after my sister May." The woman pulled the infant close to her breast and drifted into sleep.

Jacob, Thomas, Clarence Oesterreicher, c. 1903

Jacob Oesterreicher, born 1823, Okaty River, South Carolina (Hugie's grandfather)

Oleta Brown with cat, c. 1915

Pablo Beach Elementary School, 1921 (Oleta is first girl on left in second row)

Oleta Brown, c. 1921

May and Asbury Brown, c. 1918

Asbury Brown, c. 1927

The Oesterreichers, home from a hunt, c. 1923 (Standing left to right, Hugie, Clarence, Ida Brown Oesterreicher, Thomas, George; sitting, center, Tom Oesterreicher; 3 little boys in front on left, Richard, Ira, and Fred Oesterreicher; others are unknown)

Annie Sadler Brown, c. 1922

Hugie Oesterreicher, holding Annie Mary, 1928

Oleta Brown Oesterreicher, holding Annie Mary, 1929

Annie's Death

We would go back up there to see her, and I could hear her, she was on the
third floor. It was room 333, I believe. And you could hear her moaning
all over that floor. You could. The most pitiful sound, that moaning.
And we looked at her, and she would just be laying there, her face red.

—Oleta, 16 March 1984

NINETEEN TWENTY-NINE. The country had been riding the crest of a great
wave that was about to crash and recede, breaking and sucking into it
everything in its path. That particular year is infamous in the collective memory
of the nation, and for Hugie Oesterreicher and his young wife living there on
the edge of the great Durbin Swamp in northeast Florida, 1929 brought one
blow after another.

The first week of September in 1928, Oleta returned to her little frame
house beside the cypress cabin. She had been in St. Augustine with the midwife
for one month. After the birth of her first child, she remained in bed for ten
days, the custom in those years. When she finally began slowly to leave the bed
and move around the bungalow, she found she had no strength. Over and over,
her thin legs would knock and buckle beneath her. Her loss of blood during
and after the child's birth and the inactivity of her convalescence had seriously
weakened her.

Once she was home and had resumed her responsibilities, her normal chores
took on nightmarish proportions to her. Scrubbing the white pine floor, washing and pounding Hugie's heavy work clothes, and even the daily task of boiling her baby's diapers exhausted her. And when she stepped into the warm fall
sunshine of the back yard to stretch the washing on the clothesline, it took all
her strength. Even lifting the diapers to the line made her arms seem like heavy
weights. And in the bright sun, often the ground seemed to undulate before
her, rising and falling as the atmosphere around her went black and the blood
in her head pounded, surging and ebbing away, as did the ocean on the coast
ten miles away—no vitamins in those days, and no doctor with enough sense
to give her a tonic.

Also during this time, things were not going well for the Browns. After
Oleta married, Annie had let the dairy go. She had sold most of the stock, and
the few remaining cattle had wandered off to the savannahs and marshes. The
fields were unplowed and unplanted. No more stands of white cane waved in
the sea breezes that swept in across the palmettos, no more vats of cane syrup.

The beehives were gone, no more jugs of dark rich honey. And although there were still a few hogs bearing the Brown mark in nearby woods, there were no more sides of pork curing in the hickory fumes of the smokehouse. The Brown place lay fallow.

Every Sunday after Hugie and Oleta visited with Annie and May, when it was time for the young couple to start home, Oleta would put her long thin arms around her mother and hold her closely. And deep within the young woman, some small voice warned her that Annie was slipping away. Oleta wanted to cradle her mother as she cradled her own infant in her arms. She wanted to hold onto Annie, keep her. And as the young couple began the rough trip home over dirt roads and beach dunes, Oleta cried. Every time she left her mother standing on that front porch gazing after them, Oleta cried for the mother she knew she was losing.

In the weeks before the presidential election of 1928, the city council of Jacksonville Beach fired Asbury Brown from his job as chief of police. Whether because he had supported Al Smith for president, as all the Browns believed, or because of his drinking, as the city council claimed, the loss of this job was a blow from which the young man never recovered. In the election, Democrats by the thousands crossed over party lines and voted for the Republican Herbert Hoover rather than put the Catholic Al Smith in the White House. Hoover was elected, and in the minds of the Oesterreichers and the Browns, he forever bore the responsibility for the events that took place that first year of his presidency in 1929.

In the late fall of 1928, influenza struck Asbury Brown and his family. Since there were only a few chickens for May to tend, Annie could leave the Brown place now, so she went to her son and his family and stayed for days. After the influenza turned into pneumonia, Annie put Bubba and Lovey in St. Vincent's Hospital and took one of the sick children home with her. The next Sunday when Hugie and Oleta came for their visit, they found May tending Annie. Annie was down with influenza. She burned with fever for days, and when the infection turned into pneumonia, they took her to St. Vincent's.

Doctors had no penicillin in those days, and no sulfur drugs. The treatment of choice was a poultice, which was supposed to pull the infection from the lungs. But on a large person, like Annie, the layers of fat over her lungs lessened any effect the poultice might have had. As a result, Annie's infection raged unabated for weeks. Trips to St. Vincent's in Jacksonville became a part of Hugie and Oleta's life.

Christmas of 1928 passed, and Oleta's twenty-first birthday in early January of 1929 passed, as Annie wavered between states of semiconsciousness and delirium, agonizing groans and incoherent ranting. One dark evening in mid-January, Hugie and Oleta bundled up their five-month-old baby and drove the twenty miles to the hospital. The cold was so intense that Oleta wrapped herself and her baby in a large overcoat and huddled next to Hugie in the little Model T as it bumped down the dark narrow road between St. Augustine and Jacksonville.

When they reached the hospital, the sound of Annie's moaning could be heard over the entire third floor, where she lay dying with pneumonia. Her round face blazed red with fever as her great chest heaved, gasping for breath, and each time she exhaled, she moaned. Hugie kept Annie Mary in the hall, away from the contagious disease, while Oleta sat staring into the glazed and fevered eyes of her mother. Presently, Annie became aware of her daughter. "Baby!" she said. "Where's the baby?" And Oleta motioned for Hugie to bring the child to the door for her mother to see. Annie turned her head and with great effort managed a cooing smile at the child. The blond infant with her great brown eyes beamed back at the dying woman. "My baby's baby," Annie said. She turned her gaze to Oleta. "Have you been by to check on May?" she asked.

"Not tonight, we came by way of Phillips Highway. We'll go back by way of the Beach to make sure she's all right, Ma."

Annie sighed, closing her eyes.

"Ma? . . . Ma?"

No response came from Annie, only her labored breathing and deep moans.

And as the young couple left the Riverside area and crossed the Acosta Bridge, Oleta buried her face in the pale wispy curls of her infant and wept. This time, not as it had been with her father, she recognized death, knew the sight, the sound, the feeling of it hovering over her mother. And Aunt Jane's words whispered at Tom Brown's bedside eight years before echoed in Oleta's mind, "It won't be long now . . . it won't be long now . . . it won't be long now."

That night Annie Sadler Brown had spoken her last words. With Oleta standing there calling to her, Annie had slipped into a coma and never regained consciousness.

In the early morning of 24 January 1929, a loud knocking awakened Oleta and Hugie. When they opened the front door, Julian McCormick, Dora and Benny McCormick's son, was standing there in the circle of light emanating from the kerosene lamp Hugie held in his hand. "Leta," the young man said, hesitating, "Ida called. Word's come from the hospital. Mrs. Brown's gone on. Your ma's dead, Leta. I'm sorry."

Oleta just nodded. Not surprised but unable to speak, she sank slowly into a nearby chair, weighted down by a great sorrow in her heart.

"What time?" Hugie asked. "Do you know?"

"Between midnight and one A.M. is what I understand," Julian answered. "Is there anything I can do for you folks before I go?"

Oleta looked up, "No, Julian, thank you for coming." And then to her husband, she said, "We better get to May, Hugie, she'll be beside herself."

On that day in January of 1929, in the afternoon of the morning that Annie had died, she was buried beside Tom at the little Beach cemetery. Oleta stood beside Hugie and May, watching as her mother's casket was lowered into the ground.

Annie Sadler Brown was gone.

"Ma! Ma!
Ol' Reni said there would be a man
driving a buggy pulled by a white horse.
Ma, she told me to watch for him.
She said he would be my husband.
Ma, do you think it's so?"
"Annie, honey, don't put no stock in it."

The Bank

In '29, the banks all failed and took all the money we had. It
left me and her with a dollar and a half . . . I mean, that was it!

—Hugie, 3 March 1984

O N A DAY in July of 1929, as Hugie and Oleta sat at their kitchen table
eating their noon meal, they heard voices calling to them from their front
door.

"Yeehoo! You two in there?" Ida and Clarence called. "Hugie? Oleta?"

"Yeah!" Hugie called. "Come on back! What y'all doing out here in the
middle of the week?"

"It's the Beach bank!" Ida said as she rushed into the kitchen. "Word's
out they're closing the doors today. Leta, I know you got your money from
Ma's estate in there. You better get there and see if you can get it out before
it's too late."

"Oh no! Ida where did you hear that?"

"Garland was in there this morning, and the place was in an uproar."

Hugie looked at Oleta. "Let's go. Get your passbook and the baby. I'll go
crank the car."

Within minutes, the young couple was racing down the dry dirt road in
the Model T, leaving a cloud of white dust behind them. Oleta held Annie
Mary on her lap, dressing the child and lacing the little black leather high-top
shoes, while Hugie drove, still clothed in the muddy canvas trousers and riding
boots he had worn into the swamps that morning.

Rumors about banks failing had been circulating for months, but stead-
fastly, the government and banking institutions had sworn to the stability of
the economy. Perhaps this was just another rumor, the young couple hoped.
Although losing Oleta's small inheritance would not seriously hurt them, the
money in the Beach bank was all the young woman had from her mother's
estate, aside from one-sixth of the Brown house and land.

When they reached the bank, the front door was wide open. Oleta walked
in holding the passbook to her savings account. The room seemed empty. Overhead, an electric fan turned slowly, stirring papers strewn on the tile floors. She
walked to the teller's window and knocked. "Hello! Is anyone here?" she called.
"Hello!" And to an empty room, in a soft voice she said, holding up her passbook, "I want my money! Is anyone here?"

A door to a room behind the counter slowly opened, and Cecil Brown, a tall thin man with a kind face, stepped into view. He was dressed for a regular business day in a dark suit and tie, but his pale face and hunched shoulders answered the young couple's question before they asked. Oleta stood there in her voile dress with a strawhat pinned hastily askew on her short dark bob. A line of perspiration wet her hairline and neck as she held her passbook out to the little bank's president. Hugie stood behind her holding the baby.

"I've come for my money," she said in a trembling voice.

"It's too late, Mrs. Oesterreicher," Mr. Brown answered in a whispered voice. "I'm sorry to tell you, but your money is gone. This bank is closing its doors. I'm sorry."

"Too late." Oleta lowered the passbook slowly and turned to Hugie. "Too late." And then terror filled her eyes. "Hugie!" she cried. "Your money! What about your money? Do you think it's safe?"

Hugie looked at her, "My God, Leta! I don't know!"

Cecil Brown interrupted, "Mr. Oesterreicher, do you have money in another bank?"

"Yes, sir, I do. Every penny I own is in the St. Augustine bank," Hugie answered.

"Well, I would get it out of there if I were you. Or buy government bonds. Today!"

The hot air whipped against Oleta and the sleeping baby she held in her arms as the Model T made its way south on the winding dirt roads through Palm Valley. The little head against Oleta's breast was wet with perspiration. "What in the world is going on, do you suppose, Hugie?" the woman asked.

"God, I don't know, Leta. But we've got to get that money. If banks around here are going to start failing, all hell is gonna break loose."

The thirty-mile trip to St. Augustine took them over an hour. As they drove down the narrow sandy streets lined with whitewashed buildings gleaming in the sun, it was a little past two o'clock. They stopped in front of an eight-story cream-colored stucco building with a red-tiled roof, a more prosperous looking bank than that of Jacksonville Beach.

Leaving the blinding brightness of the full sunlight, Oleta blinked, trying to adjust her vision to the cooler, darker shadows of the indoors. The marble columns reaching from the marble floors upward to the high ceilings dwarfed her. A few customers stood in line at the teller's window. To their right, a young woman sat at a desk. Behind her was the door to the bank president's office.

Seeing the prim young woman behind the desk reminded Oleta that she probably looked a mess. Balancing the sleeping child on one arm, with her free hand, she ran her fingers through her damp and windblown hair, straightened her strawhat, and pulled at the cotton dress that was sticking to her wet body. She sighed. The dress was hopelessly wrinkled from holding the baby against her on that dry dusty trip. Waving her hand across her face, she tried to create a breeze as she blew out and up. She looked at Hugie. Sweat was streaming down his face beneath his strawhat and soaking the back of his shirt. He pulled off his hat, took a handkerchief from his pants pocket, and wiped his face. A few men stood by in their white summer suits. He walked to the line at the teller's window and waited his turn. Oleta joined him, listening to the business of the other customers. Nobody seemed in a panic.

"May I help you, sir?" a young man with glasses asked when Hugie reached the counter.

"Yes, sir!" Hugie responded with his usual broad smile. "My name is Hugie Oesterreicher, and I would like to close out my account and my father's account with you folks. Here's the necessary papers." Hugie had handled all of his father's business for several years. If his money was in danger, so was his father's.

"Of course, Mr. Oesterreicher," the teller said, "But tell me, is there a problem?"

"No, sir, no problem. I just want my money, that's all."

"Of course, sir. I'll be right with you."

The young man walked across to the prim young woman behind the desk and whispered to her. She rose and stepped to the door behind her, stood there for a moment, and then came back to the young man, who returned to the window where Hugie and Oleta waited. "Would you mind stepping this way?" he said. "Mr. Puller would like to see you. It's customary for our president to handle the closing of all accounts."

They followed him to Mr. Puller's office behind the young woman at the desk. The president stood as they entered the small room. A large man. Tall, a head taller than Hugie. And broad. His countenance, to the young couple, exuded a friendly self-confidence.

"Mr. and Mrs. Oesterreicher," he said, extending his hand to Hugie, "have a seat there."

Oleta sat, glad to rest from standing and holding the child, but Hugie remained standing.

"What can I do for you folks today?" the bank president asked, sweat forming across his brow and around the collar of his stiff white shirt.

Oleta noticed, thinking, "He's real hot in here." Outside the open window, with its half-drawn green canvas shade, she could see the sun reflecting on the white cobblestones of the antiquated streets of St. Augustine.

"We just want to close out our account, Mr. Puller."

"Well, of course, Mr. Oesterreicher, but may I ask if you are unhappy with our service here? We hate to lose a good customer, and if you have not been happy, we would like to rectify that."

"Well, no, we don't have any complaints. It's just that, you know, the bank in Pablo Beach failed today, and my wife lost all the money her mother left her, and we don't want to risk that happening again. My family has been working and saving a lot of years, and we don't want to lose it all."

"Well, of course you don't. But you can't compare this bank to the bank in Jacksonville Beach. Of course that little old cracker box failed. This is a real solid bank. It won't fail." Mr. Puller wiped his face.

"Well, I hope not, Mr. Puller, but I would like my money just the same," Hugie said with a broad smile.

Mr. Puller straightened himself. "Well, Mr. Oesterreicher, if you folks are afraid, if you're bent on doing this, then that's the way it's got to be. We here at the St. Augustine bank like to keep our customers happy." Mr. Puller walked over and put his hand on Hugie's shoulder. "But I tell you," he went on, "you can't put that much money in a cookie jar. As one business man to another, let me suggest how you make your savings absolutely secure."

"How's that?" Hugie Oesterreicher asked.

"Buy bonds. We can order them today, right now from the Chase Manhattan Bank in New York. They will be here in three days' time. You can come down here, withdraw your money, and pay for them. Then your money will be safe."

Hugie and Oleta looked at each other.

"Well, what do you think, Leta?"

"Mr. Brown said the same thing. I guess we could do that," Oleta said, shifting the weight of her child.

"Okay, Mr. Puller, let's order the bonds. We can go ahead and pay for them now. Wire the money to the bank in New York."

"No sense in doing that, Mr. Oesterreicher, you pay for them when they get here. You just order the bonds today, and you can get your wife and child on home. They look worn out."

Hugie ordered the bonds. As he and Oleta emerged into the afternoon sun, Mr. Puller stood tall, assuring the couple again that their bonds would be there in three days' time. The door to the bank closed behind them, and the tall broad man wiped his brow again and walked, shoulders hunched just a bit, back into his office, where he sat long and quiet behind his desk.

Three days later, on 23 July 1929, Hugie and Oleta drove back to St. Augustine. As they approached the bank, they saw something was wrong. The street and sidewalk in front of the bank were filled with people and cars. They parked the car across the street and hurried toward the front door.

"It's happening here too, Hugie. Listen to those people. They're talking about not getting their money," Leta agonized as they pushed through the crowd. "Oh Jesus, no! Don't let us be too late."

"Come on, honeybunch, we might be all right. We ordered those bonds. If they came in, and they went ahead and paid for them the way they said, we'll be safe."

Inside, throngs of people pushed against the teller's window. One man stood pounding the desk of the prim young woman outside Mr. Puller's office. She sat crying. Through the door behind her, Oleta could see a crowd of people pushing around the bank president. In one corner of the main lobby, an old man stood dazed and mumbling to himself. Papers were strewn on the floor. Hugie took Oleta's hand and walked sideways through the people mobbing Mr. Puller. The tall broad man was ashen. And somehow across the crowd, the man caught Hugie Oesterreicher's eyes, clear and blue, staring at him as he maneuvered his young wife through the people toward him. Mr. Puller could not look away. God knows, he wanted to look away.

Hugie finally reached him. Oleta stood to the side, just behind him. "Mr. Puller," the young man said, "I've come about the bonds I ordered. You said they would be here today. All we want is our bonds."

"God, man! There is no money to pay for them. Your money is gone. Your father's money is gone. This bank is closing. We're finished."

"Why didn't you pay for them when you ordered them, like I asked you to? Three days ago, you could have paid for them."

The man said nothing.

Hugie went on, anguished, "You didn't pay for them, and now you lost it all. You gave it all away to folks that got here before me. My God, I should have put a gun to your head that day and got my money."

Mr. Puller shook his head, beaten. "It wouldn't have done any good, Mr. Oesterreicher. It was already gone. The bank would have closed three days ago if you had demanded your money."

The Oesterreichers had been a frugal people, living out of the woods and maintaining a simple rustic lifestyle with few needs. For years, most of the money they made from selling livestock, cutting palms, and trapping had been saved in the St. Augustine bank. The Oesterreichers lost thousands of dollars that day. Mr. Puller had lied to them. Had they insisted on withdrawing their money three days before, the bank would have closed then, and he had known that.

Oleta and Hugie turned away and stumbled outside to their car across the street. Inside the Model T, they sat stunned for a moment. Finally, Hugie said, "Well, that's that. It's gone." And he reached into his pocket and pulled out a dollar and a half. "That's it!" he said. "That's all the money we've got in this world!"

The Fast

I bit into that sandwich and the thought struck me: "It's Friday, here I am, my baby is dying, and here I am eating meat on Friday." I took the mouthful of sandwich out of my mouth, laid the sandwich aside, and from that time on . . .

—Oleta, 3 March 1984

O N 29 OCTOBER 1929, the stock market crashed, and the nation, the world as a whole, faced what Hugie and Oleta had faced as individuals in July, total financial ruin. And before 1929 had ended, Hugie and Oleta had faced yet another crisis of a different nature.

In mid-November of that year, Oleta sat in a cane-seated rocker on the front porch of their home holding her baby, Annie Mary, comforting her. The child's round face turned upward to her mother's, eyes closed, almost asleep. Oleta put her own cheek against the blond curls and then lowered her lips to the little girl's forehead. Like soft velvet, the afternoon sun warmed Oleta's arms as it cast an amber light across Annie Mary's face and reflected in the pale wisps of her curls. Across the field, the leaves of the blackjack oaks waved like tiny yellow flags against the purple-blue of the autumn sky. Oleta sang softly, "Bye baby bunting, Daddy's gone a hunting . . . ," as she imagined Hugie somewhere in Durbin Swamp checking his line of traps. "He'll be past dark getting home tonight." And again she envisioned Hugie high on his horse, traversing the bogs and hammocks of the swamp, following his trapline. She could see him deftly guiding the horse, eyes searching the terrain, listening.

Her husband's ways in the woods had become familiar to her. Often, she accompanied him when he hunted or cut palms. Going with Hugie was recreation to her, listening to him repeat the lore of the northeast Florida woods he had learned as a boy atop the front of his father's horse. During that first year or so of marriage, the young woodsman taught his wife to shoot and bought her a 410 shotgun. But Oleta had not gone to the woods with Hugie that day. Her baby girl was sick.

At noon that day, Oleta had warmed venison stew. She had poured the gravy over a biscuit and coaxed the child to take a few mouthfuls. But for the last few days, Annie Mary had not been eating well. And that morning, the little girl had opened her eyes whimpering and hadn't stopped all day.

Oleta rocked and sang. The child dozed and then slipped into a heavy peaceful sleep against her mother's breast, the soft autumn breeze soothing her. Then slowly, the woman stood, gently holding the child against her own body, still swaying rhythmically as she glided to the mahogany four-poster in her own bedroom. Carefully, she placed the sleeping child on top of the covers, pulled a light flannel blanket over her, and left the room.

Later, in the kitchen, Oleta stirred the coals in the wood stove and stuffed in another log. From the smokehouse, she took a side of bacon, and with a long kitchen knife, she sliced a few thin pieces of the heavily salted meat and laid them in the bottom of a large cast-iron pot. But at the moment that she lifted the pot from the table to place it on the stove, she heard the baby coughing in the bedroom. Dropping the pot to the table again, she rushed to the fifteen-month-old girl. But Annie Mary wasn't coughing. She was gagging, still half-asleep as vomit projected out of her mouth onto the covers and the pillow beneath her head. Oleta gasped as she grabbed a towel from the bedpost and held it beneath the child's mouth. Gradually, the vomiting stopped, and the young mother washed her child's face and hair, wrapped her in a blanket, and placed her on a daybed in the living room. Later, Oleta was in the kitchen preparing supper when a sound came from the living room. Oleta rushed to her baby girl. The child was vomiting again.

When Hugie came home after dark, he found his wife holding the baby in her lap, spooning tiny sips of sweetened tea into the child's mouth. "She's vomited twice this afternoon. I'm just trying to get something down her to strengthen her," Oleta said.

Hugie walked to the child and put his hand to her forehead and then to her wrist. "She doesn't seem to be feverish," he said as he took his little girl in his arms and tried to coax her to take a few more sips of tea. The child shook her head and turned her cheek to the spoon.

That night, Annie Mary curled between her parents in the four-poster bed, and in her sleep, she softly moaned.

The next morning, Oleta held her child and tried to feed her. But again, Annie Mary turned her cheek and there, on her mother's lap, began to heave and gag. Oleta grabbed a nearby pan as the child emptied her stomach of everything. Clear liquid. The child fell limp in her mother's arms. Holding the child, Oleta stepped to the pump on the porch. With one hand, she moved the pump handle up and down, then thrust a cloth under the stream of water, and wiped the child's face. "Come on," Oleta said to the child, "we're going to Grandma's." The young woman wrapped the baby in a blanket and rushed out into the cool autumn air.

"Ma!" Oleta cried as she approached the old couple rocking on the front porch of the cypress cabin. "The baby's sick. She can't keep anything on her stomach."

Tom and Ella rose to meet the young woman. Strands of Ella's silver hair fell loosely from the bun at the back of her head as she took the baby in her own arms. She carried the baby to a rocker and sat holding her, examining the child with the confidence of a physician. Tom bent over her, participating in the procedure with the same assurance. Tom and Ella had used doctors occasionally in raising their nine children, but for the most part, they had doctored their family themselves. And the truth is, in the early days of the twentieth century, home remedies were often as effective as the treatments used by those trained in medicine, often but not always.

"I believe I have something that will help her, Leta," Ella said, handing the child to Tom. The young woman followed her mother-in-law through the cabin to the porch leading to the kitchen. Once inside the kitchen, the tiny little woman pulled a chair to the center of the room, awkwardly stepped on to its seat, and reached for several dry and dusty objects hanging from a string from the rafters. Stepping down from the chair, Ella blew at the dust and cobwebs collected on some shriveled things attached to the cord. "The dried inside peeling of chicken gizzards," Ella answered Oleta's unspoken question.

"Chicken gizzards?"

"Yes. You make a tea with them. It's wonderful for settling stomachs." Ella smiled.

"Aren't they a little dirty to use for a baby?"

"Oh no, they'll be fine after I wash them off," Ella said blowing at the inner peelings from the gizzards again and then wiping them on her apron.

She stepped to the back porch and dipped the objects into the bucket of freshly drawn water, swishing them around. She took a brush hanging from a nail and scrubbed at them for a moment. The little woman then drew more water from the well, put it in a kettle, started a fire in the wood stove, and set the kettle on top to steam. After that, she placed a dried gizzard peeling in a cup, poured the boiling water over it, covered it with a plate, and let it steep.

With only minutes having past, Ella returned to the front porch where Tom was holding the sick child. The old man carefully placed his ailing grandchild in his wife's arms. Ella sat cradling the little girl, spooning the brownish yellow liquid into her mouth, very slowly, very gently. Annie Mary kept it down; her eyes brightened. Finally, Ella rose and handed the little girl to Oleta. "Here," she said, "take these peelings home with you and, after two or three hours, try to give her more. The broth should settle her stomach, and if she keeps it down, it will strengthen her."

That day and the next, the child seemed to improve. She was able to keep small portions of Ella's special broth in her stomach. But on the third morning, Oleta woke to hear the little girl gagging and vomiting more violently than with the first siege. When she picked up her child, she realized Annie Mary was burning with a fever.

Only the gray light of early morning filtered in the windows, but Hugie had already left to check his trapline in Durbin Swamp. Oleta lit a kerosene lamp and began to wash down the child, but every movement brought on more violent vomiting. And even when the little girl had emptied her stomach, she continued to lurch and heave as convulsive waves swept over her tiny body. "The tea!" Oleta thought. "She needs that tea." Frantically, she stoked the stove and boiled water in which to soak the last dried inner peeling of the chicken gizzard. Although she carefully spooned the liquid into the child's mouth, the little girl still heaved it up. "Water! Maybe some plain water will stay down." No, the child vomited and fell limply against the woman.

At midmorning, Oleta lifted the child and ran to the cypress cabin. "She's sick!" she said, handing the child to Ella. "Bad sick! We've got to get her to a doctor. I'm going to get Hugie out of Durbin!" And the young woman raced back to her house, where she grabbed her 410 shotgun from the wall of her bedroom and ran out again to the Model T. She hand-cranked the engine, jumped into the sputtering vehicle, and rammed the long skinny stick shift into first gear as she turned north on Old King's Road.

Over the bumps, she skirted the edge of Durbin Swamp for a quarter of a mile and then stopped and leaned on the horn. She climbed from the car with the shotgun and fired it several times into the air. If Hugie heard her, she knew he would answer with a return shot. She stopped and listened. Nothing.

Again, she climbed into the car and drove deeper into the woods, blowing the horn as she went. She stopped, fired the shotgun several times, and waited. This time in the distance, she heard him, a single shot and then another. She answered with another shot. He would come, she knew. Turning the car in the narrow ruts of the road, she headed back for the cypress cabin. By the time she had picked up Annie Mary and hurried back to her own front porch, Hugie came on his horse, galloping out of the trees into the field in front of their houses.

"Hugie! She's bad!" Leta cried as the man halted the horse. "Nothing's working! She's burning up with fever and vomiting every fifteen minutes. Hugie, there's nothing left in her to vomit up. We've got to get it stopped."

Hugie jumped from his horse and looked at his child in his wife's arms, her eyes glazed with fever. "We've got to get her to a doctor! Who do you think?" he said to his wife.

"I've heard about a doctor for children in Jacksonville, a Dr. Love. His office is in Riverside."

Down the white sand road they sped, past the yellow-leaved blackjack hammocks, through the stands of wintergreen pines, across the palmetto scrubs, past the marshy swamps with their islands of cabbage palms, up the Acosta Bridge and across the wide St. Johns River, and down into the unfamiliar maze of streets in Riverside, searching for the office of Dr. Love. All the time, Oleta was holding her child, patting her, soothing her, and, without consciously realizing it, making silent prayers to God.

Finally, amid the elegant homes along the river, they saw Dr. Love's office.

Hugie stopped the car, got out, and walked hastily around to open the door for Oleta and the baby. One look at his young wife's weary face told him Oleta was on the verge of fainting. He figured she hadn't eaten that day, and he knew neither of them had slept since the baby had been sick. "Here, let me carry her," he said as they crossed the manicured lawn to the office entrance. When Hugie knocked on the door, a young woman opened it. "We have a sick baby," he said, "we need to see Dr. Love."

"I'm sorry, but Dr. Love just left on a call. He won't be back for an hour. You're welcome to come in and wait," the young woman answered and then, noticing the child lying limply in her father's arms, eyes half-open and glazed, repeated, "Please, do come in."

"No!" Hugie said. "I think I need to get my wife something to eat," and then turning to Oleta, observing her washed-out color, he asked, "You haven't eaten today, have you?"

She shook her head. No, she hadn't.

"We'll be right back. Don't let Dr. Love leave again!" Hugie told the woman.

Since they had passed a drugstore several blocks back, Hugie drove his young family there. Leaving Oleta and the baby in the car, he rushed up to the fountain, reached into his pocket, and found just enough money for two sandwiches. When Hugie returned, he climbed into the car and handed his wife a ham sandwich. The woman folded back the thin sheet of waxed paper enveloping the sandwich.

Oleta bit into the sandwich. But then, something happened. She bit, she chewed, she looked into the face of her listless child, and then she looked at the sandwich. And suddenly, a flood of realization poured over her. It was Friday. Here she was, fearing for the life of her baby and eating meat on Friday. In her mind, this was sin; to a Catholic, eating meat on Friday was a sin. How could she even ask? How could she even pray for her child? Two years had passed since she had bothered abstaining from meat on Fridays. And Sundays came and went without the young couple attending church. All their energies were spent in merely surviving. "Oh God," she thought, "I've been wrong. I've been wrong. Forgive me, forgive me, and God, help my baby girl." The young woman slowly raised her hand to her mouth and quietly spit out the bits of bread and ham. She folded the waxed paper back over the sandwich and set it aside.

Oleta Oesterreicher fasted that meal.

When Hugie and Oleta arrived back at Dr. Love's, he was pacing the front porch, waiting for the young couple. "Bring her in!" he called to them. "Bring her in!"

"Put her here on this table," he directed Hugie, who gently laid the child on the doctor's examining table as Dr. Love began to question them about her symptoms. The doctor observed the little girl's half-open eyes rolled back in her head, checked her pulse, noticed her limp arms and legs. And while he examined her, she began to heave and gag. Presently, he looked up at the young couple and said, "She is a very sick child. If we can't stop this vomiting, she could die."

Although Dr. Love had medication that would have quieted the convulsive waves of nausea and vomiting that seized the little girl, she could not have kept that down long enough to do any good. So he started applying allspice poultices to her stomach. And when the nausea seemed to settle, he told the frantic parents how to make the poultice, directing them to keep one on the child's stomach and to provide only barley water as nourishment for the next several days.

The Oesterreichers took their little girl home and began to treat their child according to Dr. Love's prescription. And that night, after Oleta had told her husband about her fast, they knelt beside their bed, held each other's hands, and prayed together, as they did every night for the rest of their lives. Hugie and Oleta were never the same after that fast. They had turned to God, become people of faith.

The poultices did their work. Gradually, the child kept down the spoonfuls of barley water and began to improve. And one morning in late December, almost a month later, when Hugie lit the kerosene lamp on the table beside the mahogany four-poster and the little girl sat up amid the pillows and quilts of her parents' bed, giggling and talking happily in an incoherent language, the lamplight glancing off her tousled golden curls and sparkling in her great dark eyes, Oleta and Hugie, in their hearts, were thankful. They were very thankful.

Oleta said, "Hugie, why don't you cut a tree when you're in the woods today. Tomorrow's Christmas."

He smiled, "I almost forgot."

"So did I."

"Well, then, I'll get us a tree. We need to remember Christmas."

That night, when Hugie came in from the woods, he was carrying the top of a young pine tree. And after supper, the young woman pulled from the trunk in her bedroom a package wrapped in old newspaper. Unfolding the paper, she gazed at a few colored glass balls and a strand of gold paper garland, and she remembered Annie Sadler Brown's round little hands pinning those ornaments to greenery in the Brown house. And for just a moment, kneeling there beside the trunk, tears filled Oleta's eyes. Later that evening, while Annie Mary slept quietly in the four-poster bed, Hugie and Oleta sat mesmerized by the magic of the firelight dancing on the glass ornaments hanging from their tree. And as they sat, they remembered the year just behind them. It had been like a decade to the young couple.

And 1929 drew to a close.

The Lost Trap

After the banks failed, I had to go to catching rattlesnakes and selling them, and alligators and such stuff as that, anything that I could make a dollar out of.

—Hugie, 3 March 1984

"GOD!" HUGIE THOUGHT, "God! Where the hell do you suppose that thing is gone to? Just disappeared!" And panic started crowding at his heart. Somewhere in there, in that tangle of trees and underbrush, he had tied a trap to a stake just two days before, but since that, heavy rains had flooded the Diego Plain, and now all of Durbin Swamp was under water. "Wet enough to bog a duck!" Hugie exclaimed to himself as he guided the horse slowly across the mucky terrain. All the while, his eyes were searching intently for the stake he hoped might still be poking above the foot-deep water. He had to find that trap.

In that December of 1931, Hugie was desperate. He had no money. No money was in circulation. Buying and selling had almost stopped, and there were no jobs, but a good fur might bring fifteen or twenty dollars from a furrier in the North, enough to buy the supplies necessary to get his family through to palm season in the early spring. So Hugie needed the animal he hoped might be in that lost trap.

In the year and a half since the young Oesterreichers had lost all of their money, banks had continued to fail across the country at the rate of eight or ten a day. In Florida alone, eighty-seven banks failed in 1929 and 1930. The state comptroller's office reported that six state banks had failed in the Jacksonville area by 30 June 1930, a number that did not include the string of national banks that had also failed.

In the big cities, bread lines were forming to feed thousands of hungry and homeless people, but Hugie hadn't been forced to beg food for himself, for his wife and children, or for Tom and Ella, who had been dependent on their youngest son since they had also lost their life's savings. Somehow, Hugie had managed to grind a living out of the woods that was sufficient for all of them.

The last year had become a blur of backbreaking work for the young man. He had done anything to make a dollar and had not considered himself above any kind of work. He had risked his life catching rattlesnakes and selling them; he had strained his back cutting and hauling cross ties for the railroad; he had wrestled alligators, dug ditches, and spent sweltering days in the swamps cutting palms.

124

Almost everyone he knew dealt in illegal whiskey. Either they made it in their own stills, or they sold what other people made, or they helped smuggle it in from the islands. Hugie hadn't wanted any part of it, yet during those Prohibition years from 1919 to 1933, bootlegging was a quick way to make a dollar, and dollars were hard to come by.

However, Hugie's great fear in those years was not that of failing to provide for his family. He had a strong back and a sure aim; he could always put food on the table. However, the enormous fear that seemed always before the young man was that of losing Oleta. Her life, her health seemed such a tenuous thing. At times, the woman appeared so fragile that the possibility of her death loomed before him, haunting him like a great dark specter.

But on that December morning in 1931, as he pushed deeper and deeper into Durbin Swamp looking for that trap, Hugie remembered the hard times he and Oleta had faced but had somehow managed to come through. The year before, Oleta had developed hayfever, an allergy that had plagued her relentlessly into the early spring of 1931. The small bit of weight she had gained under Dr. Wilkinson's care had begun to fall off her. Tom and Ella had tried all their home remedies on her, but nothing had worked. Then they had heard of a Dr. Farrara in Jacksonville who might be able to help her, but Hugie and Oleta hadn't had the funds necessary for even one visit to a specialist. Although it had been palm-cutting season, the profit Hugie would have made when he sold those palms later that spring had had to be used to pay Dr. Wilkinson and the hospital for delivering their second child, which had been due toward the end of May. He wouldn't have had an extra dollar for Dr. Farrara's treatment.

So in the early spring of 1931, Hugie had been looking for a way to pay for a visit to the hayfever doctor. One day, he had taken a horse and wagon into Cabbage Swamp to cut palms. He had been there since before daylight, walking from cabbage palm to cabbage palm. He would stand beneath each tree, reach with his long tool into the top fronds, hook the bud, give a quick yank, and let the pale green sliver of a palm bud fall to the ground beside him. Then he would move on to the next tree. Every so often, he would stop and retrace his steps, gather the cut buds into bundles of twenty-five or fifty and carry them back to the waiting wagon. By three o'clock that afternoon, his shoulders had been aching from reaching and stretching over and over again. And even though it was only March, the swamp had been steaming hot, and Hugie's sweat had soaked his head, his face, his neck, and every inch of his clothing. Nevertheless, he had figured he would cut palms until it got too dark to see, since every bundle of buds he could pack and get to the docks by the Palm Valley Bridge meant another dollar.

The sweat had streamed into his eyes, and he had stopped for a minute to wipe his face with a dirty handkerchief before moving on. And all the time he had been snipping away at the palm buds, he had been thinking about Oleta and the way she had been looking lately. Here she was six-months pregnant and losing weight, and nothing Dr. Wilkinson could do would stop it. The bit of color that had come to her cheeks the summer before had drained away, and a gray-blue hue encircled her great brown eyes. He had moved on to the next palm, sweat almost blinding his view of the top of the tree. Again, he had pulled the dirty handkerchief from his pocket and wiped his blurred and burning eyes.

And then, it seemed, the earth had moved beneath his feet. He had felt it as a wave, soft and swirling, and for one split-second, he had thought he might be fainting. He had never fainted before, but he had known this sudden swaying motion must be like fainting. He had looked to the top of the tree through the blur of sweat and then at the pile of moving earth beneath his feet. And then he had heard that sound . . . rattles singing. A rattlesnake had moved beneath his feet.

His reaction had been instantaneous. He had jumped three feet up and back into the air, and with one movement, he had dropped the pole in his hand, reached for the pistol in a scabbard at his side, and fired at the flared head of the snake coiled at the base of that cabbage palm. As his feet had hit the ground, the head of the snake had dropped. He had killed it, a big one. Hugie had laughed as he pulled out his knife, snipped the row of rattles from the snake's tail, and put them in his pocket. After skinning the rattlesnake, he had stretched its six-and-a-half-foot skin across the wagon to dry in the sun.

That was not the first time Hugie had stepped on a rattlesnake, nor would it be the last. But the snake Hugie had killed that March afternoon in 1931 served him and Oleta in a particularly beneficial way. As the sun was dipping beneath the horizon, Hugie had driven the wagon loaded with palm buds to the edge of Cabbage Swamp. There he had unhitched the horse from the wagon, mounted him bareback, and rode to the house of a man who dealt in skins. "You interested in a rattlesnake skin?" he had asked the man.

"Sure," the dealer had said. "What you got?"

Hugie had pulled the skin from across the back of his horse and had held it up so that the man could see the full size of the piece he was getting. "What you give me for this?"

"Well, if he was alive, I would give you five dollars for him. But I'll give three for his skin."

"It's a deal!" Hugie had said, handing the man his merchandise.

The man had walked into his house, got three dollars, and placed it in Hugie's hand.

"Thank you very much!" Hugie had laughed, tipping his strawhat as he climbed back onto the horse. "I just happened to step over him in Cabbage Swamp today."

"Well, you was damn lucky you lived to tell about it."

"Yeah, I know," Hugie had agreed as he rode off into the twilight, feeling as though the weight of the world had been lifted from his shoulders. He had reached in his pocket and pulled out the three dollars, knowing he could now take Oleta to see Dr. Farrara.

Dr. Farrara had helped Oleta's hayfever. And on 29 May 1931, Oleta had had her second child, another little girl whom they named June Francis. But this time, Hugie had insisted that Oleta go to the hospital. He had used the money he made from selling palms to pay Dr. Wilkinson and St. Vincent's Hospital.

By December of 1931, though, they were out of money again. "Yes," Hugie thought as he pushed on into Durbin, relentlessly searching the rain-drenched woods for his lost trap, "we're in hard times and no end in sight." He slid from the horse and stood there in knee-deep water, wondering which direction to take or whether to give up the search altogether until the woods had a chance to drain. No, he couldn't give up. He had no choice but to find that trap and whatever he had caught in it. Money could come from no other source. That was it. Hugie had nothing else to sell, nothing else to do that could earn him a dollar in those winter months of 1931.

So he tied the horse to a young pine sapling that rose up from the standing water and waded away, skirting the edge of a bog where he knew the water would be neck-deep after yesterday's deluge. And then Hugie stopped. Searching was useless. With everything under water, he could walk all day and not spot that trap. "Useless!" he thought, falling to his knees, kneeling in waist-deep water. "Useless!"

And for that moment, he was beat, whipped by hard times and bad luck. He just knelt there, yesterday's rain swirling around him, mixing with black waters from the sloughs of Durbin Swamp. "God?" he prayed finally. "God? Please. . . . " And then lifting his eyes above the flooded underbrush and the little islands of palm trees lining the horizon to the white fleecy clouds moving across the western sky, he whispered, "Let me find that trap. I've got to have it, God."

He stood and started walking, once more sloshing through the waters. "That stick was long enough," he thought. "The water ain't so deep that it shouldn't be sticking up somewhere out here." And then he saw something black jutting up all by itself in a pool of clear rainwater trapped in a low place beside a palmetto thicket. "That's it!" He hastened toward the slender black thing.

And then bending over it, he saw beneath the surface of the pond the fur of an animal caught in his trap, still attached to the stake. "An otter!" he exclaimed, scooping the animal and trap into the air and wading off to his waiting horse, tied to the pine sapling in the flooded waters of Durbin Swamp, "an otter!"

The fur of that otter brought the Oesterreichers twenty dollars. And they had grits and flour and sugar and coffee that December of 1931.

Moonshine

*That was in the depression . . . was terrible times. People living today don't know.
They have no idea what a hard time is. We have lived through it! I mean, if you
could get hold of a dollar, you could buy something with it. But you couldn't get
hold to it. There was no money in circulation.*

—Hugie, 3 March 1984

OLETA LINGERED AT the window, peering through the sheer curtain at
Hugie and his brothers, who were talking in the front yard. Their voices
rose and fell, and although she could not hear exactly what they were saying,
she knew what they were discussing. She knew, and she was afraid. The four-
teen-month-old girl Oleta carried on her hip whimpered, rubbing her big green
eyes. Oleta returned once more to the window, watching the anguished face of
her husband as he wrestled with the decision she knew he was making, even as
he stood there gesturing emphatically with his hands.

For the last three months, Hugie had cut cross ties for the railroad. Every
morning, he would drive his team of oxen into the high pine flats of the northeast Florida woods, where he chopped down trees and carried them, one after
another, on his own back to the wagon. When he had a full load, he would
drive the oxen-pulled wagon out of the woods. After this, he would move the
logs from his wagon to his truck. Once he had the logs at home, Hugie would
use a foot adze to shape the logs into cross ties. When he had a truckload of
ties, he would drive to the docks in Jacksonville, where he was paid fifteen cents
apiece for them. Most of the time, Hugie did this by himself in the heat of
the summer months. He would work all day, and if he cleared a dollar, he considered himself lucky. Being resentful never occurred to him. As long as he
could work, he didn't care. But the day before had made a difference for the
young man.

The day before had been a good day. He had come out of the woods with
a wagon full of cross ties. But after he got home, he realized he had to do
something different. He had unhitched the oxen, led them to the barn, and
climbed into the loft, where he raked the last bit of feed to the huge animals.
"An animal's got to eat if it's going to work," Hugie thought to himself as he
trod toward the house. Without the oxen, there could be no cross-tie business. Many of the logs were so large only an ox could move them, and no
truck could pull a load of cross ties across the mucky earth of those woods and
swamps. "I just gave the last bit of feed to the oxen," he told his wife, "and

we don't have the money to buy any more. If we can't afford to keep the oxen, I can't run my cross-tie business." And after they had settled their two little girls to sleep, Hugie and Oleta climbed into bed and talked in long low tones about a solution to their problem. They talked about moonshining.

That had been the night before. So now, while Oleta hesitated at the window, slowly swaying her second child to and fro and watching Hugie, she knew he was working out a deal with his brothers. After George and Clarence had climbed into their car, Hugie came in and faced his young wife. Her dark eyes questioned him. "Well, I guess I'm in the moonshine business," he said.

"Shhh! Don't even say it so loud." Oleta shuddered. "I'm scared to death."

For his wife's sake, Hugie lowered his voice. "George and Clarence can find customers for as much as I want to make. Whiskey or wine. I figure I'll make enough to buy feed for the oxen."

"Hugie, I'm so scared. We're breaking the law. What if you get caught?"

Hugie held his wife's worried stare. "Leta, I've done everything I know to do. Everything. I'd work for anything anybody would pay me, but nobody will hire me. Nobody has any money to hire me with. There ain't no jobs. Leta, the cross-tie business is finished if I can't feed them oxen. And it's seven or eight months before I can hope to make anything cutting palms. We've still got the winter to go through, and what if you get sick or if one of the babies get sick. Leta, we don't have any choice. I've got to try it, at least long enough to get feed money for the animals. Leta, God knows, I don't see any other way."

Oleta glanced away for a minute, away out the window, across the sunlit field, and into the dark woods crowding around it. "All right," she said, reaching back to her husband to take his hard square hand into her long slender hands. Gazing down at that hand that worked so hard for her, she turned it over, running her fingers across his palm. It was leathery and streaked with grime embedded in the pores, as if that dirt from all that work were a part of his hands, inseparable. "All right, we'll do what we have to do. And we'll come through it, somehow."

So in the summer of 1932, Hugie Oesterreicher started making illegal whiskey. He did this on and off until the end of Prohibition in December of 1933. During this time, he had to buy corn and rye and hundreds of pounds of sugar. In the beginning, he and Oleta could go to a wholesale house in Jacksonville and buy fifty- and hundred-pound bags of sugar. But later, when the government started cracking down and such large orders of sugar became suspect, the couple went from store to store in Duval and St. Johns counties, buying five pounds of sugar here and ten pounds of sugar there.

When Hugie made moonshine, he started by covering a little whole-kernel corn and whole-grain rye with six inches of water in the bottom of a fifty-gallon barrel. After the ingredients had soured within the lidded container, a process that took two or three days in the summer and a week in the winter, Hugie mixed in fifty pounds of sugar that had been dissolved in water. The resulting chemical reaction released heat and made the mixture boil for about two days. When the boiling had stopped, Hugie ladled the liquid, or buck, as moonshine is called at this stage, into a fifty- or seventy-five-gallon copper pot, which he would cover with the cap, or horn, that is, a lid with a tube or condenser. Then Hugie put a fire under the copper pot, so that the ingredients would begin to steam. As the steam passed through the water-cooled condenser, it turned back into liquid and flowed into the jug or barrel. When Hugie was finished, he would have five gallons of ninety-eight- to one-hundred-proof moonshine.

He could sell the moonshine at that point, or he could age it in a white oak barrel for a month or two. Sometimes, he put charred peaches in with the aging whiskey to give the liquid a red color and eliminate the strong taste. Had Hugie moonshined in the early days of Prohibition, he could have sold that five-gallon jug of whiskey for fifty or sixty dollars, but by the early 1930s when Hugie took up the business, there were so many people running moonshine that the market was glutted and the price deflated. Moonshine straight from Hugie's still sold for about a dollar a gallon; the aged whiskey sold for about two dollars a gallon.

At first, Clarence and George handled most of his whiskey, but after awhile Hugie and Oleta started delivering it themselves to customers in Jacksonville. They would hide the five-gallon jugs in the trunk or beneath the seats of the Model T, and then, as a family, they and their children would make the rounds delivering the whiskey to private homes. The young woman never got over being afraid.

During these months, Hugie did not produce moonshine consistently. He would make enough to pay off bills, to meet basic needs, and would then stop. But then hard times would come again, and he would once more resort to that illegal business.

During the year and a half from the time he made his first batch of whiskey to the end of Prohibition, Hugie had several close calls with the law. One cold damp fall day, he was out in Durbin Swamp running off a batch of whiskey. He knelt beside the kerosene burner, resting and warming his calloused hands, quietly, thoughtfully. And in that crouched position, his feet fell asleep, so he stood for a moment and stomped around, crunching bits of damp leaves and twigs beneath his boots. When he moved back beside the kerosene burner to warm his legs, he heard something, lifted his head, and turned to the direction from which the sound seemed to be coming. An engine, a Model T, probably out on Old King's Road, approached the edge of the swamp. Now with full attention, he listened as it grew louder and nearer. Then it stopped.

"Revenue men!" he gasped softly to himself as he pushed himself through the underbrush, away from the clearing and the still. He crouched on his hands and knees on the muddy earth, waiting for some voice or sound confirming his suspicions. After awhile, he cautiously crawled back to the clearing. He was almost at the still when he heard voices, and suddenly, there, a mere five feet from him, was not only Sheriff Boyce of St. Johns County but also federal men, two of the government agents who always called the local authorities when they received a tip about a still in that area. Their faces were turned away from Hugie as they lifted their axes to the still. He crawled slowly back into the swamp, ever so carefully, while the noise of the ax blades tearing into the metal resounded in his ears and echoed against the tall cypress of Durbin Swamp.

Oleta was outside hoeing at the soft earth in her fall garden when she heard the terrible noise ripping across the woods and fields. She knew her husband's still was being torn to shreds. "Hugie's out there! What if they've found him!" she exclaimed aloud. Dropping the hoe, she ran to the front porch and stared out across the woods in the direction of Hugie's still, listening, pacing, waiting for the horrible noise to stop. And from the cypress cabin around the bend, Ella and Tom came rushing as quickly as their aging frames would carry them, terror for their young son flaring in their old eyes.

"Leta! Leta! Where's Hugie?" Ella cried when she reached the front yard.

"He's out there, Ma, at the still!"

"God, no!" Tom said, putting his hand to his long gray beard and then to his mouth as his eyes scanned the edges of the swamp beyond the field. "But they may not have him. Hugie's no fool. If he heard them coming, he got outa there. We'll just wait and see."

Finally, the sound of ripping metal ceased, and after a few minutes, in the distance, Oleta heard an engine turn and move away into the woods. Minutes passed with no sign of Hugie. "You don't suppose they would take him off to jail and not even bring him by to tell us, do you?" she asked, pleading for Tom to reassure her.

"God! You don't know what they would do. You don't think they care about you here worrying yourself to death, do you? Hugie's breaking the law. Breaking the law, I tell you! I told him to stay out of this bootlegging business. Damn it all to hell, anyway. I told him, didn't I, Ella?" Old Tom Oesterreicher sat down on the step, scared to death for his son. Then scanning the field through his dim eyes, Tom saw a movement in the shadows at the edge of the clearing. "What's that off there?" he called to Oleta, pointing toward the edge of the swamp.

Oleta stared across the field where, through a misty rain, she too spotted something skirting the edge of the field, staying in the underbrush. "I see Hugie," she said. "He's trying to stay out of sight, making sure it's clear for him to come up to the house." The young woman jumped off the porch, wildly waving her arms. "It's okay! It's okay!" she cried. Her husband stepped out into the field.

"Whewee! That was a close call!" Hugie exclaimed, stomping the mud off his boots before climbing onto the porch.

"We were worried to death! Where have you been?" Oleta asked.

"Staying out of sight! And after they left, I went back to see what damage they had done. They chopped it up and hauled the whole thing off, kerosene burner and all. Chopped up several barrels of whiskey I had aging."

"Well," Tom said, standing up and hobbling down off the porch, "let that be the end of it then. You need to stay out of it. What good you going to do Leta and these babies if you get hauled off to jail? Tell me that, now, Mr. Bootlegger."

The young man knew his father was right. But Hugie made moonshine again. Times got hard, and he built himself another copper still, a beautiful one, he thought. And the revenue men came again. This time, they chopped up Hugie's still and left it scattered on the muddy earth of Durbin Swamp. The man gathered the copper pieces and took them home. He would not make moonshine again, he thought.

However, in the spring of 1933, Oleta became pregnant with their third child. The baby was due in November, and by the early fall of that year, the money Hugie had made from cutting palms was gone. He had raked every dime he could from the woods, cutting cross ties. So he went to the shed behind his house, pulled out the bits of copper, and carefully began to weld the shattered still together again.

Meanwhile, Oleta had determined she was not going to the hospital to have this next baby. She was not going to be away from Hugie and her children for two weeks. She just couldn't stand that again. So she talked to Dr. Wilkinson about having the child at home. Was it safe, she wondered, and would he consider coming out there to deliver her baby? Yes, he had said, he felt it would be safe. She was not likely to have another breach birth. And if he kept close watch over her in the weeks to come, should the baby go into breach position, he would know to put her in the hospital. And yes, he would come out there to deliver her baby. So arrangements were made that, when Oleta went into labor, Hugie would go to Bayard and call Dr. Wilkinson, who would then take the train to Durbin Station, where Hugie would pick him up and bring him out to the house.

Several weeks before the baby was due, Hugie loaded his Model T with five-gallon jugs of whiskey and drove to Dr. Wilkinson's house in Jacksonville. Pulling to the back door, he stopped the car, unloaded the moonshine, and carried it into the doctor's kitchen. When the car was empty, Hugie shook hands with the doctor, smiled, and drove away. He had just paid for his third child.

That day, he didn't drive home by way of Phillips Highway but drove east on Atlantic Boulevard, across the Intracoastal Waterway, and south to the Brown place. Pulling into the shade of the oak trees, he saw May sitting on the front porch of the old white house, waiting for him, a small suitcase beside her. She rose, strands of graying hair falling from the bun at the back of her head down her slender neck and shoulders, watching Hugie's car approach. As it entered the shadows of the old oaks, May turned, pulled the white wooden door shut, inserted a key, and twisted it until she heard it click. She was ready to leave, ready to close the door of that lonely house.

Annie Brown had been dead for almost five years. On the afternoon her mother had been buried, May had returned to the Brown house alone. And although May had spent the weeks before her mother's death by herself while Annie was tending Asbury's sick family and then while Annie was in the hospital, she had been comforted to know that Annie would come home soon and that she would have work for May to do. Annie always found more work to do. But those weeks alone had not prepared May for the emptiness of life without Annie Sadler Brown. And perhaps nothing could have readied her for the absolute lack of purpose with which she was confronted after her mother's death, the apparent pointlessness of her existence.

May only knew work. Her labor was her only value, she felt, and now that was no longer needed. For as long as May could remember, all her strength had been spent tending the needs, the desires, the demands of Annie Brown. Even the work she had done for her father was really done only to ease the burden on her mother. And now she was gone; all Annie's needs, all her desires, all her demands were gone, leaving in their place a terrible hollow.

So in the fall of 1933, when Oleta had asked her to come stay with her for a few weeks as it grew time for her to have her third baby, May was happy, happy to be of use to someone again. And on that afternoon in early November when Hugie came to pick her up, she walked out of that old white frame house and never glanced back. May was ready to leave.

Several weeks after May had come to stay, Oleta went into labor, and as had been agreed earlier, Hugie drove to Bayard and called Dr. Wilkinson, arranging to pick him up at Durbin Station. By the time Hugie had returned with the doctor, Oleta was in bed, Tom and Ella were keeping vigil in the living room, and May was tending the two little Oesterreicher girls in the second bedroom. A kind of festivity was in the air. Late that night, Oleta gave birth to another baby girl, whom she named Sylvia. And after she had held the child and examined her, she handed her to May. And as May stood there, cradling the infant in her arms, something warm and living filled the hollow in her heart.

A few days later, on 5 December 1933, Prohibition was repealed. Hugie's days of moonshining were finished. So he loaded his copper still onto the back of his truck and drove to a Jacksonville junkyard, where he sold it for scrap. Folks in town stopped on the sidewalk and stared, amazed at the brashness of this woodsman who was hauling his moonshine still right down Bay Street, the busiest thoroughfare in the city. Hugie Oesterreicher was not proud he had run moonshine during the days of Prohibition, but neither was he ever ashamed of it.

Fences

FOR THE THREE years after the end of Prohibition, Hugie managed to scrape a scant living out of the woods for himself, Oleta, his three daughters, his parents, and May. The forty-year-old spinster had stayed with Hugie and Oleta after little Sylvia's birth because she had not been able to face going back to the Brown place alone. Besides, she found purpose not only in tending the Oesterreichers' children but also in helping the young couple survive those depression years. She often worked alongside Hugie as would another man.

However, by the mid-thirties, things were changing in northeast Florida, where large tracts of land were being fenced. Because of the Texas tick fever, the state had mandated an eradication program that required the regular dipping of cattle, and ranchers began stringing barbed wire around their own land to keep their herds within manageable range. Also, several attempts had been made to pass a fence law to keep cattle off the highways. Fencing their stock seemed logical to the big cattlemen in the area; rounding up the cattle was easier at dipping time, and their cattle would be less likely to cause automobile accidents, for which the owners might be held responsible. But as a woodsman, Hugie often would be in the woods tracking a hog or a deer and would have to come to a dead halt at a barbed-wire fence. Few places were left in which he could lay his traps, nor could his own cattle wander freely in neighboring swamps and woods. Everywhere Hugie went, he was confronted with signs that read, "No Trespassing."

The new dipping law, which required that all cattle be dipped twice a month to kill the Texas tick and other parasites, made it almost impossible for a man such as Hugie to keep a sizable herd. Rounding up the cattle every two weeks for dipping was too hard. Then, increasing his problems, game began to disappear from places still open for hunting. And finally, a law was passed that restricted hunting to only a few months out of the year. For the first time in

Hugie Oesterreicher's life, he could not make a living. Progress was crowding him out of the woods.

Then, on 2 December 1936, Tom Oesterreicher died of stomach cancer. Ella said she would not spend a single night in the cypress cabin without Tom, and so, on the night of his death, Ella moved into the two-bedroom house with Hugie, Oleta, their three girls, and May. But Tom's death opened another avenue to Hugie, an avenue he would not have considered thinkable ten years before, an avenue Oleta had deemed forever closed to her from the day she had chosen to marry the woodsman Hugie Oesterreicher. With the closing off to Hugie of large tracts of land on which he had hunted and trapped, with the death of his father and his mother's own willingness to go anywhere but back to the cypress cabin alone, and with the destitution of those depression years, Hugie became open to the possibility of moving himself and his family closer to town, where he might find work. Toward that end, in the early spring of 1937, Hugie and Oleta began negotiations with the Brown heirs to buy their shares of the family homestead from them.

It was during those days, when the Oesterreichers were making their decision and when Hugie was contemplating a more domesticated kind of life, that he found Nanny. One day in early spring, he was in the woods cutting palms when he came across a new fawn, nestled in the shadows of a palmetto thicket. "Brand new," Hugie had decided as he peaked beneath the pointed fronds at the little thing, still camouflaged with white spots and unable to stand on its own legs. On and off during the day, Hugie checked on the tiny animal, waiting to see whether the mother had returned. At twilight, when there was still no sign of her, he knew the mother had most likely been killed, and so he scooped the little thing in his arms and carried her home.

When the three little girls saw their papa coming, holding the little deer in his arms, they ran to meet him. "I've got you something," he said to them, grinning. "Now, you going to have to take care of her," he warned his daughters as he placed the tiny animal in Annie Mary's arms, " 'cause she's lost her mama." Hugie taught his little girls to feed the fawn with a baby bottle. They named her Nanny, and she became their special pet, sleeping in the bed with them or behind Oleta's treadle sewing machine.

Several weeks later, Oleta's siblings agreed to sell the house and land to Hugie and her. So Hugie went to the St. Augustine bank to borrow money to buy the Brown place. He explained to Xavier Pellicer, the banker handling the loan application, that if he bought the land, he was going into the hog business. The arrangement that Hugie proposed to the bank was that once a year, in the spring, he would borrow money to pay the Brown heirs, and in the summer, after he had sold his hogs, he would make one big yearly payment to the bank for the mortgage. After he and the banker had struck a deal, the Oesterreichers went to Judge Brennan to obtain the necessary legal documents for such an agreement. When they told the man of their plans, the judge said to Hugie, "You are a very brave man to take on this kind of debt in hard times like these."

But of course, Hugie did not see his actions as particularly courageous. His motives were those born in the hearts of desperate men, men left with no choice but bravery.

For there were fences then, and Hugie was leaving the Diego Plain.

The Rattlesnake

A rattlesnake that had killed five dogs bit a six
year old child at Jacksonville Beach yesterday.

—The *Jacksonville Journal*, 7 April 1937

JUST BEYOND THE shade of the oaks that sheltered the old Brown place, the
sun warmed the grassy earth. Beneath the palmettos that crowded themselves
toward the white frame house, in the tunnels the hogs had hollowed out beneath
their silver-green fronds, a great snake moved sluggishly toward that sunny spot.
The snake would sleep there stretched in the sun hidden in the grasses. He had
been there before. Those palmettos, with their dark juicy fruits, were his palmettos, and that grassy place beyond the oaks was his grassy place. And once,
after a bad storm, when fierce little rivers ran through the hollowed-out places
beneath the palmettos and a lake of water stood a foot deep around the roots
of the oaks, he had sought refuge on the porch of the Brown house, safe beneath the sill of the front door. And there had been dogs intending to interfere
with his travels beneath his palmettos, across his grassy spots, and through his
patches of blackberries, five different dogs on five different occasions, but he
had killed them all. On this crisp April morning, though, the snake once again
found the grassy place and stretched himself in the warming sun.

That year, before Hugie and Oleta moved to the old homestead, the Brown
house was being rented to a woman with eight children. And on that April
morning of 1937, one of those children, a six-year-old girl with long blond
curls clambered down the steps and danced across the yard. The light filtering
through the mossy branches overhead flecked her sea blue eyes. "I can spin
longer than anyone," the little girl called back to her twelve-year-old brother,
sitting on the front step of the house. "I can spin and never fall down. Watch
me." And she danced and turned until the morning sun hit her full in the face,
her head tilted back as she moved across the grassy place.

The earth beneath the serpent vibrated. He was disturbed. Something was
approaching, careening toward him. Instinctively he drew himself into attack
position, coiled, rattles singing.

The little girl danced, and then she stopped. The sky, the trees, the palmettos seemed to swirl around her. Her ears were ringing, she thought. Then,
leaning forward to regain her balance, she looked up and stared full into the
face of the killer rattlesnake, fangs bared, head swaying over its coiled body.
The child staggered. She lunged to get away from the snake, and as she did, a

hot pain coursed through her body. "Robert!" the little girl screamed to the boy who watched her from the front step. "Robert!"

The snake crawled away. He had dealt with the intruder.

"Robert," the little girl gasped, crumpling into a heap as the boy reached her side, "a snake, Robert." She pointed to the warm grassy spot. "A big snake."

"Did it bite you, Mary?" the boy cried, scanning his little sister's body. "Did it bite you?" Then he saw it there on the little girl's thigh—the wound, the strike, a little horseshoe array of teeth marks and, above it, two punctures where the snake's fangs had pierced the child's skin and sent enough venom surging through her veins to kill a two-hundred-pound man. "Ma! Ma!" the boy screamed. "It's Mary. Oh, Mary, I think it's a rattlesnake bite." He was not a country boy, but he recognized those wounds. He had seen them on the dogs.

"Oh Jesus God!" the mother sobbed, running to where her children crouched in the front yard. She reached for her wounded child, held the little girl to her breast, and then wailed in bewilderment to the heavens, "Oh Jesus God, no! I don't know what to do! I don't know what to do!" The renters had no car, they had no horses, they had no telephone. It was the depression. She was lucky to have a roof under which she and her children could sleep. "Oh God, Robert, I don't know what to do!" the woman cried helplessly to her son.

"We gotta get her to a doctor, Ma! There's one at the Beach." And then he glanced out across the wide expanse of palmettos and declared, "I'll carry her, Ma. I can do it."

"Do that, Robert. Take her, run as fast as you can. Oh, Mary, honey, I think a rattlesnake's bit you. Oh Jesus, Robert! Run! Run!"

And Robert scooped his little sister in his arms and began to run down the overgrown road that wound through the acres of palmettos. He ran, all the time talking to Mary, tears streaming down his cheeks. "It's all right, Mary, I'm gonna get you to the doctor!"

His side started aching, but he pushed on across the scrub. Little Mary began to vomit, and the vomit spilled over the boy's arms as they clutched his sister's body and down on his bare feet as they made their tracks in the ruts in the soft sand road. But Robert kept running. He glimpsed the wound on the girl's thigh and noticed that the flesh around it was turning black, either because of the poison or because of the force with which the snake had struck her. When the boy reached Highway A1A, he slowed and looked in both directions, hoping for an approaching car. There was not one. So he took off running down the middle of the highway, running for the doctor's office in the heart of the beach settlement, over a mile away.

Mary started to cry, "I can't see, Robert. It's so dark."

And Robert looked down in the vacant eyes of his little sister, who was staring full into the morning light. "Just hold on, honey, maybe we can flag someone down if they come by." But on that morning in 1937, in the time it took Robert to run that mile carrying his sister, he didn't pass a single automobile. When he finally reached Pablo Avenue, the boy was sobbing, and Mary was unconscious, limp in his arms. A man leaning against the open door of the Bamboo Bar saw the boy and called to him across the street. "My God, son, what's the matter?"

"Snakebite! Got to get her to a doctor!" the boy panted.

The man ran to the sad little pair and pleaded, "Come on, son, let me carry her for you!" But the boy would not release his sister to him, and so the man ran ahead to the doctor's office on the second floor of the old bank building on the corner of First Avenue and First Street. "Doc! Doc!" the man yelled from the open door. "We got a snakebite out here!" And the doctor took the flight of stairs in three steps to the sidewalk in front of his office, where the boy placed his sister in Earl Roberts's arms and sank to the ground, sobbing.

"My God!" the doctor exclaimed to his wife as he stretched the child on a table and examined the blackened wound on her thigh. "My God, Lois, he hit her hard! Get on the telephone and get Ed McCormick over here!"

By the time Ed McCormick, the chief of police, had arrived, Earl Roberts had pumped his only dose of rattlesnake serum into the veins of the child, slit the deadly wound with his scalpel, and was furiously sucking the child's blood from the incision with his own mouth, hoping to remove some of the venom from her body. The doctor looked up, a drop of blood at the corner of his mouth. "Ed, you got to find me some more serum. I only had enough on hand to treat one adult. A child needs twice that amount. Ed, find another dose and get it to me. And Ed, this happened out on the Brown place. You might want to let Hugie and Leta know."

The chief rushed to the telephone, lifted the receiver, and spoke authoritatively into the mouthpiece. "This is Ed McCormick. Get me the sheriff in Jacksonville." He waited for his call to go through. Then came a voice from the other end of the line. "This is Rex Sweat."

"Rex, this is Ed McCormick at the Beach. We got a snakebite out here. A little girl. We need another dose of serum. Can you get your hands on some and get it out here quick, to Doc Roberts's office?"

"Yeah, I can do it, Ed! My men will have it there in the hour. A little child, Ed, that's awful."

Ed McCormick looked at Earl Roberts, who was bending over the unconscious body of the little girl, sucking on the rattlesnake wound, and spitting the blood in a pan Lois Roberts was holding for her husband. "The serum will be here within the hour, Earl. You need anything else?"

The doctor shook his head.

"Then I'll be back directly."

Ed McCormick turned to leave, but as he passed the hunched figure in a chair in the corner, he put his hand on the tousled head of the boy and said, "Son . . . son!" He shook his head as he descended the stairs; he wanted to offer the boy hope, but he had none to offer. And he muttered to himself, "I'm going to kill that goddamned snake!" He drove the short distance to his office and blew his automobile horn. When one of his men came to the door, he ordered, "Get some men together and get out to the Brown place. We're going snake hunting!"

"How's the little girl, chief?"

And again, Ed McCormick shook his head, "She ain't got a chance in hell, Chuck. I'll see you out there!"

The chief drove south on A1A until he reached the home of Garland Strickland, who was outside working on a well.

"What's up, Ed?" Garland asked as he hurried toward the car.

"That damned snake, the one that's killed those dogs, has bit one of those children renting out at the Brown place. Damn it, Garland, I should have gone out there and found him after he killed those dogs, and now he's got a little six-year-old girl. Her brother carried her on foot all the way to Doc Roberts's place. Rex Sweat has his men bringing serum down here right now. And Earl is up there sucking the venom out with his own mouth. But Garland, she's gonna die. There ain't no hope for her. But anyway. . . . " Ed McCormick cleared his throat and shook his head once more. "Anyway, I'm getting a posse together to go look for the snake. Could you run out to Hugie and Leta's and let them know what's happened. I think Hugie would want to be in on the hunt since he's going to be moving his family to the Brown place in two months' time. Those little girls of his—God, Garland—those little girls of his will be playing in that yard in two months' time."

Garland had an hour's drive over bad roads to the remote area of Palm Valley where Hugie and Oleta lived. When he arrived, Hugie had just come in from the woods for his noon meal. The couple greeted him on the front porch, anxious to know the reason for his visit. May came out holding one of the little Oesterreicher girls on her hip. "What's wrong, Garland?" Hugie asked. He knew something had to be wrong; only bad news brought a person out that far in the middle of a workday.

"A rattlesnake bit one of the little children staying out at your folks' place, Leta. Ed says he doesn't think the child will make it. He's getting a posse together to go look for the snake, Hugie. He thought you might want to help out. Oh God, Hugie, he thinks it's the same snake that's been killing those dogs. And now he's got a little girl." And Garland looked at the little girl on May's hip and added, "You ought to come on up to the Beach and help find that son of a bitch, Hugie."

"I'm right behind you, Garland," Hugie answered as he rushed into his parlor, where he took a pistol and holster hanging from a set of antlers on the wall, strapped it around his waist, then reached for his shotgun, and shoved some shells into his pants pocket.

At that moment, little Annie Mary came to the front porch. "What's wrong, Mama?" the girl asked.

And Oleta, putting her slender arms around the little girl as though to protect her from some unseen threat, said to Hugie as he stepped off the porch and lunged toward his Model T, "Hugie, find that snake. Find that snake and kill it!"

"I will, Leta. I will find him," the man assured his wife.

Oleta knew if the snake could be found, Hugie would find it.

By the time Hugie had arrived at the Brown place, it was almost one in the afternoon, and Ed McCormick and his men had fanned out over the palmetto scrub looking for the killer snake. Close to the house, palmetto roots were smoldering where the men had set fire to the brush in an effort to smoke the killer out. Ed McCormick called to Hugie as he climbed from his automobile, "Not a sign of him yet, Hugie. Come on over here and let me show you his crawl."

Hugie stared down at the marks left that morning by the snake as it crossed the road. "It's a big one!" he thought.

"Her mama says he got her right over there." Ed pointed to the grassy place beyond the oaks.

A few minutes before two o'clock, Hugie looked out across the scrub and saw the black top of a sedan moving toward them on the dirt road leading from the highway. All the men stopped their hunt and moved together, waiting to converge on the driver, whom they knew would have news of the little girl. Earl Roberts, with the twelve-year-old boy beside him on the front seat, brought the car to a halt just beyond the oak trees. All the men watched him silently. He climbed from the car, glanced at the men, and then turned away, shaking his head. "She's gone," he finally said. "Sweat's men got the serum to me, and I gave her the second injection. I tried to suck the venom out, but I was just too late. The poison had already got to her. I'll go on in and tell her family. Poor little thing. God, I hate it . . . I hate it." And he walked toward the house.

"Hugie," Ed muttered, "I should have come out here and found that snake after he started killing those dogs, but I didn't do it."

Hugie studied the chief. "Yeah, Ed, you should have. We both should have, but we didn't."

Garland Strickland approached the two men, "We might as well go on and leave these people alone with their grief. That snake could be to Palm Valley by now."

"Yeah," Hugie said, "he could be, but he ain't. He's right out there some-where." And he pointed to the palmetto scrub. "He'll be back. And so will I."

The Move

He took all our palm money for that year to make the payments, the down
payments for the place. We left over there, I think, with one dime. Papa had
a few old razorback hogs, tame ones. And we had a few head of cattle that
he had driven down here, on foot, from all the way over there. And we had
our furniture on a truck, and we were loaded up in the car and had the
little deer in our laps, holding her, and we come down here to the Beach.

—Oleta, 24 March 1984

ONLY A SLIVER of a moon hung in the sky that July night in 1937 as Hugie
and Oleta strolled together arm in arm down the white sand road that
glowed faintly before them in the pale light of the new moon. Each understood,
without expressing it, the mixture of emotions the other was experiencing.
And Oleta knew, without asking, where her husband was leading her. The dim
outline of the cypress cabin appeared before them, dark and vacant these last
months. Past the porch, past the grapevine, past the well with its ancient cypress
curbing, past the smokehouse, they crept silently to the edge of the field that
sloped down into the thick black shadows of Durbin Swamp.

They stood still for a moment facing the field. Then, slowly raising his right
hand to the headlamp strapped to his head, Hugie whispered, "Look at this."
And as the light of the lamp flooded the field, a hundred eyes, it seemed to the
woman, reflected back at them, blue and green and yellow points of light, float-
ing just above the ground, rising and falling in the mist that drifted up from
the warm earth into the cool breeze of the summer evening.

Hugie and Oleta paused for a long time, caught in the magic of the tiny
lights that drifted softly across the field. Finally, Hugie whispered, "There's
nothing like the eyes of a deer, no other animal. They like stars fallen to the
ground." Quietly, they turned and headed back to their house, and as they
rounded the corner of their yard, they saw the black hulk of the truck, loaded
with all their possessions, waiting to be driven to the Brown place.

When Oleta had married Hugie ten years before and had moved away from
her mother's house, it had been in perfect repair. Annie had always kept everything, house, barns, and fences, painted and in working order. But since May
had moved out, the place had been rented to several families, and when Oleta
went back a few days before the move, she found that the last tenants had left
the place filthy, so filthy she suddenly dreaded moving back. The day before
moving day, she and May had left the children with Ella and had driven to the
old house. All day, the two women scrubbed walls and floors with boiling water

and potash. Utter filth—human excrement rubbed into floors and walls, infestations of roaches and fleas—the two women could almost vomit at the sight and smell of it. But they labored that day, sweeping, mopping, scrubbing, boiling, trying to make the place decent enough for their family. And when they finished, they sat on the front porch late in the afternoon gazing up into the tangle of oak branches overhead and out across the palmettos that stretched to the white sandy beaches of the Atlantic coast.

They were waiting for Hugie. He had left well before daylight, on foot, to drive their few cattle the twenty miles north from the Diego Plain. Long before this, he had given up his horses and oxen; keeping them in feed in those days was impossible. Finally, they heard, coming up from the savannahs, the sound of Hugie's whistle and the crack of the long whip he used for driving cattle.

After he had penned the stock, he turned toward the two women waiting in the shade of the porch. "Well," he asked, "did you finish it?"

"Everything except the candles," Leta replied. They entered the house, tightly closed all the windows, and placed sulfur candles in each room. After lighting the candles, they closed the door and returned to the waiting Model T, with hopes that the sulfur would kill the vermin infesting the place.

The next morning, the family finished loading their possessions. Hugie climbed into the truck, and the family climbed into the Model T, with Oleta slipping into the driver's seat. May held Sylvia, the youngest girl; Ella held June. And Annie Mary held Nanny, the family's pet fawn. The little caravan pulled away from the house and the cypress cabin, down the dusty roads, across the coastal canal, and north to the Brown place.

"Leavin' the woods," Hugie thought to himself as the overburdened truck creaked along the hot white road.

"Leavin' these woods," Oleta thought, glancing back at the darkness of Durbin Swamp looming behind her.

Although Hugie had cut palms that spring, all of that money had been used as a down payment on the Brown house and its forty acres. On that July morning in 1937, at the start of a new life with his family, as he headed north on the winding dirt road through Palm Valley, he felt in his pocket. He had one dime.

They had been weeks without rain. Everything was so dry that all the muck ponds were burning. But that night, as Oleta and Hugie climbed into the mahogany four-poster, ready to sleep for the first time in their new home, the rain started. And when it rained, the water poured through a hundred holes in the tin roof. Oleta lay next to her husband, listening to the water pinging as it hit the pots that had been placed beneath leaks in every room of the house. As she drifted off to sleep, she thought of the filth she and May had scrubbed from the walls and floors of that place, and she shuddered, longing quietly for the clean solid little house she had just left. And when she slept, she dreamed of the deer that feed in the field at the edge of Durbin Swamp.

Justice

"A Killer Is Killed"

—The *Jacksonville Journal*, 19 August 1937

DURING THOSE FIRST weeks after their move back to the Brown place, Hugie, Oleta, and May scoured the grounds for any evidence of the rattlesnake. Hugie cleared the grounds around the house and burned back the palmettos again, but the snake was not to be found. Rattlesnakes were always a danger in Florida, and one never tramped through those woods without a certain amount of caution. But this was different. This snake was a proven killer; he would strike an intruder rather than seek refuge in a hiding place.

And then one morning in August, shortly after Hugie had left for work and after the summer sun had risen above the horizon to glisten on the sea of silver-green fronds that stretched toward the coast, the rattlesnake moved from the palmettos toward the grassy spot just beyond the shade of the oaks.

Inside the house, the little Oesterreicher girls were eating their breakfast at the family's big oak table. "I can dance faster than you," Annie Mary taunted June.

"No you can't," responded her little sister, pushing herself back from the table. "I can spin and never get dizzy. I'll show you."

"Finish your breakfast first," Oleta said to the child.

The rattlesnake stretched itself in the sun there in the soft grassy place.

The woman walked out the back toward the fowl yard, where she fed the chickens and checked for eggs beneath the hens. As she finished that chore, she glanced toward the house and noticed the girls dancing in the front yard. Annie Mary and June danced and spun out toward the edge of the oaks. Sylvia trailed behind them, laughing at her older sisters' antics.

The earth vibrated beneath the belly of the snake. It was disturbed.

The little girls danced, and the morning sunlight filtered through the branches, flecking their hair and eyes, glistening on the drops of dew still clinging to the grass, and sparkling on the diamond patterns adorning the rattlesnake's back. Spinning out across the warm grassy earth, the girls danced, laughing, until the sun hit them full in the face.

But then they stopped. Bullet, Hugie's hog dog, was barking viciously at something over in the grass. At that moment, Bear, another dog, shot from beneath the house toward the object of Bullet's anger. The dogs were moving

144

in and out, barking furiously, circling something. The children couldn't see. They moved closer.

Oleta hastened to see the cause of the row in the front yard. She stopped, almost frozen on the front porch. Her girls were rushing toward the dogs. "Girls!" she screamed. "Get back! Get back now!" Instinctively, she knew what the dogs had bayed, and she rushed to the children. "Go in the house. Go!" she ordered as she ran toward the frantically barking dogs. She stopped on the edge of the grassy place. She saw it there, coiled, its flared head raised and swaying, and above the barking of the dogs, she heard its rattles singing. Over and over, the great snake struck out at the dogs, and over and over, the dogs darted out of the way of its poisonous fangs.

For only an instant, Oleta was confused about what to do. And then she turned and ran wildly back to the house and into her bedroom, where she reached for her 410 shotgun on the rack above her chiffonnier. She found shells in the top drawer and shoved several in her apron pocket. On her way out the front door, she yelled to May, who had rushed in from the garden, "It's the snake, May!" and to the girls, "Stay on the porch!" May grabbed the hoe and followed Oleta out to the road.

The snake was still striking viciously at the furious dogs that danced frantically around it as Oleta shoved a shell into the barrel of her gun. She raised her weapon to her shoulder and aimed at the swaying head of the rattlesnake. But the dogs were in the way; she couldn't get a clear shot. "What would Hugie do?" she wondered, and then she knew. Motioning with one hand, she commanded, "Bullet! Bear! Get back!"

The dogs fell back behind the woman with the gun. Hugie had trained them well. Again, she raised the shotgun to her shoulder, and as the little girl had done three months before, Oleta stared full into the face of the rattlesnake, its fangs bared. In the moment that the snake reared back to lurch forward and strike at the woman, she pulled the trigger. The snake's head exploded. She grabbed another shell and shoved it into the barrel of the shotgun. But the snake's head was gone. The body still swayed there, and the rattles still sang, but that malevolent head with its murderous fangs had been blown apart.

May, holding the hoe beside her younger sister, stood ready to attack that thing with that instrument, if necessary. May could not shoot a gun, but she could swing a hoe. She had killed rattlesnakes that way before. Finally, Oleta spoke. "I believe that's the one, May. I believe that's the one that killed little Mary."

That afternoon, chief of police Ed McCormick drove out and measured the snake at six feet and two inches. He was as big around as the calf of a man's leg and had nine rattles and a button. Ed made an official statement that, judging from the size of the crawl he had seen last April, this was the snake that had killed the little girl.

The next day, the little Oesterreicher girls walked out to the mailbox on the highway and picked up the daily newspaper for their mother. When they handed it to Oleta, she opened the *Jacksonville Journal* and read the headlines for 19 August 1937, "Huge Jap Army Arriving in Shanghai." And at the bottom of page one, she saw her story. The bold type heading the article read, "A Killer Is Killed." Oleta kept the newspaper out on the tea table for a few days. But then she slipped into her room and knelt before the trunk she had always kept at the foot of her bed. Having lifted the heavy lid, she placed the folded journal inside. When she closed the lid of the trunk, she closed the chapter on the rattlesnake. She never mentioned it again.

The Depression Ends

I'd work all day and haul swill for the hogs at night. Sometimes, it
would be twelve o'clock when I'd get back in. Get up the next morning,
and go to work. I have went out there on that highway in the morning,
in a little cut-down Ford I had, before day, and the ducks and the coots
would be standing up on the highway, ponds frozen over. And I didn't
have no overcoat. Cold! Good God Almighty! Freezing to death!

—Hugie, 3 March 1984

IN THE LATE thirties, the decade of the Great Depression, the Oesterreichers
had moved closer to town, hoping that somehow Hugie would be able to
make a living for them, that somehow things might ease for them.

Gradually, Hugie managed to repair parts of the broken-down place they
had bought. He repaired fences, painted the house, and replaced the old roofing
with new tin from Sears and Roebuck. Those first few years after the move,
Hugie worked all day digging palm trees, carrying them out of the swamps,
loading them onto his truck, and then replanting them in the yards of homes
and businesses around the Beach. Also during that time, he took up carpentry
and worked on and off for twenty dollars a week.

Hugie had brought some hogs with him to their new home. He penned
them and installed a hand pump to get fresh water for them, because hogs need
a great deal of water. Shortly after that, he contracted with the Atlantic Beach
Hotel and the Ponte Vedra Inn to collect their swill, the leftovers from the
restaurant, to use for feeding his hogs. He worked all day digging palms or
doing carpentry, and then at night, he drove his truck loaded with fifty-gallon barrels to the backdoors of the exclusive hotels and collected their leftover
scraps of food. Often, it was midnight before he finished driving to the pens
and heaving the huge barrels of swill to the hogs, and he would be up before
the sun the next day, going to work in his cut-down truck, which had no cab,
only a windshield.

Some mornings were so cold that when he drove past the run of water at
Sixteenth Avenue South, the ducks and coots would be standing out on the
highway, because the pond was frozen over. Hugie remembered being cold,
with no overcoat in the cut-down truck, the icy wind off the ocean whipping
at him as he drove to work in the early hours of day.

During all of this time the little fawn, Nanny, had become a regular member of the family. The little deer lived in the Oesterreicher home and played in

the nearby forests. If Hugie and Oleta climbed into his truck and drove to the woods, Nanny would run playfully beside them. When Hugie planted a garden and fenced it, Nanny jumped the fence and nipped away at the tiny buds poking their heads above the soil. Hugie raised the fence; Nanny jumped that one also. This was repeated several times, but not one fence Hugie built was tall enough to keep Nanny out of the garden. However, as drastic as it might seem to have an animal destroying a garden in such difficult times, Nanny's pranks didn't seem to bother any of the Oesterreichers. They loved her.

What did worry the family was the way Nanny had started wandering away. If she headed to the Beach, she might be run over by an automobile. If she went too deeply into the woods, a hunter might mistake her for a wild deer and shoot her. Finally, when it became apparent that Nanny was no longer safe wandering the woods and highways near the Oesterreicher home, Hugie took the animal to the Alligator Farm in St. Augustine, where she would be protected from automobiles and hunters.

Later, Hugie and Oleta heard a story about their little deer. When filmmakers were casting for the movie of Marjorie Kinnan Rawlings's novel *The Yearling*, they came to the Alligator Farm looking for a tame deer that was a good jumper. They used Nanny. She was thoroughly tamed and excellently trained from jumping Hugie's fences.

Before the end of the decade, Hugie and Oleta had bought five more acres of land beyond the savannahs, which Hugie fenced for keeping his hogs. All this time, he had been hand-pumping enough water daily for seventy-five to a hundred head of hogs. He decided to order a windmill from Sears and Roebuck. The machine arrived in pieces, with a big bucket of bolts. Hugie read instructions for a week, figuring exactly how to go about putting this new wind-powered pump together. Finally, he set to work on this project. When it was finished, he hoisted it up on a tower in the southwest corner of the new five acres he had fenced, and the wind did his work for him, day and night, pumping fresh water to his hogs.

All during the late thirties, since the move to the Beach area, although Hugie had other jobs, and although Oleta added to their income by selling fresh eggs from her hens and fresh peas from her garden to local markets, Hugie's hog business had been the main source of income for his family. One night, when he pulled up to the kitchen door of the Ponte Vedra Inn, the cook met him and told him the hotel had contracted someone else to haul off the swill. Without warning, the biggest supply of food for his hogs had been taken from him. His hogs would starve, unless he found new sources. He went to bakeries in Jacksonville and got their old bread. He hauled Irish potatoes thirty miles from Hastings in his truck. Then, one day, he heard that the city of Jacksonville Beach was looking for a new place to dump its garbage. Hugie approached officials about dumping on his five acres west of the savannahs, where his hogs, he knew, could root through the mounds of garbage and find plenty of food, and soon the garbage trucks were rolling across the palmetto scrub and down the old wagon road through the savannahs to Hugie's hog pen.

Things did get better for Hugie Oesterreicher. He no longer had to work all day and then go out late into the night picking up swill and delivering it to his hogs. He no longer had to hand-pump water for them, since the windmill took care of that. And so the hog business thrived.

In spring of 1939, when Oleta was expecting another child, one of her sisters said to her, "You must be crazy, in these times, having all these babies and nursing all of them." Oleta smiled and thought to herself, "I guess this isn't the modern thing to do." But in May of that year, their fourth daughter was born.

Those were hard times, the thirties, but they passed. The depression that had racked the world, the nation, and Hugie Oesterreicher started to ease. And often, at night, the family would gather on the front porch, and there beneath the great oak branches, by lamplight, Oleta would read to her husband and children. Or sometimes Hugie would draw from the store of songs and poems he always carried in his head:

> O Captain! my Captain! our fearful trip is done,
> The ship has weather'd every rack, the prize we sought is won . . .

Hunting Squirrels in Small's Hammock

I was out there, just before dark. I heard someone calling . . .
and I jumped in my truck and made a dash back to the house.
And I went in there and said to May, "Where's Leta?"

—Hugie, 16 February 1984

ALTHOUGH THE HOUSE Hugie and Oleta moved to in 1937 was closer to town than the one they had lived in for the previous twelve years, it had no modern conveniences. Without electricity, the family still used kerosene lamps for light and heavy irons heated on the stove for ironing clothes. Clothes were still washed the old-fashioned way, by boiling them in a big pot outdoors or scrubbing them by hand on a ribbed board. They had no telephone and only a wood stove for cooking. They used an outhouse because they had no indoor toilet. And until 1940, when Hugie put down an artesian well that supplied the house with running water, all of the water for bathing, cooking, cleaning, and washing clothes had to be retrieved with a hand pump on the back porch.

Nevertheless, it was all so familiar to Oleta that she was comfortable there. The old house with the porch wrapping round it, the oak trees blocking the summer sun and fending the winter winds, the once-tilled fields stretching into the stands of stately pines, the hammocks and woods surrounding the place of her childhood, she knew them all.

In February of 1941, the fire in the wood stove blazed as May stood at the kitchen table straining the cream from milk. The three older girls chattered in a corner, lost in some imaginary world. The youngest child was stretched across Oleta's pregnant belly, sleeping. Oleta stood, heaved the little girl up in her arms, and carried her to a bed, where she gently laid the child down and covered her with a quilt. Oleta went to her room and pulled Hugie's old hunting jacket over her thin arms, straining to button it over the bulge of her stomach. Returning to the kitchen, she said to May, "I'm going squirrel hunting."

She had cabin fever. Hugie had been away all day, and she needed to get out of the house. Picking up the 410 shotgun Hugie had given her when they first married, she headed for Small's Hammock, a grove of trees north of the house. She felt perfectly safe. The air outside of the old house was cold, and as she emerged from the protection of the oaks onto the white sand road, the winter wind hit her with full force. She continued toward the hammock, the dark entrance of which, with its thick overhanging trees, looked more like the door to a cave in the side of a mountain than a roadway into a wood. In the fall, the blackjack oaks and hickory trees in this hammock blazed with yellow and red, but by February, the branches of many of these trees stretched naked, their black-webbed fingers etched against the cold blue sky. As she entered Small's, the spirits of the place danced round her and cut her off from everything except its own magic life. The Indians, the Spaniards, and the early settlers had traveled that road and camped in those woods. Their ghosts seemed hidden in the trees, calling her on. She headed northward, only half-aware of the squirrels scampering above her.

Later, when the sun started to sink and the hammock darkened, Oleta suddenly remembered her girls, Hugie, and their supper. "He will be hungry," she thought. She turned to circle back, heading south in the hammock but at some distance off of the road. Something was different, though. Maybe it was just the shadows of late afternoon, but the hammock suddenly became strange to her. That slough, she had never seen it before. She walked beside it for awhile, pushing back the underbrush as she made her way across increasingly moist earth. She looked beyond the bulge of her belly and noticed her feet were sinking in the thick black mud of the bog. Beyond the run of water, she knew, was the familiar road, but she couldn't get to it. "Oh, this is foolishness," she thought, "I'll wade across."

She hiked her skirt round her thighs, lifted the shotgun shoulder high, and waded into the slough, slowly feeling her way along the bottom with her feet, trying the soft ground beneath her with each step before trusting it with her full weight. The bog kept getting deeper. The icy black water reached the tops of her legs. Panic rose in her throat. Beyond the hammock, she could hear the roosters crowing. Dark was settling over the homeplace. "Hugie," she whispered. "Oh, Hugie." Then she screamed, "Hugie, Hugie!"

A mile from that place, Hugie was working on the windmill he had built to pump water for his hogs. Earlier, he had seen the setting sun reflecting on the smoke streaming from the chimney in the distance, and he had thought of Oleta and his girls and the baby she carried. He hurried to feed the hogs, for the sun was beneath the trees in the west and the light of day was fading fast.

Then he heard something. Was someone calling? Probably just that old panther. He had seen its tracks in Small's Hammock. He heard it again. It sounded like Oleta. He dropped the bucket of slop, jumped into his truck, and drove bumping over the dirt roads to the house. As he pushed the backdoor open, he called to May, "Where's Leta?"

"She went squirrel hunting. She's not back yet," May answered, startled by the obvious worry in Hugie's voice.

Hugie ran back to his truck and frantically drove over the roads to Small's Hammock, tires whirring in the cold white sand of the road. The hammock was dark by the time he had stopped the truck and jumped out calling, "Leta!

Leta!" She answered from somewhere across the hammock, west of him. He ran toward the sound, palmettos and vines and brush cutting like whips across his face.

A thin light broke through the treetops, glistening on the slough. She stood there almost up to her belly in black water. One look told him she was bogging down. "Stay there! I'll get you!" he cried.

He waded in, reaching for her. As he did, the shotgun she held accidently went off, blasting between them, resounding in the shadowy trees. His hand touched her hand. His strong bearlike arms encircled her, and they clung to each other, weeping.

"I was so worried about you, Leta! God knows, when I heard you calling, I knew it was something bad."

"I don't know what happened to me, Hugie. I know these woods. And I just got turned around out here. And then I tried to cross this slough and started sinking."

"Well, it's all right now. I've got you." Hugie lifted his pregnant wife into his arms and carried her to dry ground.

A month later, in March of 1941, Oleta had a son, whom she named Hugh. He was Hugie and Oleta's fifth child and only boy.

The War Years

I used to tell Henry Jackson, "No, we ain't going to get
whipped, Henry. They against God. Anyone that's against God,
can't stand. We'll come out of it all right. We might lose some . . .
some might get killed. But they ain't going to take our country.
Everybody there is here would go to fighting before they could take it."

—Hugie, 24 March 1984

IN SEPTEMBER OF 1939, when Germany invaded Poland, war broke out in
Europe. To the Oesterreichers, the threat of this war seemed far greater than
that of World War I because of the vivid firsthand accounts in newsreel pictures
and radio broadcasts. They watched and listened, aware their nation could be
drawn into the conflict. However, into the early 1940s, life for the family continued as it had been before, when their greatest challenge was not fear for their
nation but the daily quest for their own personal survival.

Then one day in early December of 1941, Annie Mary and June walked to
pick up the newspaper from their mailbox on the highway. When they saw the
headlines, they ran with the paper all the way home to their parents. The Japa-
nese had bombed Pearl Harbor; America was at war.

If the sleepy little settlement of Pablo Beach on the northeastern coast of
Florida had managed to slip through World War I without notice, this was
certainly not the case with World War II. Possibly more than other sections
of the United States, the little beach community, because of its location, was
drastically affected by the war. Almost immediately, the numbers of troops stationed at nearby army and navy bases increased. In 1941, the new naval air station at Jacksonville was training one hundred cadets a month, but by 1944, over
ten thousand men were stationed there. An auxiliary field was opened by the
navy at Mayport, at the mouth of the St. Johns River, and by 1945, this field had
approximately two thousand men. Also between 1940 and 1945, over eight hundred thousand men had received all or part of their training at Camp Blanding,
the army training center in nearby Starke, Florida. Suddenly, the quiet little
beach community was flooded with those troops, young men from all over the
country pouring into the streets and businesses, onto the boardwalk and beaches,
seeking to fill their off-duty hours.

And while the community was flooded with young men from all over the
United States, one by one, the local boys were enlisting and leaving. Hugie and
Oleta had known no one who fought in World War I, but now Jake's sons, Ida

and Clarence's sons, Jean's son, Ada's son, and Asbury's sons and daughter were gone. Oesterreicher boys, Mickler boys, Brown boys, McCormick boys were all gone off to the war. It was as though the people of the Beach had given up their own precious sons and received back a hundredfold the sons of the nation: sons of midwestern farmers, sons of New England fishermen, sons of Detroit factory workers, sons of Oregon loggers spilled onto the white sandy shores of Jacksonville Beach.

On the night of 10 April 1942, the firemen were having a dance on the Jacksonville Beach pier. The swing music of the forties drifted across the ocean air. The pier was illuminated with festive lighting, and up on the boardwalk, the Ferris wheel and the merry-go-round were casting spinning circles of light out over the waters of the Atlantic.

Suddenly, a loud explosion shook the pier. The music stopped, and the frightened crowd ran to the edge of the pier, where they saw flames leaping from a ship just off the coast. They could plainly see men running around on the burning ship and hear the sound of machine guns that seemed to be mowing down the survivors on the deck of the tanker. A German U-boat had torpedoed an American tanker a few miles offshore. Against the lights of the pier and the lights on the amusement rides, the tanker's silhouette had been easily spotted by the U-boat. Residents up and down the coast heard the explosion and ran to the beach, watching the war on their front doorsteps. Some of them set out in rowboats to help rescue the men on the burning tanker.

After this incident, the coastal area went on permanent blackout, since lights along the shore made the ships that passed in and out of the St. Johns River easy targets for a submarine. All houses had black curtains; the lights on cars were painted black on the top three quarters of the headlamps. Streetlights weren't allowed, and even way out at the Oesterreicher place, the east side of the house had to have blackout shades. Jacksonville Beach was a dark place after sundown, and to keep it that way, the Civil Defense rode up and down the beach at night on watch for houses with lighting that might endanger the residents or shipping in that area.

On 16 June 1942, a German submarine deposited on the shore south of Mickler's pier four saboteurs, invaders who had come prepared to damage places strategic to the war effort. Not only did they bring with them munitions and explosives and carry in their pockets seventy thousand dollars in cash, but they were also proficient enough in English to travel around the states undetected. At the same time, another group of four Nazi spies had landed on Long Island, New York. Although their plan had been to meet to begin their work of sabotage, this didn't happen because one of the men confessed the plot to the FBI. All the saboteurs were subsequently apprehended. Two testified against the others and received long prison terms, but the other six spies were executed. After that, the Coast Guard had men on horseback patrolling the shore day and night, and the story of the Nazi saboteurs became part of the local folklore. Everyone had his or her own particular version to tell: "I was on the bus with one of them. I thought something was peculiar," or, "I saw one of them in the little grocery store on Tenth Avenue South, and I put in a call to the FBI," or, "I was on the beach that night, fishing, and all of a sudden I saw. . . ." Often, right off the shore, pilots practiced dive bombing and target shooting. The children of the area would line the beaches, fascinated by the display. Sometimes, the airplanes would zoom down fifty or sixty feet above the waters along the coast, and the pilots, with their leather hats and their yellow scarfs flying behind them, would flash a smile and wave at the children below. Meanwhile, only a short distance away, the army had bivouacked right in front of the Oesterreichers' forty acres. World War II had come to Jacksonville Beach, Florida.

During this time, there was little chance that Hugie could have been drafted. He was over forty years old and had eight dependents—Oleta, the five children, May, and often his mother. Also, Hugie raised hogs; the government needed that pork to feed the boys who were defending the country.

During those war years, meat, coffee, sugar, flour, gasoline, tires, and other staples were rationed. The rationing of meat was not a hardship for the Oesterreichers because Hugie could always hunt meat for their table. However, for anyone residing in outlying areas or who made a living with a car or a truck, the rationing of gasoline and tires sometimes presented problems. And even though people in these circumstances were given special allowances, this didn't always make it easier. Once during this time, Hugie needed tires for his truck, and even after going through all the necessary paperwork, he could not get them. With no tires for his truck, he was in a fix; he had a big family to provide for, a brood that now included their sixth and last child, a little girl they had named Angela. So he went to the garbage dump and dug through refuse until he found four old tires. He took them home, patched them, and put them on his truck. Hugie drove on those tires until the end of the war.

Meanwhile, Oleta's brother Bubba and his wife Lovey, had divorced. After that, Bubba, almost fifty years old and floundering for purpose, had enlisted in the navy and had been shipped to the South Pacific with the construction battalion. Sometimes, letters came from Bubba, and when Oleta opened them, they were almost impossible to read because they were so full of holes; the censors had cut out large portions because Bubba had written such descriptive passages that they were afraid he would give his battalion's position away.

By 1944, the war had touched every facet of the Oesterreichers' lives. Staples were rationed; young men from all over the country flooded the streets of the small town; airplanes held target practice just offshore; guardsmen patrolled the beach; the army bivouacked right in front of their homestead; there were blackouts and dark streets. But nobody seemed to mind any of those things. Sacrifice was part of the war effort. A tremendous sense of patriotism inspired the people. And when the national anthem came across the radio, the whole Oesterreicher family stood, often with tears glistening on their cheeks as those last words rang out, "Oh, say, does that star-spangled banner yet wave, O'er the land of the free and the home of the brave."

The war went on. And word came that T. C. Oesterreicher and Asbury Kelly had been killed in the Pacific; Bob Brown was declared missing in action; and the last word from Ira Oesterreicher was from a gunboat in the north Atlantic. Oleta and Hugie grieved for the young men in their family.

But then, toward the end of the war, in 1944, Oleta became restless.

The Grocery Store

"Mama, do you love me?"
"Do I love you? I'd go through fire for you."
"Does Papa love me?"
"He'd go through fire for you too."

—Michel and Oleta, summer of 1944

THE FIRE BLAZED as dark smoke curled round the contours of the big black pot. Like her mother and grandmother before her, Oleta was boiling clothes outdoors over an open fire; steam billowed upward, wetting her face and hair and dress. She was soaked, and when she moved from the warmth of the fire, she shuddered in the chilly air of that autumn morning of 1944. But on that day, her mind was far from her own particular discomfort and far from the laborious task of washing clothes. Oleta had an idea, and it was time to broach this idea to her husband.

She heard his vehicle round the last bend on the road emerging from the savannahs. She stirred the clothes, waiting for him. Hugie pulled his truck beneath the oaks, parked, climbed from the open cab, and walked toward his wife. They talked together softly about their morning, and then Oleta said, "Hugie, I've been thinking. Maybe we should build a grocery store. I think I would be real good in a store, Hugie, working with people."

"Well, you've never done it before. Neither have I. Don't know the first thing about running a grocery store."

"We could learn."

"Whew! What a undertaking, borrowing all that money, building a place, learning a business. We could lose everything."

"We could. It would be a big risk," the woman admitted.

That evening, she and Hugie sat deep in thought, gazing into the glowing embers of the fire. "Yes," they both were thinking, "a grocery store would be a big undertaking, but it might be possible."

Within weeks, they had found on the south end of the Beach a lot that they thought might be a good location for a store. Hugie and Oleta went to the bank. They would mortgage their house and land to buy the lot and build the store, and money from the hog business would make the payments on the mortgage until the store started making a profit.

By early 1945, Hugie had started work on the building. The lot on Sixteenth Avenue South sat on the east side of First Street, which ran parallel to the ocean, one block inland. Across the street was a run of water where ducks and coots often swam in and out of the cattails that lined the banks. During a strong easterly wind, the ocean would rise, sweep down the street in front of the lot, and flow into that run of water, and so he planned to build the store a foot and a half off the ground.

As Hugie and Oleta were facing this new challenge, with thousands of dollars running through their fingers, all of it borrowed, all to be paid back somehow, the war was still raging. Rationing continued. Off-duty soldiers and sailors flocked through the streets. The blackout continued, and when, at night, the Beach people looked out onto the dark waters of the Atlantic, they did so with the sure knowledge that lurking out there were German submarines waiting to torpedo some troop ship or tanker making its way along the Florida coast.

Word came through that Bob Brown was in a German prisoner of war camp. Nothing had been heard from Ira Oesterreicher since he had shipped out on a gunboat to the north Atlantic months before. Young Flavian Mickler was somewhere on an aircraft carrier, and Bubba was still in the South Pacific. Oleta wondered if she would ever see her nephews again, ever see her brother again, ever see the other boys from the Beach, the sons of her lifelong friends, soldiers who were away fighting in the war.

A few weeks after Hugie had started construction, a setback occurred in the Oesterreichers' plans for their store. Hugie and Oleta were already committed to the business venture, the money had been borrowed and half spent, and the building was half finished when, one block west of their place on Sixteenth Avenue, a family opened a grocery store in their home.

"All those years," Oleta thought, "all those years there was nothing on that end of the Beach, and now another grocery store almost next door to us."

"Well," Hugie had said, "we have no choice but to go through with it. We'll lose some business, but we can't back out now." He continued building, working against a deadline, for the store was scheduled to open on the first of May.

Now, all of this time, the couple knew absolutely nothing about running a grocery store, or as Oleta said years later, "We walked into it blind." She had never used a telephone; she had answered the telephone at Jean and Arthur's grocery store, but she had never put through a call. She and Hugie had certainly never operated a cash register or an adding machine. They had never lived in a house with electricity, and therefore, electrical devices were strange to them. After all, it had only been a couple of years before when Hugie had put an indoor water-flushing toilet in their home. Furthermore, they didn't know how to order stock or how to conduct themselves in business transactions without being intimidated by certain forms of salesmanship. It was as though Oleta and

Hugie and their children had been living on an island in time. Time continued to flow past them, but they, on their little island, had managed to stand still, almost untouched by the changes all around them. And they didn't know that, on the day they stepped into that grocery store, they would be stepping into the present.

One day in the first week of April in 1945, Hugie was on horseback driving a herd of cattle away from the highway toward the marsh. He was running the horse hard across a scrub when the animal stepped in a hole, flipped, and fell on top of Hugie. The frightened animal regained its footing and bounded off, but when Hugie tried to move, he couldn't. His leg was broken.

Well, Hugie was down. He had never been down a day in his life, but he was down then. And he couldn't build the store on a pair of crutches. Sitting in the mahogany bed with his leg in a cast, he said to Oleta, "We'll have to hire some men. I'll ask McCormick's to send some hands to finish the store. I can at least oversee it." He shook his head and added, "More money."

"Yes," Oleta said, nodding, a bit overwhelmed.

Having Hugie incapacitated with a broken leg was a blow to the couple as they struggled to make a new start; however, only days after Hugie's accident, the Oesterreichers received a blow of another kind. Franklin Roosevelt, from the earliest days of his presidency, had been almost a father figure to the couple. They believed his reforms during the depression had made it possible for them personally to survive those hard years. When Roosevelt's fireside chats were broadcast, Hugie and Oleta gathered their children around the radio and listened to every word. And when the president said, "My friends, and you are my friends . . . ," they believed he was talking directly to them and that he meant exactly what he was saying. During the depression and during the war years, the leadership of this man, the personal way he related to the people reassured Hugie and Oleta. So on that day in early April of 1945, when Dr. Roberts drove out to the Oesterreicher place, bringing the news of President Roosevelt's death, Hugie and Oleta grieved as though they had lost a member of their own family.

Meanwhile, hired men continued working on the store. Every morning, Oleta drove Hugie to the building site, where he, on crutches, watched over the construction of his grocery store. Then, one day in mid-April, Oleta was in the kitchen when her younger children ran to her crying, "Mama, someone's coming!" Oleta rushed to her room, ran a comb through her dark hair, and puffed a little powder on her nose. The car pulled into the shade of the oak trees, and the couple who had opened the grocery store in their home on Sixteenth Avenue got out. Oleta walked onto the front porch to greet them.

"We have a proposition for you and Mr. Oesterreicher," Mr. Reed said.

Oleta offered them a seat in one of the cane rockers on the front porch.

"Mrs. Reed and I are not happy with our store. We decided we want to get out of the business. We thought you and Hugie might want to buy our stock. We'll help you move it to your store when it's finished."

Oleta was so excited; their competition was pulling out.

"In fact," Mrs. Reed added, "we don't want to work another day in that store. If you folks buy the stock, you could come on in now and start running it as if it were yours. And we would be there to show you anything you might need to know."

"I'll talk to Hugie tonight," Oleta said.

Hugie and Oleta bought the stock from the little neighborhood grocery store—cold drinks, potato chips, bread, coffee, Vienna sausages. For the next few weeks, when Oleta dropped Hugie off at the building site of their grocery store, she went on to the Reeds'. The Reeds taught her everything. She met the wholesale grocery men, the soft drink men, the bakery men. And little by little, she met the people of south Jacksonville Beach who would be her customers and her friends in the years to come.

Three weeks after her first day in the Reed store, the building on the corner of First Street and Sixteenth Avenue was ready to be stocked. The trucks started coming. Cold cuts, bacon, chickens, and sides of beef for the meat market Hugie would operate. Fresh fruit, milk, butter, eggs, cheese, canned goods, soft drinks, bread, beer and wine, suntan oil, beach towels, comic books, and cigarettes, all stacked in crates ready to be put on the rows of shelves Hugie had built. And down the street, Oleta supervised the emptying of the Reed store. All of her children, along with the neighborhood children, made a caravan carrying boxes of stock to the little white stucco building bearing the name in big black letters across the top, Oesterreicher's Grocery.

Finally, the store opened and customers came. Boys on their way to school with a little change in their pockets would stop in to buy an R.C. Cola and a Moon Pie for breakfast, and they would talk to Mr. Oesterreicher. Housewives would leave their chores to stand at the counter gossiping, Cokes in one hand and cigarettes in the other. The mailman always took his break at Oesterreicher's Grocery, and the bus drivers making the loop on the south end took a rest stop there. Little children came with pennies for bubblegum. And because Hugie gave fine cuts of fresh meat at a fair price, the meat market was very popular. Some of the customers did all their shopping with the Oesterreichers, but for most, it was a place close by to get a loaf of bread or a quart of milk. Tourists came in the summer time. People from all over the world came to Jacksonville Beach in those days, and many of them passed through the door of the little grocery store on Sixteenth Avenue South.

Then, in August of 1945, the war ended. The young men of their family, the ones who had survived, came home.

Bubba's son, Bob Brown, had been captive in a German concentration camp during the last year of the war and had almost starved, but then, so had his captors. One morning, he and his fellow prisoners of war looked out to see that the guards had fled and that the gates of the camp were open. The freed prisoners then staggered hundreds of miles through snow to meet the Allied troops. Ada's son, Raymond Strickland, also came home. Word came that Flavian Mickler was safe. Ira Oesterreicher came home. As a gunner on a boat in the North Atlantic, sometimes he had stood in the freezing wind, blasting the thundering guns for thirty-six hours at a time. When the war ended in Europe, he was shipped to the Pacific, where he had fought until the end of the war.

One night after the Oesterreichers had gone to bed, a car pulled under the oaks. Hugie peered out his bedroom window. "It's a taxi cab!" he exclaimed to Oleta.

For a just a moment, she had no breath. Then she cried, "Bubba's home!" Almost tumbling from the bed, she scrambled to the front porch, calling her brother's name.

Hugie and Oleta ran to the uniformed man climbing from the car. The children clambered from their beds, and after tears and hugs and kisses, Bubba handed Oleta a package wrapped in brown paper. "Here," he said, "I thought you would like this." She opened the wrapping and found a book bound in blue linen. *Evangeline*, she read on the cover. Oleta's brother was home now. For the Oesterreichers, World War II was finished.

However, the grand adventure of the grocery store was just beginning. During those years, the children were often awakened early in the morning with the sound of Oleta playing the piano and singing, her unique way of rousing her young ones from their beds. And they would tumble sleepily into the kitchen, where Hugie had prepared his family a breakfast of eggs, grits, sausage, hot cocoa, and bread or biscuits toasted brown in the iron frying pan.

Because Hugie and Oleta kept the store open from eight in the morning until eight in the evening, seven days a week, it was necessary to make it into a sort of home. The store had a small backroom. They bought an automatic washing machine, and May did all the laundry there, hanging the clothes on a line behind the building—no more scrub boards and big iron pots over outdoor fires. Oleta had a hot plate on which she made stew or roast or perlow or fried chicken. Also, she had an electric oven in which she baked biscuits, cornbread, cakes, and pies.

The store was a family enterprise. Everyone worked. The children swept floors and kept shelves stocked. Oleta taught even her youngest children to use the cash register and how to make change. Often, when things were busy, one of the little ones with bare sandy feet, fresh from playing on the nearby shore, would climb on a stool in front of the cash register and begin to punch in the prices of items placed on the counter by a customer.

When the grocery store did not make enough to support them, Hugie would take outside jobs to supplement their income. To prepare for these absences, he taught his children to do some of the simpler tasks in the meat market. When a customer would come to the meat counter, from behind the high display case he or she would hear a little voice say, "May I help you, please?" And the customer would peer over the counter at the wind-tousled head of some child and say, "Uh, yes, I would like a pound of bologna." And the little Oesterreicher would place the bologna on the big sharp slicer, asking, "How would you like it sliced?" Then, *swish, swish,* the child would slice the bologna, climb atop a stool in front of the scale, weigh the luncheon meat, and then wrap it in paper and string for the wary customer. But when Oleta didn't need the children to help in the store, they were running on the beach or hiding in the dunes, or resting in some corner with a comic book, or even sleeping in the stockroom on a pile of boxes.

Often in those days, May would walk home from the store with the little ones in the late afternoon. In the hot summer months, the children would run from tuft of grass to tuft of grass because the blacktop pavement of First Street and its sandy shoulders burned their bare feet. And if a child cried enough, May would take that child on her hip as she trod along the white road, across the palmetto scrub to the cool shelter of the old oaks surrounding the homeplace. And when Oleta heard her sister had carried one of the children all the way home, she would say, "May, you're spoiling those children." And May would act as though she hadn't heard Oleta.

Most nights, the store closed at eight o'clock. The Oesterreichers climbed in the car, bringing with them the supper Oleta had cooked in the little backroom. Sometimes the family didn't finish their evening meal until after nine o'clock; yet, every night, they circled the big oak table, said the blessing, and ate together.

One day, shortly after the grocery store had opened, Sylvia walked up to her mother and said timidly, "Mama, I think I need a pair of shoes." The Oesterreicher girls did not like asking for things, because they knew how hard times were for their parents. But she lifted her foot so that her mother could see that a hole in the sole of her shoe had worn through to her socks. Oleta opened the cash register, took out three dollars, and said, "Here, baby, go buy yourself a pair of shoes." She could do that. For the first time in her life, Oleta Oesterreicher had a little extra money.

Owning the grocery store was a turning point in the lives of Hugie and Oleta Oesterreicher. In that place, they managed to acquire a certain amount of financial stability. Also, the daily business of running that place, the people they met, and the ideas to which they were exposed changed their lives. Yet their substance, what they were inside, remained unspoiled.

Hugie was always that kind of man Oleta had perceived him to be when she was a mere girl of eighteen—a man of boundless physical strength, a man of infinite endurance, a man of great and gentle heart. Because Hugie continued to do manual labor, his hands too never lost their particular character. They were always as hard as leather left too long in the sun and rain. But when one of his children was ill, Hugie would sit beside the sickbed all night, comforting, watching, wiping that child's brow or holding that child's hand in his strong hard hand.

And Oleta never lost that proud determination she had found in herself after Tom Brown's death. During those early years in the store, Oleta had a black strawhat. Although she sewed most of the children's clothes in the backroom of the grocery store, every year at Easter time, she would go to Jacksonville and outfit her children in new clothes, complete with hats and gloves for the girls. But at that time, Oleta never bought herself anything new. Every Easter Sunday morning, the Oesterreicher children would arrive at St. Paul's Catholic Church for seven o'clock Mass decked out in their new clothes, but year after year, Oleta would wear her black strawhat. One year, she would turn the brim up, sailor fashion, and put a ribbon on it. The next year, she would turn the brim down and pin a flower on it. The next year, she would cock the brim to one side and stick a feather in it. And when Oleta walked with Hugie into church, the children trailing behind her in their new Easter outfits, she walked with the bearing of a queen in her old strawhat.

Into the Present

THE YEARS IN the grocery store were not easy for Hugie. He was an outdoors man. Wading up to his neck in snake-infested waters, working in the blazing sun with sweat streaming in his eyes, riding in a cut-down truck with the freezing rain pelting his face, and breathing the fall air just as the morning light is flooding the woods, all were sustenance to that man who had only worked with his hands, and always freely and always out of doors. Oleta understood this about her husband, so in 1954, after almost ten years, they leased the grocery store to a Syrian man. Years later, my father said that working in the store "was too confining to me . . . got next to me . . . I missed going in the woods, working."

The fall of 1954 through the spring of 1955 was the year my mother didn't work. It was a good year. I went straight home after school. No more stopovers at the grocery store. In those months, the school bus would drop me off out on the highway, and I would walk the mile home across the palmetto scrub. Mama would be waiting there in the house we had both grown up in, rested. But she was not content to do that for long.

In the summer of 1955, Hugie and Oleta had the opportunity to buy a twenty-eight-unit apartment house in Jacksonville Beach, one of several big complexes the McCormicks had built in the late 1940s to house the area's burgeoning population. The plan was that the couple would temporarily manage and maintain the complex with the option to buy at some future date. Hugie and Oleta rented out the Brown place and moved their family into two adjoining two-bedroom units at the apartment house.

Again, the Oesterreichers went to work. Everyone did what he or she could, sweeping, mopping, and waxing floors, cleaning units for rental, and painting walls. Hugie did all the repairs, but most of the work was left to Oleta and May. The older girls were married or away, and the younger children were busy with high school activities and after-school jobs.

In 1963, they gave up the apartment house; it had not been a successful endeavor. They sold the Brown place with its forty acres and bought the home they would live in the rest of their lives, a carefully built house in a quiet neighborhood of Jacksonville Beach, with large rooms, cedar-lined closets, hardwood floors, and French doors partitioning some of the rooms. And because it sat on three lots, the yard was big enough for Hugie to keep a garden and big enough to accommodate the play of the increasing number of Oesterreicher grandchildren.

Hugie and Oleta had opened the grocery store when he was almost fifty; they had tackled the apartment house when he was almost sixty; and in about 1973, when Hugie was in his seventies and Oleta in her sixties, the Oesterreichers decided to liquidate most of their assets—the grocery store, the five acres of land west of the savannahs, and a couple of life insurance policies. The Syrian man got a wonderful deal on the grocery store. In the 1950s, when he had leased it, Hugie had promised him first option to buy and had named the price he would ask should he ever choose to sell. Twenty years later, the land had at least tripled in value, but Hugie and Oleta sold it at the original price they had quoted. Hugie had given his word to the Syrian man; they had shaken hands on it. Hugie would not violate that.

With the money from these three assets—the land, the grocery store, and the insurance policies—they went to the bank. Remembering his losses in 1929, Hugie asked the bank president if his savings would be secure in that institution. After the official assured him they would be, Hugie and Oleta put the money representing the accumulation of their years of work in various kinds of accounts, the interest on which provided a comfortable life for them after that. They made several trips abroad. Every week, Oleta went to the beauty parlor and had her thick mass of silver hair swept elegantly into luxurious curls crowning her head. And even in Jacksonville's best stores, if she saw a dress or a pair of shoes or a new strawhat that she liked, she could buy it. Nevertheless, they both continued to work.

Oleta always found ways to make extra money. She worked once in a bakery and once as the cook in a parochial school cafeteria. Occasionally, she would keep a child for a young working mother. To Oleta, it was all adventure—preserving jam at her kitchen counter, riding high atop a camel in the deserts of Morocco, or watching faces of little children in the school cafeteria spy her strawberry shortcake. She seized life in her later years with enthusiasm; everything she did, she loved.

Hugie also worked; the salary was no longer necessary to his survival, but the work itself was. When I was a teenager, I used to go to weekday Mass. On my way home on some cold dark mornings, warmly wrapped in an overcoat and enclosed in the family car, I sometimes saw my father driving down the highway in the open cut-down truck on his way to work. I hurt for him. He was almost sixty then, and I remember worrying about my father and wondering if he would ever get rest from his hard way of life. I was much older when I finally realized he had always been doing exactly what he loved. He worked that way for almost twenty-five more years and retired when he was eighty-two.

May always stayed with Hugie and Oleta, adding her shoulder to all their efforts. She lived long enough to spoil three generations of Oesterreichers, Hugie and Oleta's children, grandchildren and great-grandchildren. She watched over us all. When we were teenagers, we could fool Mama and Papa, but we could never fool Aunt May. When she caught us creeping in late or sneaking cigarettes, we wondered, "Doesn't she ever sleep?" She saw everything.

When she was very old, she liked to go shopping. She wouldn't tell anyone. She would just dress herself and walk to the store. The shopping center wasn't far away, but it was on the other side of a busy highway. This was dangerous because May liked to cross at the place of her convenience, not at a traffic light, yet she never stopped to check for oncoming cars. She would just step out into the traffic flow, eyes straight ahead, oblivious to the horns blowing and people shouting at her. She was totally deaf by then. No hearing aid really helped her.

The family could not dissuade her from venturing to the shopping center on her own. These trips were her statement of autonomy. When she returned from these excursions, she had gifts for all of us. Boxes of matches and bars of soap for Hugie and Oleta's grown children and a stash of candy for the grandchildren. She kept the candy secreted away and when the parents weren't looking, she would take a piece of candy from her apron pocket and slip it to one of the children. She always had this look on her face that silently communicated a message every child instinctively understood: "You don't tell on me, and I won't tell on you." They always smiled back knowingly, sealing the terms of the secret transaction. They would never tell.

When Aunt May was in her mid-seventies, she fell off one of the grandson's bicycles and broke her elbow. She mended quickly. When she was in her mid-eighties and I was in my thirties, she would wrench a load of laundry from my arms because she thought it too heavy for me to carry—still spoiling me. And then in 1982, when she was eighty-nine years old, after a brief illness, Aunt May died in her own room, cared for and surrounded by the family to whom she had given herself.

This book has been about the long and fruitful life Hugie and Oleta led together. It does not seem the time or place to discuss the details of their deaths. Nevertheless, there are a few things that should be said. Their final illnesses and deaths took place over a sixteen-month period, first Mama in 1986 and then Papa in 1987. During that time, we took care of them. We spent days and nights in critical care waiting rooms, and days and nights tending them when we brought them home. The granddaughters, to whom Oleta had revealed in every aspect of her nature what a woman is, fed her and fixed her hair with ribbons and made her pretty hospital gowns. The grandsons, with whom Hugie had shared the secrets gleaned from a lifetime in the woods, lifted him and carried him tenderly where he could no longer take himself. We held on to Hugie and Oleta. I do not believe any of their children or grandchildren had ever faced the mortality of those two people. We thought they would be with us always. Giving them up was hard. They were the last of that generation. All their brothers and sisters had died before them.

The northeast Florida described in the stories of this book no longer exists. The features nature formed in this locale eons ago are under constant threat from the needs of an ever-expanding affluent population. Marshes have been filled, swamps have been drained, forests have been hollowed out, and sand dunes, those barriers the ocean itself creates to contain its own fury, have been crushed beneath houses and high rises. No end is in sight.

The woods and beaches have also been altered. The Oesterreichers sold the Brown place in 1963. Shortly after that, the house burned down, taking with it the old scarred oak that was home to the big blue lizards with the scarlet heads. The orange trees must have died in a freeze, for they are no longer there. A housing development crowds itself beneath the oak grove, but the builder was kind. He saved all of the trees, and some of the oaks still have nails in them from the ladders Hugie had made to our tree houses.

The savannahs are crisscrossed with paved streets and dotted with houses. Small's Hammock has disappeared. Bulldozers have plowed down many of the trees, flattened the Indian mounds, and turned into a lake the slough where Oleta bogged down. Evidence throughout the community reveals that the residents and politicians of Jacksonville Beach have not been good stewards of the place nature and the early settlers of Pablo Beach left them.

The cypress cabin still stands and the woods and swamps around it are untouched because J. T. and Ben McCormick bought it in the late 1930s. They added thousands of acres to the original thirty-six-acre plot that had belonged to Tom Oesterreicher and turned it into a game preserve. Similarly, when the city of Jacksonville wanted to put a landfill in Durbin Swamp, it was stymied by public outcry and the efforts of individual private citizens such as J. T. McCormick. After months of wrangling in the courts, the plan was finally abandoned, and Durbin Swamp is safe for now.

Hugie's last job was in the Durbin woods he loved so much. Until he was eighty-two, he went several days a week to feed the animals in McCormick's game preserve. He traversed the old wagon roads in his cut-down truck, stopping at regular intervals to leave corn for the hogs and deer still proliferating in that place.

Toward the end, I think, part of him wanted to leave the rattlesnakes alone. He seemed to have gained an empathy for his old natural enemy, as well as for the bears, the hogs, and the deer. They were all being crowded from the Florida landscape. Yet a lifetime habit is hard to break; when he saw a rattlesnake, he killed it, "because that's what you're supposed to do to a rattlesnake."

On one cold November morning in 1981, when Hugie was eighty-three years old, he took one of his grandsons hunting. The air was biting cold, but the gray light of dawn gradually gave way to a bright sun. The boy, wrapped in an old hunting jacket, sat shivering at the base of a tree on the edge of a clearing. In the branches above his head, Hugie sat on the pine planks of a hunter's blind, watching the quiet woods, deciphering the minute signs, reading them knowingly.

The boy slipped into sleep only to be awakened when his head nodded to one side. Then out of the corner of his eye, he saw something move on the far edge of the clearing. He stopped breathing momentarily, his eyes fixed on one particular vague shadow in the tangle of swamp surrounding him and his grandfather. The shadow moved—glided—and then bolted full into the sunlight. The boy's heart pounded in his chest as he watched the animal bound across the field.

"It's a buck! It's a buck!" he wanted to scream, but he didn't dare. Instead, he slapped his hand to his mouth, quieting even his own gasps as he waited for some word, some acknowledgment from his grandfather. There was nothing. "Why doesn't he shoot?" he agonized to himself, not daring to move. The deer reached midfield and headed toward the shelter of the densely underbrushed forests. "Doesn't he see him? He's getting away?" Not a sound or movement came from the blind above his head. The boy was in torment over what he should do. Had his grandfather fallen asleep? Had his old eyes failed him? Should he quickly climb to the blind and shake the old man, or should he cry out? But he had been told not to move or make a sound.

Then, suddenly, above his head, a shrill whistle pierced the cold thin air of the field. Simultaneously, the deer stopped as though in midair, threw back his head, and spread his ears. Another sound, cracking like thunder, reverberated across the clearing. The boy jerked. The deer fell. The child jumped to his feet screaming.

"You did it, Grandpa! You did it! You got him!"

Clear blue eyes twinkling, chuckling with delight, the burly little man, gnarled with his eighty-three years, scrambled down the ladder from the blind and walked with quick agile steps straight to the animal. The boy followed alongside him.

"How did you know, Grandpa? How did you know he would stop when you whistled? How did you know that?" the boy asked, tugging at his grandfather's leathery old hand.

"I just knowed, that's all! I just knowed. . . . " And the man's voice trailed off because the question had triggered a flood of recollections from deep within his soul. Memories invaded his consciousness—images transposed upon the reality of the surrounding cypress swamp—voices speaking louder than the crunching noise of the icy blades of grass crushed beneath their footfall. The man whispered in conversation with himself. His words were unintelligible to the boy, but he said nothing because he knew his grandfather was experiencing a daydream.

The man continued, caught in the images of the past. In his mind's eye, he saw them there—deer leaping over fallen trees and disappearing into dark impenetrable underbrush, deer feeding silently in the dewy morning of the forest, deer rushing headlong before the pursuing dogs, and deer staring blinded and paralyzed in the beam of his headlamp.

And in his mind's ear, the old man heard the voices of his past.

"That Hugie. He got himself an old buck last night."

"What you gonna do, boy, clean out the woods?"

"I know Durbin Swamp like the back of my hand."

"Here you take this gun, boy. You put away that BB gun."

"You old enough to shoot it, you old enough to butcher it."

"Hugie! Come here, son. Your daddy's coming with the cattle."

"What you doing with that doll, boy? What are you, a sissy?"

The burly little man bent over the deer. Its leg quivered. A thin stream of blood trickled from the clean hole behind its ear. The boy warmed his hands against the body of the fallen animal.

And Hugie looked at his grandson and said again, "I just knowed. . . . " And with a hand like some bear's paw, rough and leathery, he pulled a knife from his pocket, opened it, and inserted the blade in the throat of the deer, making a large gash. The blood spurted onto the cold grassy earth. Kneeling, he hoisted the animal on his shoulder. And the man Hugie Oesterreicher stood and turned toward the road leading to the cypress cabin where, at night, hundreds of deer still feed at the edge of Durbin Swamp, their eyes shining in the mist, like stars fallen to the ground.

Notes On Interviews

The Doll

The story of the cattle is taken from an interview with Hugie Oesterreicher, taped on 4 February 1984. The story of the doll is from an interview taped on 16 February 1984. Like most of the stories in this book, the story of the doll is one I've heard all of my life. I heard Hugie's older sister make reference to this story at her house in St. Augustine in August 1983 on her ninetieth birthday.

The Fever

The story of Ella's fever and the trip to Bayard for ice is from an interview with Hugie Oesterreicher, taped on 16 February 1984. The story of Hugie's baby sister is from an untaped interview made the summer of 1986. After hearing the story, I immediately wrote "The Fever" and read it aloud to Papa. He said wistfully, "That's exactly the way it was." In August of that summer, Hugie Oesterreicher had a stroke and never spoke another word.

Hugie's Education

Interviews with Hugie, 4, 7, and 11 February 1984.

The Hunt

Interviews with Hugie, 4 and 11 February 1984.

The Woodsman

This chapter is based on interviews with Hugie, 4 and 16 February, 16 March, and 23 July 1984. Reference to Hugie's reputation as a marksman is in Ed Smith, *Them Good Ole Days in Mayport and the Beaches* (Neptune Beach, Fla.: E. Smith, 1974), 19.

The Browns

Interview with Oleta, 3 February 1984. The story of Annie's shoes is part of our family lore.

The Kittens

Interview with Oleta, 16 February 1984. The original terminal mentioned in this chapter was built in 1897 but was replaced in 1919 by the station standing today. See Wayne Wood, *Jacksonville's Architectural Heritage: Landmarks for the Future* (Jacksonville: University of North Florida Press, 1989), 94–95.

Armistice Day

Interviews with Oleta, 18 February 1984, and Hugie, 3 March 1984. For armistice celebrations in other Florida cities, see the *Florida Times-Union,* 12 and 13 November 1918. A notice in the *Florida Metropolis,* 12 November 1918, stated that questionnaires from the draft board need not be returned.

The Donkey

Interviews with Oleta, 18 February and 3 March 1984. The story of May is part of the Brown and Oesterreicher family lore.

Tom's Death

Interview with Oleta, 3 March 1984. The *Florida Times-Union,* 26 October 1921, reported that a tropical storm passed through northeast Florida on 25 October 1921, the day Tom Brown was buried.

The Dance

The graduation story was taped on 18 February 1984; the New Year's Eve dance, on 3 March 1984; Annie and her gun, on 9 March 1984.

The Onion Poultice

Interview with Oleta, 23 July 1984.

Hugie and Oleta

Interviews with Oleta, 18 February and 3 and 9 March 1984; interviews with Hugie, 11 February and 3 March 1984. For information on construction of the Intracoastal Waterway, consult George E. Buker, *Sun, Sand and Water: A History of the Jacksonville District U.S. Army Corps of Engineers* (Washington, D.C.: Government Printing Office, 1981).

The Decision

Interviews with Hugie, 3 March 1984, and Oleta, 9 March 1984.

The Klan

Interviews with Oleta, 9 and 16 March 1984, and Hugie, 7 February 1984. Carleton M. Burr, in "The Jacksonville Beach Story" (Jacksonville Beach, 1965), compiled old newspaper articles and minutes of town council meetings. This manuscript can be found in the Florida Room of the Jacksonville Public Library. Carleton Burr states that A. B. Brown was found convicted of unspecified charges and removed from office in December 1928. Oleta, however, said that Asbury Brown was wrongfully charged with drinking on the job.

The Birth

Interviews with Oleta, 16 March 1984, and Hugie, 3 March 1984.

Annie's Death

Interview with Oleta, 16 March 1984. On St. Vincent's Hospital, see Marian J. Rust, *The Healers: A History of Health Care in Jacksonville, Florida, 1791–1986* (Jacksonville: Memorial Health, Education and Research Foundation, 1986), 56.

The Bank

Interviews with Hugie, 3 March 1984, and Oleta, 16 March 1984.

The Fast

Interviews with Oleta, 16 March 1984, and Hugie and Oleta, Thanksgiving, 1982.

The Lost Trap

Interviews with Hugie and Oleta, Thanksgiving, 1982; with Hugie, 4 December 1983 and 3 March 1984; and with Oleta, 16 and 24 March 1984. Bank failures in Florida are discussed in Charlton W. Tebeau, *A History of Florida* (Miami, Fla.: University of Miami Press, 1971), 394; and in Ernest Amos, *Annual Report of the Comptroller of the State of Florida, Banking Department* (Tallahassee, 30 June 1930).

Moonshine

Interviews with Hugie, 3 March 1984, and Oleta, 24 March 1984.

Fences

Interviews with Hugie, 4 February and 3 and 16 March 1984, and Oleta, 24 March 1984. The fencing of the Florida range was primarily a result of the cattle dipping law of 1923, an effort to eradicate Texas tick fever. Cattle were to be penned and dipped every two weeks, a mandate that caused many cattlemen to go out of business. See Joe A. Akerman, Jr., *Florida Cowman: A History of Florida Cattle Raising* (Madison, Fla.: Florida Cattlemen's Association, 1976).

The Rattlesnake

The details of this story are based on articles published in the *Florida Times-Union* and the *Jacksonville Journal* on 7 April 1937.

The Move

Interviews with Hugie, 3 March 1984, and Oleta, 24 March 1984.

Justice

This story is based on an article published in the *Jacksonville Journal* on 19 August 1937.

The Depression Ends

Interviews with Hugie, 3 March 1984, and Oleta, 24 March 1984.

Hunting Squirrels in Small's Hammock

Interview with Hugie and Oleta, Thanksgiving, 1982.

The War Years

Interviews with Hugie, 16 March 1984, and Anne Burnett (Annie Mary Oesterreicher), 21 October 1985. Untaped interviews with Fred Allen of Atlantic Beach and James Messinese of Neptune Beach.

The Grocery Store

Interview with Oleta, 23 July 1984.

Into the Present

This chapter is based on my own memory. The sources for the story of the hunt are my sons, Tony and Greg Nettuno. The daydream sequence is based on my own experiences with my father. He often spoke audibly as he reminisced with himself about the past. His children and grandchildren always respected his right to exclude us from that.

About the Author

Michel Oesterreicher earned her bachelor's degree from the University of North Florida, where she won the 1984 History Award and Department of Language and Literature Award. She currently lives in Florida and teaches English in Duval County. *Pioneer Family* is her first book.